HOW TO PROSPER
AS AN INTERIOR DESIGNER

HOW TO PROSPER AS AN INTERIOR DESIGNER

A BUSINESS AND LEGAL GUIDE

ROBERT L. ALDERMAN

JOHN WILEY AND SONS, INC.

New York ■ Chichester ■ Weinheim ■ Brisbane ■ Singapore ■ Toronto

This text is printed on acid-free paper.

This publication is designed to provide accurate and
authoritative information in regard to the subject
matter covered. It is sold with the understanding that
the publisher is not engaged in rendering legal, accounting,
or other professional services. If legal advice or other
expert assistance is required, the services of a competent
professional person should be sought.

Library of Congress Cataloging in Publication Data:

Alderman, Robert L.
    How to prosper as an interior designer : a business and legal
  guide / by Robert L. Alderman.
      p.   cm.
  Includes index.
  ISBN 0-471-16223-X (cloth : alk. paper)
    1. Interior decoration firms—United States—Management.
  2. Interior decoration firms—Law and legislation—United States.
  I. Title.
NK2116.2.A39   1997
729'.068—dc20   96-43760F

Printed in the United States of America

10 9 8 7 6

For my mother, Freida B. Alderman, and my aunt, Dorothy Y. Ben

CONTENTS

PREFACE

THE CHALLENGE OF THE NEW MILLENIUM:
HOW TO PROSPER

This book is a journey into the labyrinths and recesses of the interior design business. Come, and take it with me. I think you'll find that it's worth the trip.

My intention is not to outline rules of law and business. My intention is not to write a book to give you answers about business and design. Instead, it is to teach you how to ask questions in these areas. I think that's far more important.

I have presented most of the material as case studies, although four chapters provide outlines on how to prepare contracts and proposals. Each case is based on an actual business or legal problem that has confronted an interior designer. In each situation, I have provided a strategy to solve the problem.

You may not relate to each and every problem. However, if you read this book from cover to cover, you may be surprised how it may affect your perspective in dealing with your own problems. Ideally, you will identify with the experiences of other designers. A thought-provoking process may encourage you to create your own brand of common sense.

After you've finished the book, put it aside. Read through it again sometime later. You may be surprised to find that some of the decisions you've made in your business since the first reading were affected by the cases in this book.

Many of you are old friends of mine. We may have become acquainted in a number of ways. My first book, *How to Make More Money at Interior Design*, published in 1982, was so successful that it was reprinted four times. If you were an interior designer during that era, there is a good chance that you already own it. You may also remember my magazine columns from *Interior Design* and *The Designer*. I wrote for those publications about business and law for interior designers for many years. I have also been a continuing education instructor for the American Society of

Interior Designers and have lectured nationwide for many years. Some of you may have become acquainted with me as a teacher.

Since I published my first book, two factors influenced me to write this one. First, a whole new generation of designers has emerged in the nearly 15 years since my book was published. Second, I have developed, year by year, new material that should also be helpful, on a financial and legal basis, in guiding interior designers to operate their practices. Some of it has appeared in magazine articles, and some has been consolidated in my audiocassette series, *How to Make More Money at Interior Design*.

This book will, I hope, achieve two goals. First, it will revisit selected material from my first book, which I feel is still relevant today. Second, it will introduce new material, developed subsequently, that I feel is essential for designers to know.

The role of designers in society is greatly influenced by the era in which they function. Interior designers, to some degree, are a product of their age. When I began writing for designers in the mid-1970s, our economy was on the verge of an era of prosperity that was unprecedented in our generation. Business was excellent and continued to grow. The stock market reached new highs, and the real estate market exploded. Commercial and residential real estate development became target areas for investment by financial institutions, such as banks and mutual funds, and by individuals.

A by-product of this development was an overwhelming demand for interior designers and interior design products. The design business boomed and prospered, along with many other businesses. The concept of hiring interior designers was not a new one, but the demand for their services entered a whole new dimension.

It was quite common in the past for commercial, and even residential, developers to rely on architects to design interiors. In fact, many architects became interior designers for two reasons. First, once the building boom began to subside and the need for architectural services declined, there was still a considerable demand for designing interiors. Second, some architects began to avoid designing buildings due to their malpractice liablity. Architects have been sued for malpractice, as a result of design defects in buildings, for staggering amounts. Many of them simply decided to turn to designing interiors to reduce their exposure.

The interior design field became populated by many different types of designers. There was, and always will be, the classic interior decorator. Although there are those snobs who sneer at the term "decorator," the decorator is an essential part of the design community. Decorators focus on style, comfort, and tradition. Borrowing from the past, they lend a human element to interior design. Interior decorators understand period furniture, fabrics, and antiques. They are frequently consulted for architectural projects where life-style and hospitality interiors (such as restaurants, hotels, condominiums, etc.) are involved.

A newer breed of designer, known as an "interior designer," evolved. In addition to decorating, the interior designer understands the architectural ramifications of design and creates interiors based on architectural criteria. The designer understands architectural working drawings, unlike the decorator, who relies on floor plans. The designer can prepare reflected ceiling plans and confer with lighting designers to prepare complex lighting designs. The decorator usually selects lighting fixtures. In other words, the interior designer's architectural approach is a departure from decorating, and the designer takes pride in this image as a professional.

Some architects protest, claiming that interior designers are trying to use their methods of design without being properly trained and licensed. However, the interiors that are created by this new breed of designer are much more exciting and dynamic than many architectural interiors. The interior designer has the "cutting edge." The rest is history.

Depending on a project's sophistication, whether residential or commercial, interior designers are often the first to be consulted by owners and developers. They plan the interior from the "inside out" instead of the "outside in." Now it is the interior designer who frequently selects an architect for a client's project. It is the interior designer who is consulted about lighting, cabinetry, and even landscape architecture. The interior designer is the pivot, and a whole new generation is scrambling for business and recognition.

When I began writing for designers, business was reaching fever pitch. If a designer was talented, it was usually possible for him or her to find a niche in the design world to earn a living. Of course, some designers became more successful than others. This is always the case, regardless of the economy. However, the stock market crash in the 1980s depressed the design business. The financial markets experienced recession, and the real estate market tumbled in the years that followed. The demand for design services and design products declined considerably. It was a frightening and terrible time for the design community.

This downturn forced the design economy to restructure. Many manufacturers and showrooms that produced expensive, fine quality products disappeared; others consolidated. Interior design centers in major cities lost many of their tenants. In some cases, design centers were converted to office buildings or warehouses. To survive, many designers left the business to find other kinds of employment. Major design periodicals, formerly as thick as books and laden with advertising copy, became skinny and, in some cases, disappeared.

Regardless of the turmoil, however, the interior designer who survived was a newer, tougher breed. The image of the designer as a professional, as opposed to an artist and dilettante, became paramount in the
world of interior design. Interior designers lobbied for licensing in various states, forcing legal recognition. National organizations, such as the
American Society of Interior Designers and the International Interior
Design Assocation, gained importance and helped secure further recognition for designers.

Finally, the economy began to revive. The stock market was resuscitat-
ed, and soared to new highs. Real estate development resumed. Things
have returned to normal—or have they? Not really. For many reasons, it
has become harder for designers to become successful as entrepreneurs.

The cost of doing business has become greater, and the competition
for clients is stiffer. Important commissions for commercial and contract
design seems to be drifting toward large, established firms. It is harder for
smaller firms to compete and stay alive.

Residential design has been affected by the big retail stores. They offer
home furnishings to the public that had previously been available only
through professional sources. The public seems eager, on a certain level,
to bypass the interior designer in order to save on commissions and
design fees. The entrepreneurial design movement has become more anxious. Do these trends threaten the success of the independent, creative
interior designer?

Absolutely not. All this means, the experts agree, is that many designers must learn how to repackage their services to meet the demands of the
public. To some degree, they conclude, it is more a marketing problem
than a trip to oblivion. In fact, design products have become more sophisticated and specialized than ever. Educated and trained professionals are
required to cope with every phase of interior design.

One fact remains undisputed. It is definitely more difficult for smaller
firms to survive today because of intense competition and the need for
specialization. It is hard for solo practitioners to be a jack-of-all-trades.
Some designers are more adept at promoting business and finding clients;
some are excellent designers; and still others excel at job supervision and
managing their offices. Regardless, it is crucial that designers equip themselves with the best legal and business skills they can find.

Designers must learn about all financial aspects of their business as
early in their careers as possible. Knowledge creates awareness; awareness develops skills and expertise. Knowledge also dispels fear. Designers
should acquire basic financial skills when their careers begin. Then their
business abilities and acumen will mature progressively as their creative
talents continue to develop.

Business is a science, just as design is an art, and accounting is a vital area of this science. The principles of accounting teach cash flow. An understanding of one's expenditure patterns leads to financial responsibility. Helpful courses other than those in accounting are those in basic business management. They analyze general principles of business and teach management techniques.

Another method of learning about the design business is to gain hands-on experience by working for a company. Good jobs are often hard to find, and salaries for newcomers are, typically, shockingly low. Often, employers do not devote much effort to teaching designers all phases of their business. It is then the designer's responsibility to acquire a complete overview of a design firm's financial operation.

I think the challenges of this era are more difficult for experienced designers than for newer ones. New designers start out with a clean slate. Having no prior experience, they adapt to their immediate reality. Experienced designers, on the other hand, must reshape their attitudes and learn to handle financial and legal matters to cope with today's demands. Once they establish a new pattern and incorporate business into their careers, the light at the end of the tunnel will allow them to see the rewards.

Regardless of their particular niche in their profession, I believe that all designers should understand certain basic legal and financial concepts that apply to interior design. Keep in mind, however, that this book does not provide specific legal or financial advice. It discusses concepts and case studies that should offer some guidance. Before taking any irrevocable steps, share your conclusions with your business partner, accountant, or attorney.

Although nothing can substitute for a good financial education or years of experience, I have provided a detailed guide to help you become smarter and more financially informed in most residential and some corporate markets. This book covers such areas as the following:

Preparing Letters of Agreement—General and Commercial
Preparing Design Proposals—Contract and Residential
Charging a Client
Professional Analysis for Charging Clients
Contracts, Contractors, and Liability
Working with Architects
Designers and Industry: Expectations and Ramifications
Purchases and Deliveries
Financial Management for Residential Interior Designers
All of these topics are discussed in the light of specific examples.

Some are explored by using a summary of a "past history." Examples of common problems are introduced and followed with complete explanations, which include other related points. If a question demands a legal response, it is fully answered. All alternatives are explored; legal remedies are tempered by business policy.

Do not attempt to read this book as a novel, absorbing it as a one-time experience. Read it once to become acquainted with all the information. Then refer to those areas of the book as needed in your own business. Reread the entire book some months later. Repeating the process over a period of time will result in learning and developing new insights.

After my first book was published, I received two types of responses from designers. One was, "I read your book, and I enjoyed it." The other was, "I keep your book in my office. Whenever I have a problem, I check it for advice." Designers have also commented, "I refer to your book before I charge a client or prepare a letter of agreement." That is how I would like you to use this book.

The information in the following chapters can be extremely important to a designer. Of course, if you are experienced, you will realize that an infinite number of variables can change the outcome of a decision. Obviously, all these variables cannot be discussed here. You will learn general principles and the rationales for their development. These axiomatic rules did not evolve in a vacuum but developed from application, adaptation, and reuse.

Designers tell me that most books offering legal and financial advice for designers are not very helpful. I think mine will be different. I will communicate with you. When the subject matter is contracts and proposals, I provide a step-by-step guide. You may not agree with it, but you will have an opportunity to examine a viable approach with a complete explanation. In Chapter 6, "Contracts, Contractors, and Liability," I tell story after story, illustrating various points of interest. You might forget some rules, but you won't forget the stories. They are all true-to-life situations that happen to designers every day. Remembering them will keep you from forgetting how to handle analagous situations.

If we are old acquaintances, I am thrilled to renew our friendship after many years. If we are new friends, I appreciate the opportunity to develop a new relationship. One promise I can easily make. If you use this book as I have intended, it will not only provide guidance and help with your career, it will also help you prosper!

1

PREPARING A LETTER OF AGREEMENT

One of the first things a client is likely to ask is, "How much do you charge?" and then, "May I see a copy of your contract?"

Young designers are stunned by the frequency of these questions at such a premature level of the designer-client relationship. "They want to know how much I charge and what my contract is like," they say, "before they even take a look at my portfolio."

But consider these questions in a different light. I once asked a client of mine, a well-known architect, why certain run-of-the-mill architectural firms are selected over established architects who are known to be geniuses. "Because," he told me, "corporations are mainly concerned with having their buildings finished at budget and on time. As long as the building fits the purposes for which it is intended, the overall quality of design does not have the highest priority. These firms deliver as promised. Their clients know this and trust them."

Most interior design clients, especially those retaining the services of a professional for the first time, are usually unsophisticated about the field of design. Of course, they have varying tastes and preferences. They might know, for example, that they prefer some colors and textures to others or that they want a modern look, not a traditional one. But very often the decisive factor for these clients is whether you look "professional." I assume that you are capable of discussing your philosophy of design with a prospective client, but a professional should also be able to present his financial posture in a positive way. Charging a client is discussed in depth later, but now, let's prepare a letter of agreement.

I will show you how to make this letter look professional, how to present a business format while still preserving your design image, and how to protect yourself from financial loss as a result of unforeseen circumstances.

Samples are provided for various segments of your letter of agreement. Professionals use different techniques to suit their particular needs.

Some will be suitable for your use; others will not. A presentation of possible approaches offers hints on the psychology involved in preparing a letter of agreement. This information will protect you and make you look professional even if you have never operated on a free-lance basis before. If you are already conducting a business, you will receive confirmation in certain areas and will question others. You may realize that you have been operating without sufficient protection and see what you can do to limit potential liability from certain risks. If you are in the early stages of setting up your business, it may not be possible to compel clients to agree with all your demands. However, as a more secure financial base is developed, you will then be able to gradually add more protection. Leverage with clients is important, and the letter of agreement is one of your most important levers. It defines responsibilities and obligations and can often make or break you.

Caution: Throughout this book, I will be providing you with various model agreements. Do not submit your own agreements to clients or third parties based on these models without consulting an attorney in your local jurisdiction. Federal, state, and/or local legislation may affect the way you prepare all documentation. In certain states, licensing statutes for interior designers may also affect what your agreements should provide, including how they should be worded.

The model agreements are presented to help you think and to structure your ideas. Use these models on a conceptual level. Don't reproduce them as legal documents.

WHEN DO YOU PRESENT A CLIENT WITH A LETTER OF AGREEMENT?

Before discussing *how* to prepare a letter of agreement, it makes sense to talk about *when* to produce it. There are two schools of thought on this subject. You can have a "standard letter" ready to show a client, with blank spaces to fill in the name and other details, or you can prepare each letter individually and delay showing it to the client until it is worked out and completed.

You have a strong advantage with a standard letter. If the client is faced with a "fill-in-the-blanks" contract, he or she may think, "This agreement is standard for everyone. It must be all right. I suppose if I want to hire the design firm, I have to agree to the same terms the rest of its clients do. I may as well sign it."

Yet there may be problems with this technique. Although you may develop a standard letter, it is most unlikely that you will have standard clients. Each will be different. If you show a client a standard letter but then decide to make changes for the project at hand, you may encounter some heavy objections. Your client may feel that your changes are discriminatory and unreasonable deviations from your standard policy.

Timing is very important. Even though your letter of agreement will contain many standard clauses, many others may depend on the project. It takes time, thought, and perhaps the help of another professional to prepare a letter of agreement, especially for a project of any size, which can cost money. Before going through all of this, you should be fairly sure that the client will actually be doing business with your office.

Generally, a prospective client will meet with you at least twice before deciding to hire you. Get as much "job input" as possible before supplying information about fees or letters of agreement. In some instances, this won't be a problem. You'll know exactly what you have to do, how much it will cost, and how you'll need to operate. You'll be able to talk business right away. But at other times, you won't be so sure.

When you are faced with a financial question you can't answer, stall. Remember, your client will always be more familiar with the particulars of his project than you will. He may, for example, approach you with a set of floor plans or drawings and say, "OK, I want this, this, and this. How much do you charge? How much will the project cost? When will it be finished? Do you have a letter of agreement?"

This is a typical rapid-fire "businessman's approach." Everything you say will be remembered. When you are caught in these circumstances, it is wise to say, "I really have to give this some thought. I have a business manager (or lawyer or accountant) with whom I have to discuss this before I can give you an answer."

After the client has left your office, you can decide the fee you want to quote. Review things carefully, and perhaps talk it over with another professional.

At the next meeting, advise your client about financial and other business terms orally. If those terms are acceptable and the client agrees to hire you, then prepare your letter of agreement.

Designers have frequently called me with this complaint: "I showed your letter of agreement to my new client," they say. "Before we prepared it, I told her about all the terms, and she agreed. Now, she's objecting to everything all over again, and she doesn't want to sign it."

Nothing is foolproof. Some clients are tough. They'll say yes one minute and no the next. Generally, you should sound out a client thoroughly before submitting a letter of agreement unless you are absolutely positive about how you will operate in a given situation. Present the letter only when you're prepared and ready.

NATIONALLY STANDARDIZED AGREEMENTS

There are national professional organizations for interior designers and architects that have developed standard contracts, as well as other documents, to be utilized in the practice of architecture and interior design.

Many designers, who belong to these organizations and subscribe to their theories and principles, use only those standard agreements in the course of their practice. When discussing their contracts with clients, these designers state, "I use only the (design organization's) contract."

Even if all interior designers utilize standard agreements, I still believe it would be important to understand how to prepare a basic letter of agreement. Although these agreements are "standard" for the designer, they are totally unfamiliar to clients. It is important for you to understand what they mean and to be able to explain how they operate. Therefore, even if you use such standard contracts in your practice, it is, in my opinion, crucial to understand my analysis to prepare letters of agreement.

Of course, as it happens, not all interior designers use standard contracts. I have often asked designers who prepare personalized contracts why they don't use standard agreements. Their reasons vary.

Some designers don't belong to the national organizations that have developed these contracts. Usually, it is the members of these organizations who are the strongest advocates of such agreements.

Some designers have told me that the standard contracts don't meet their needs. I have heard such comments as, "The clients don't understand them, and I can't explain the language" or "I prefer to develop my own agreement based on the client and the project."

Many designers have asked my personal opinion about use of standard agreements. I have always given the same answer. To my knowledge, there are no laws or rules compelling designers to use any specific standard agreements. If you like a particular standard agreement and feel that it meets the necessary professional and legal criteria, then use it—it's a matter of personal choice.

However, regardless of whether you use a standard agreement or prepare your own, be sure you understand each clause thoroughly. This includes all professional, legal, and business ramifications. Once you submit an agreement to a client, you must be able to answer any question about its language. Otherwise, you will appear unprofessional.

WHY USE A LETTER AS A FORMAT?

The use of a letter of agreement as opposed to a contract can be a key to your relationship with your client, especially in residential projects. A designer-client relationship is often very personal. Many clients expect not only an attractive series of rooms but a new life-style. They may long have harbored fantasies about the way they want to live and work. The designer is the "genie" who is to fulfill their wishes. Accordingly, the first written encounter must provide all the elements necessary to define the new relationship; it should be presented in a very personal way. Therefore, a formal legal format is inappropriate. The language should not be stiff or legalistic—it should sound like you. Don't use "party of the first part," "whereas," or "forthwith." Dispose of that terminology. Talk to your client in layman's language.

A letter format does not affect the legality of your agreement. A letter of agreement is a contract with a different presentation. A more personal approach, however, does not have to sacrifice thoroughness, clarity, and a comprehensive treatment of the necessary areas. Say what you have to say, but in the right way.

Specify the Area to Be Designed

In the introductory paragraph of your letter of agreement, state the name of the client and the address of the space. For residential projects, list the number of rooms to be designed and describe them by name:

> Dear Mr. and Mrs. Smith:
>
>   We are pleased to submit our letter of agreement describing our design and planning services for your apartment. The areas of your residence, 2000 Fifth Avenue, Apartment 19D, New York, New York, which relate to this agreement are the following:
>
>   1. Entrance foyer
>   2. Library
>   3. Living room
>   4. Dining room
>   5. Master bedroom and Bath

This situation is a perfect example as to why it is important to be so specific. Obviously, the apartment is larger than the number of rooms listed. There would also be a kitchen, pantry, other bedrooms and bathrooms, and so forth. However, the Smiths are interested only in working on these rooms with their designer. If they wanted the entire apartment designed, you could omit specifically designating the rooms, as shown in the next example:

>   We are pleased to submit our letter of agreement describing our design and planning services for your entire residence at 2000 Fifth Avenue, Apartment 19D, New York, New York.

These distinctions can save you money, depending on how you charge. If you charge a flat fee or a design fee plus a percentage of purchases, the amount of compensation is totally fixed in the first case and somewhat fixed in the second. Obviously, if the Smiths don't want the entire apartment designed at the start, you don't want other rooms, such as a kitchen, to be added on later for no additional fee.

My clients who charge strictly "retail" or on a percentage basis often argue, "As my fee doesn't relate to the number of rooms, I don't have to be specific. If they buy, I make money. If they don't, I make less." Designers who charge on an hourly basis also make a similar argument. They determine that they are paid for their time, regardless of the scope of the project. That may be true. But there's still another reason to be specific on a "room count."

Frequently, clients try to pin down designers about completion dates. Presume that you told the Smiths that you could complete the five rooms in six months. If you had not been specific about the number of rooms and half-way through the project they decided to add the kitchen to the project, at the end of six months you might not be finished. Yet the Smiths might object, because you initially promised a six-month period, and may even decide to withhold part of your fee until the work is finished.

This sounds terribly unreasonable, but "fee withholding" is not uncommon. List rooms specifically unless you are designing the entire space. If an additional room is included later, the client will understand why the project will not be completed within the initially projected period.

This kind of precision is vital for commercial ventures. Identify the space that is being designed in every reasonably possible way. The following example is a typical description for a commercial office:

X Y Z Corporation
5000 Madison Avenue
New York, New York

Attention: Clinton Jones, President

Dear Mr. Jones:

We are pleased to submit our letter of agreement describing our design and planning services for your offices consisting of the entire 31st floor at 5000 Madison Avenue, New York, New York. You have advised us that your space is approximately 10,000 usable square feet, which you will be permitted to subdivide. You have requested subdivision as follows:

1. Large reception area
2. Executive board room

3. Chief executive's office with private bath and kitchenette
4. Two additional executive offices without bath
5. Two small staff offices
6. Six secretarial areas

The same reasons for identifying spaces for design in residential projects apply here as well. However, listing specific areas can be even more important in commercial cases. Some commercial designers charge a basic commercial rate by the square foot to prepare design plans. Obviously, the approximate square footage should appear in the letter of agreement. Some commercial designers charge percentages for making purchases of furniture, fixtures, and equipment. These designers frequently charge higher percentages for more heavily decorated areas such as board rooms and executive offices. For example, 15 percent on purchases may be assessed for staff offices, and 20 percent may be the rate for executive areas.

In any case, for either residential or commercial projects, design areas should usually be identified and described at the beginning of your letter of agreement. It is generally wise to lay this foundation in order to make subsequent provisions understandable and enforceable.

OUTLINE PROJECT DEVELOPMENT

After the introduction, explain in a concise, orderly manner the sequential development of design phases and your general method of operation. In other words, tell your client how you are going to run the project. This is one of the most important things the client will want to know. If he's worked with a designer before, he'll want to compare your technique with that of a previous designer. If he's unfamiliar with the way a designer works, this will assure him that you use a professional system.

Project development can be outlined in a list or described in one or two paragraphs. Avoid using a list except for large commercial projects, where more formality is expected. The following example is a typical presentation:

> As we have discussed, the project will be designed and supervised by (the designer) and other members of our staff. All plans, furnishings, and budget will be approved by you in advance.
>
> Our general method of operation shall be as follows. Initially, we will consult with you to determine the requirements of each area of your residence to be designed. All areas will be surveyed and measured. Next, design plans and materials will be presented, with a preliminary budget. Based on your final approval and signature of the designs and renderings, the following interior design plans will be prepared:

    1. Cabinetwork
    2. Reflected ceiling plan
    3. Painting and wall covering schedule

    All basic plans, drawings, schedules, and sketches will be reviewed with you and subject to your written approval. These items will then be submitted for competitive bidding to a contractor of your choice or ours. The quality and supervision of the work are the obligation of the contractor. We will provide any reasonable assistance and will visit the project, as necessary, to determine whether the contractor is conforming to our plans.

At this point, some observations are in order to help you prepare your own letter.

"Other members of your staff" may be working on the project. Even if you don't have a partner, you may decide to hire an assistant—this is always a possibility. Clients often object, however, if you don't handle every detail personally. If you warn them in advance that you may have to delegate some of the tasks to your assistant, it will help to prevent future problems.

If no detailed floor plan exists, you will have to measure the space or hire someone to do it for you. Let your client know about this. Scaled drawings look very professional; freehand sketches are for amateurs.

You will interview your client to discuss requirements of the space. Some designers ask clients to submit a list of "musts" and "likes and dislikes." These don't have to be mentioned in the agreement itself, although they could be. Usually, the designer will explain this when she reviews the contract with the prospective client.

Once a tentative design is developed—that is, a floor plan is prepared containing a furniture layout and a color scheme is selected with sample fabrics, pictures of furniture, sketches of built-ins, and so on—the designer will make her visual presentation to the client.

In the preceding example, the visual presentation is simply called "design plans and materials." Some think it is more impressive to specify how elaborate their visual presentation will be. Others don't want to commit themselves to exhaustive presentations, so they leave the wording very loose (as in the example) and then decide later how detailed they want to be.

As the example illustrates, some designers prepare a preliminary budget at the time of the visual presentation. If that's how you operate, mention it. To avoid wasting time, some designers do not prepare a budget until final selections are made. A "guess-estimate" is not considered a preliminary budget. If you want to mention general figures at the presentation, qualify your answers as uncertain. Put in writing only numbers that have been costed out with a fair amount of precision.

Once all preliminary stages are complete, prepare final design drawings or plans. The example lists three typical final sets of plans or drawings prepared by interior designers: cabinetwork, reflected ceiling plan, painting and wall covering schedule.

After the design has been completed, the drawings may have to be submitted to contractors for estimates. Many designers have their favorite general contractors and specialty craftsmen; however, in the letter of agreement, it is always smart to indicate that the plans will be sent out for competitive bidding. Clients often urge designers to work with whomever they like. However, let your client know that you have an open mind.

Sometimes clients insist on using their own contractors. Frequently, they do this for a couple of reasons. First, they think it will be cheaper than using the designer's contractors. Second, they want to eliminate the possibility of their designer getting a kickback, or undisclosed commission, from using her own sources.

Designers often complain about the contractors that their clients select. I have known several designers who refuse to work with any contractors except their own. They like using contractors with whom they have established a working relationship and who can guarantee results.

I respect the ability of any designer who has established a sufficiently good relationship with her clients to be able to insist on using specific sources and contractors. However, be advised that if you take that position, especially early in your client relationship, you are waving a "red flag" that might even cost you the job. For any number of reasons, some clients prefer to select their own contractors. If you refuse to cooperate, the client may suspect you have ulterior financial motives.

The last two sentences in the preceding example are very important. The quality of the work is the responsibility of the contractor, not the designer. It is also the contractor's responsibility to supervise his own employees as they complete the work.

You must visit the site to ensure that your drawings are being complied with, but you are not responsible for faulty construction or inadequate workmanship. Of course, you will ultimately be the middleman to correct any reasonable problem, but don't allow the client or the contractor to pass the buck to you in the case of a costly mistake by the contractor.

These suggestions on outlining project development are based on the general methods of operation of many designers I have counseled. However, every designer operates differently, and very often a designer substantially varies her procedure from one project to the next, according to their different needs and requirements.

Although the example gives you an idea of what a project outline might contain, there cannot be a standard form. Here's how I handle it with my own clients.

When new designer clients ask me to prepare a letter of agreement, their general preconception is that I will put together a model package of standard clauses tailored for their needs. I advise that I prefer not to prepare models, and that they should contact me when they have a new client ready to enter into an agreement. At that time, the designer and I, working with specific facts about the tangible project, prepare a letter of agreement.

When we arrive at the outline of the project development section, I ask, "What are you going to do on this project from start to finish?—make a list." For any new project, numerically list what you are going to do in that specific situation. Use the example at the beginning of this section as a checkpoint. Then, write it up in one or two cohesive paragraphs, generally less than 500 words. Each time you are about to prepare a new letter of agreement, check this list to see whether you will be operating in a different way. Change the list as necessary to conform with the requirements of a specific project. This process becomes easier over time.

Why place so much emphasis on a section that neither protects you against liability nor creates income? The answer is easy. Outlining methods of your design process helps to create a professional image. Without that image, you may lose clients.

When clients approach designers, they are not only considering the size of the design fee, but also the quality of advice. Many clients spend substantial amounts on goods and services and want to be certain that their money is well spent. They want their designer to weigh these expenditures carefully.

When you present a letter of agreement to clients requesting an advance retainer or design fee, the right impression must be conveyed from the outset. When clients see the method of operation outlined in the agreement, they are able to visualize how their project will develop. They see that the approach to planning their project will be businesslike as well as creative.

Many very talented designers never achieve success because they are unable to convince prospective clients that they are responsible enough to handle the financial aspects of the job. A professional presentation is essential to obtain the client's trust. Once you have that trust, you are more likely to be hired.

Insist on Written Client Approval

Always stipulate that clients must approve all their decisions in writing. In the previous section, "Outline Project Development," I used a design outline as an example. Notice that I discussed written approval at two stages of the project.

Projects usually progress in phases; don't proceed from one to the next without the client's written approval. For example, if your client approves your initial "visual presentation," (samples of merchandise and design drawings mounted on boards), have him initial it. Then, once your "final budget" is prepared and approved, have him sign it. This is particularly important if the budget exceeds the preliminary estimate, which is typically the case. You will be armed with documentation should your client attack you later for exceeding the preliminary estimate. This protection can be crucial.

When purchase orders or purchase estimates are obtained, have the client sign these too, even if he submits the deposit. Be specific in your letter of agreement. Here is a good example:

> You will be required to provide your written approval upon acceptance of the visual presentation, final budget, purchase orders, and all design plans.

Although this clause is one of the easiest to insert, it can end up being one of the most important. The significance of timely client approval will be apparent later in the discussion on dealing with responsibility.

Purchases

There are three different purchasing methods:

1. The designer is the direct purchaser.
2. The designer purchases as an agent for the client.
3. The client makes purchases directly.

Any one of the three methods may be appropriate at different times. For example, if the designer charges "retail," the client is usually unaware of the markup. In that case, the designer pays the wholesale price to the vendor directly. Then, she collects the retail price from her client. Therefore, the designer is usually the direct purchaser when charging retail

In your agreement, when charging retail, state the following:

> All purchases will be made at retail cost, and all purchasing transactions will be made by my office.

If you charge on a cost-plus basis, that is, a percentage of goods and services, you may decide to act as a purchasing agent. Designers like to use this method so that they can control the project by making purchases directly. However, since the designer is acting as an agent, instead of as the purchaser, the liability to the client for guaranteeing goods and services is more limited. Suggested language for using this method is as follows:

> All purchases will be made available to you at our wholesale cost, and our office shall act as your purchasing agent in this connection. We shall prepare all necessary purchase orders (deposit requests) and submit them to you for your written approval. Upon approval of purchase orders, payment shall be made as follows:
>
> 1. Full payment for wall coverings, fabrics, lighting fixtures, accessories, plants, and any retail items (flatware, china, crystal, linen, and other household items) and design fees thereon;
> 2. Fifty percent (50%) of wholesale cost and design fees for other furnishings and fixtures with the remaining balances due prior to delivery and installation;
> 3. Fifty percent (50%) of wholesale cost and design fees on all design services with the remaining balances due prior to completion.
>
> Payments shall include sales tax, freight, and shipping charges on purchase orders and invoices for merchandise ordered for you.

When you prepare each purchase order or "deposit request," the document will state the terms of payment. If full payment is required, the purchase order will state "full payment" and list the amount. If a 50 percent deposit is required, the purchase order will state "50 percent deposit, balance prior to delivery."

Yet if that is the case, why is it necessary to discuss terms of payment in the agreement? Why not simply state, "Payment for goods and services will be requested as per the terms of the purchase orders?"

There is a very good reason for this. If your client is unfamiliar with the interior design business, she may not understand that many items have to be purchased "pro forma", that is, in full, upon order. Clients often tell designers, "I don't want to pay in full for anything until it is delivered."

Designers are then forced to educate their clients about the design business. If the client refuses to pay as per the terms of the vendors, the designer can't buy those goods.

Some designers surmount a client's objections by purchasing the goods themselves and charging the client "retail." Usually, designers make more money on charging retail than on cost-plus. However, if the client refuses to pay for custom-ordered goods once delivered, the designer is stuck with a restocking charge, at least. Some vendors will not accept any returns, and in that case the designer owns the purchases.

Regardless of what route you decide to take, the letter of agreement is the first written document your client will receive advising him about deposits. If there are any objections, clear the air before you get started.

Some design firms want the client to make purchases directly. As designers, they need only prepare the specifications from their offices. Here is an example of how to provide for direct payment:

> All purchases will be made available to you at our wholesale cost. As you are the purchaser, all bills will be sent to you directly for payment. Although we will prepare the purchase orders, as the "purchaser" you will deal directly with the vendor on a pro forma basis. We will not be held liable for any payment, including sales tax, freight, and shipping charges, on purchase orders and invoices for any merchandise ordered for you.

There are certain problems in using this approach. Some clients refuse to pay each vendor directly. They don't like writing out many different checks and sending them to the vendors. They think the designer should handle that aspect of the job. These clients want the designer to send them a statement listing groups of purchases, with one lump sum covering many deposits. Then they want the designer to distribute the lump sum to the vendors for all their deposits.

Some vendors refuse to accept a client's check and will accept payment only from a designer. The designer is then forced to purchase certain goods for their clients.

However, in spite of these problems, many designers refuse to pay vendors directly. They believe that having a client pay vendors saves their offices a great deal of time in bookkeeping. It also establishes a direct relationship between the client and the vendor, an advantage in the event something goes wrong with an order. If goods are late or defective, the client is more likely to deal with the vendor directly if she has paid him for the goods. The designer is also less likely to be blamed by the client for problems with the vendor if he is not involved with payment.

Many commercial clients retain designers only for their creative services. Some have their own purchasing agents and handle all purchases directly. In these situations, the aforementioned clause is appropriate.

Some designers further minimize their involvement in the purchasing process, especially when purchasing on a cost-plus basis. They add the following statement:

> Our role is to expedite and double-check your purchases and to follow up in case of loss or damage. Please bear in mind that we do everything possible to keep the furniture deliveries on schedule, but we cannot answer for those vendors who do not make the promised delivery dates. Just before move-in, we compose a punch list of outstanding items and concentrate on expediting the delivery and installation of the same.

This statement may seem unimportant at first glance, but keep in mind how some clients may react when furniture deliveries are a month or more late or when workmen suddenly fail to appear to complete a job in progress. Most clients understand that such problems are bound to crop up on a project, but others become enraged and blame their designers for things that are totally beyond their control.

The preceding example is a "disclaiming statement," placed in a letter of agreement to minimize as much as possible the designer's responsibilities for purchases. Some designers refuse to disclaim, believing that it is part of their responsibility to their clients to remain somewhat liable themselves.

I disagree. A designer may place himself in a risk-free position from a legal standpoint without abdicating any of his professional responsibilities. Disclaimer statements help keep the designer off the hook in case the client decides not to pay balances on approved and ordered merchandise. This subject is discussed in detail in Chapter 14.

Outside Purchases

After purchases have been discussed, you might consider using the following optional, but interesting, clause:

> It is understood and agreed that all furnishings and design services will be purchased to implement the floor plan and other design plans submitted by our office. In that connection, we will agree to assist you in the purchase of the foregoing at our cost. However, in the event any such purchases are made or contracted for during the tenure of this agreement without our services or consultation, said purchases will be included in the total cost used as a basis on which all commissions are assessed.

The reason for this insertion is fairly obvious, but can be best illustrated by the following hypothetical situation.

Suppose you and your client decide to purchase an antique armoire for the bedroom. For two months you both scour antique dealers, furniture stores, and auction galleries but find nothing that seems to fit the client's taste or budget. Then, a month later, when visiting his residence for an installation, you see an armoire in the bedroom that looks amazingly similar to a number of pieces you had seen when shopping together. The client explains that it was a gift, or an impulsive purchase, or manufactures another story. According to the clause we are discussing, the commission is payable to you regardless of how the armoire was finally acquired.

To prevent any misunderstanding about what the client already owned before your work began, after your letter of agreement is signed, request a list of any furniture that may have a potential use in the project.

If you are charging a flat fee, obviously you won't need a clause of this nature. The client's purchases have nothing to do with your compensation, so how they are made has little to do with your financial arrangements. However, when your compensation is tied in to the goods and services bought, monitor the source of the purchases. If your client refuses to agree to a clause of this type, be wary. He obviously intends to get as much free mileage out of your ideas as possible.

When I suggest this clause to designers, they invariably ask two questions. The first is, "This clause covers only purchases made while I am working on the project. After I finish, the client can use my ideas and buy anything without paying my commission. Is there anything I can do about this?"

The answer, of course, is no. No contract, no matter how foolproof, can completely protect you from a dishonest client. However, most clients are not dishonest.

If you are designing a large project, generally, your client will want as much of your input and supervision as possible. He'll want you to place the furniture as well as select it. The more dependent the client is on your design judgment, the less likely he'll want an incomplete project before you leave.

The second question is, "Have you ever caught a client of a designer making an outside purchase, and then inserted the purchase into the decorator's budget so that he got his commission on that item?"

The answer to that question is also no. But I'll tell you what *has* happened. Many designers constantly complain about losing commissions on outside purchases. Placing this clause in their letters of agreement for new clients stopped these problems. The clause is more for prevention than to cure. When prospective clients read this clause, they are put on guard immediately. They know that their designer will be watching all purchases as they are made, which is generally enough to discourage any unsupervised purchasing.

Unfortunately, some designers have reported the following set of circumstances to me on a number of occasions. A designer, who charges a design fee for a presentation, and cost-plus for all purchases of goods, is engaged by a client and paid an initial design fee.

A visual presentation is prepared with samples and pictures of proposed furniture and furnishings, in addition to a complete floor plan. After the presentation is accepted, the client decides to engage contractors and complete design "backgrounds" (built-in cabinetry, lighting, mirror work, etc.) prior to making major purchases of goods. Budgetary reasons are often the excuse for delay. Once the backgrounds are completed, supervised by the designer for an hourly fee, the designer is discharged.

The client then uses the designer's specifications and makes all the purchases. Often, the designer has taken the client shopping to various showrooms, and the client is now familiar with the goods the designer specified for the presentation.

Usually, this type of client owns a business and has a "resale number" or other identification that qualifies the client as a purchaser for wholesale sources. Designers then complain, "My client stole all my sources for a small fee. She cheated me out of my commission. Can I sue?"

The answer is, usually, no. The client paid for a presentation, including a floor plan. Obviously, the client misled the designer, allowing her to think that she would make all the purchases and complete the project. However, the client was too smart for her.

These designers ask whether there is a clause that can prevent such situations. I don't know of one. In this case, the client misleads the designer but doesn't do anything illegal. However, I do have other suggestions to help prevent this from happening to you.

Screen clients carefully. Before providing any specifications about purchases, look for certain signs. Does your client own a business? Has she made purchases of design merchandise before? Is she an "amateur designer"? Is she pressing you to shop at showrooms without an intention to make purchases? Clients who intend to make their own purchases usually give themselves away.

If you're suspicious that a client will use you in this way, act accordingly. Don't take a client to any showrooms for major purchases unless she tells you that she's ready to buy. When showing samples of fabrics or pictures of furniture, do not identify the showroom, colors, or order numbers. If a client presses you for technical information about various items but is not willing to provide deposits, you'll realize that your client intends to make her own purchases.

Includable Items

Designers often work with architects, in both commercial and residential projects, which gives rise to a series of problems. These are discussed later when the role of the interior designer is more fully explored.

When working with other professionals, particularly if your fee is determined on a cost plus basis, it is important to clarify which items are included in your budget for commission purposes. Because architects and builders supply various standard features, list any items subject to your design fees that could possibly enter a gray area, as the following example illustrates.

> With respect to includable items for our budget, it is agreed and understood that all items for the interior that are specified by our firm are included in the budget for commission purposes. This includes, but is not limited to, the following:
>
> 1. Custom plumbing and hardware fixtures
> 2. Lighting and switching
> 3. Wall coverings and interior painting schedule
> 4. Window treatments
> 5. Flooring and floor coverings
> 6. All cabinetwork, including kitchen cabinets, custom vanities, buffets, bookshelves, banquettes and upholstery, and custom interior doors

If this list is included in your agreement, be prepared for an argument. The architect and general contractor are going to want these items in *their* budgets, not yours. An interior designer is often involved with others who have, to some degree, overlapping roles, so setting up budget boundaries may involve a power struggle.

If your client objects, for example, to including custom plumbing fixtures in your budget, then state, "If you don't want those items in my budget, then I won't design your bathrooms." But, your client may answer, "Will you confer with my architect and use your input? I'll pay you by the hour for your time."

Another example concerns flooring. Your client may tell you, "The contractor is installing wooden flooring in certain rooms, marble in others, and carpeting in the bedrooms. Will you help me select the marble and design a pattern for the wooden floors?" You might answer, "I will charge by the hour for helping you with the marble and wood floors.

However, I want the opportunity to purchase all the carpeting on a cost-plus basis, the same method I am using to purchase your furniture."

If you think you will make enough money on the rest of the job, it may be worth your while to accede to your client's wishes. It's strictly a subjective decision. However, you must clarify your position before you start. Once you begin work, it is too late to bargain for everything to which you're entitled.

Fees

Regardless of how you charge your clients, provide a direct and complete explanation of what your fees will be in the letter of agreement. If you are vague or evasive, the client might hesitate to sign because the approach appears unbusinesslike or misleading.

I advise my designer clients never to *begin* their letters with a discussion of fees. Although there are no rigid rules of sequence, I suggest the following:

1. Introduction
2. Specify design areas
3. Outline project development
4. Purchases
5. Outside purchasing clause
6. Purchases included in budget (when necessary)

First, tell your client what you are going to do for him. Then let him know how much it will cost. If you intend to charge on a retail basis, state this as follows:

> In consideration for my services, you will be charged retail or list price, quoted by vendors and craftsmen, for goods and services that I will purchase on your behalf.

When you present the agreement to your client, explain orally exactly what "charging retail" means. Explain that "retail" or "list" is the price of goods and services charged by vendors and craftsmen. As a designer, you are entitled to a professional discount or wholesale price. The discount, the difference between the wholesale and the retail price, will be your fee for services.

The dynamics of charging retail, which have changed considerably over the years, are discussed in Chapter 2. However, this method of charging has by no means disappeared as a viable fee structure used by many designers.

Here is an example of how many successful designers, who charge a percentage of goods and design services, set forth the cost-plus method:

> My fee for work under this agreement is projected at $45,000, i.e., thirty percent (30%) of a projected budget of $150,000. $5000 is payable upon signing this agreement and is not refundable. The balance is payable in accordance with our schedule of payments, attached to this agreement. In the event, during the tenure of this agreement, you determine to discontinue the use of our services on this project, all commissions will be due and payable with respect to any purchase orders of goods and design services that have been approved by you pursuant to your written acknowledgement on such purchase orders that have been issued by our office.
>
> It is understood that if the total cost of your project increases because of additions approved in writing by you, our fee shall increase proportionately, i.e., 30 percent additional design fee on all approved purchases to implement the additions to the project beyond $150,000. This written approval shall be indicated by your signature on all purchase orders exceeding the project budget.

This is a very sophisticated way of discussing your fee when charging on a cost-plus basis. It outlines the minimum cost of your services and approximates the total cost of the project, based on the client's needs and your design concept. Designers are often reluctant to be this specific so early in the relationship for fear of scaring the client away. They prefer to whet his appetite and lead him into spending money as the job continues. However, a minimum figure will dispel any notions that a design miracle can be worked for substantially less. Telling the basic truth at this time can head off any future misunderstandings once design plans are complete and the budget is prepared.

Some designers feel that although it is important to be candid with a client about the budget, it is not necessary to discuss it in the letter of agreement. If you share this point of view, modify the first sentence of the example as follows:

> My fee for work under this agreement is 30 percent of all purchases of goods and design services specified for your project by my office.

Of course, the sentence about the retainer should remain. Most designers insist on retainers or "advance fee deposits" from clients. Because a large percentage of design time is devoted to early client interviews and preparation of initial design plans, money should change hands upon the signing of the agreement. Whatever the fee structure is, don't make the deposit a "token" amount. Clients can always decide not to continue the project even after the preliminary work is done. If a sufficient deposit has not been collected to cover a good portion of time, you may end up working for free.

If you have not estimated the project cost, you cannot establish a payment schedule. If you estimate a fee and the project has a certain "life" (e.g., six months), you can establish a schedule for the client to pay your fee. Of course, if you exceed the budget with the client's approval, you can bill the additional fees as they are incurred. At least, with a schedule, you have set up a basic method of payment.

> My fee for work under this agreement is 30 percent of all purchases of goods and design services specified for your project by my office. $5,000 is payable upon signing this agreement and shall be nonrefundable. Further, it shall be credited toward subsequent design fees incurred. The balance of my fee shall be billed in conjunction with issuing your purchase orders. Payments for design fees shall be billed as deposits, and balances are required by contractors and vendors. In addition, you will receive a monthly statement.

The second paragraph of the "cost-plus" example, discussing purchases exceeding the budget, has been omitted from this clause. It is not necessary here, since a budget has not been discussed. In fact, most designers do not discuss budgets in their agreements, particulary for residential projects. Accordingly, this clause is the most popular one among my design-clients when charging on a cost plus basis.

Note in the preceding example that the retainer is being credited against commissions for future purchases. This is strictly a matter of choice. Many designers charge a retainer as an initial flat fee and do not credit any commissions against the retainer.

Always state that your design commissions are due and payable on all purchase orders that have been approved. Whether or not the budget has been projected, the following sentence is important to your letter:

> In the event, during the tenure of this agreement, you determine to discontinue the use of our services on this project, all commissions will be due and payable with respect to any purchase orders of goods and design commissions that have been approved by you in writing.

I cannot overemphasize the importance of this stipulation. The discussion of your fee has been tied in with "fee billing." Fee billing, as the examples illustrate, can be done according to a schedule of payments when there's a budget forecast or in conjunction with purchase orders when a budget isn't mentioned.

Be certain that your client understands that a regular system of billings will be provided by your office. This clause will prevent the loss of commissions on purchases as long as selections have been approved, regardless of delivery, should your client decide to dismiss you in the middle of a project.

Realistically, it's very hard to collect commissions from clients, even on approved purchase orders, once you've been dismissed from a job. Most clients will not pay legitimate bills to a designer if they've fired him from a project. These clients will devise endless reasons to justify default- ing on their obligations. Frequently, if the designer really wants to collect the fees, he will have to sue the client.

Moreover, if a client cancels an order for goods, even though they were approved, the designer will have a difficult time collecting a com- mission on the deposit.

A designer once told me how he lost substantial commissions in this type of situation. He had specified a large dining table base for a client's dining room, which was delivered and accepted. Separately, he had ordered a marble top that rested on the base. Although the top was fine, the client didn't like it. Subsequently, the client purchased a granite top. That was returned also. The client then purchased a glass top. That too was ultimately rejected, and the client finally purchased a marble top, in a different color from the original choice.

All these selections were made with the client's approval, but the client would pay the designer a commission only for the final marble top that was accepted. The designer complained, "I purchased four different tabletops, and was paid only one commission." The designer settled for one commission because he knew that if he forced the issue with his client, he would be dismissed from the lucrative project. Legally, as well as logically, the designer was entitled to four separate commissions but, for business reasons, settled for only one.

If you are charging a "fixed" or flat fee, state the amount of the design fee and the intervals at which the payments are to be made. In many cases, designers who charge flat fees insert a cutoff date for their services. If the job has not been completed by that date, an additional monthly fee will be imposed. The following is a popular flat-fee clause:

> As indicated by our previous consultations and the nature of our ser- vices as described earlier in the agreement, a great deal of our design services will be devoted to redesigning your existing interior. In view of this, our fee for work under this agreement will be a comprehensive flat

fee in the amount of $15,000. It shall be payable as follows:

$2500	Upon Signing	$2500	March 1st
$2500	January 1st	$2500	April 1st
$2500	February 1st	$2500	May 1st

Each installment shall be considered payment for services rendered when received and shall be non-refundable. It is contemplated that the project should be completed by June 1st. If you decide to continue to use our services after June 1st, a monthly fee of $1,250 will be required until you feel our design work is complete.

Note that I used the phrase "redesigning your existing interior" before leading into the "flat fee." Most designers hesitate to charge on a flat-fee basis, especially for residential projects, unless there is a good reason. In this example, the client had hired another designer previously and was unhappy with the results—not an uncommon situation. The present designer was requested to redesign the existing interior. Because all the important purchases had already been made, it would have been unprofitable to charge on a retail or cost-plus basis. Remember, when discussing flat fees in your letter, it is sometimes a good idea to offer some kind of brief rationale to clarify why that method was selected.

The preceding example specifies that each payment is "nonrefundable." Note, too, that if the job in question is not completed by "June 1st," regardless of the reason, the designer will lose money on the project. This clause protects him from any number of variables that could delay the project and keep him working indefinitely without additional compensation. It also encourages the client to make decisions to keep things moving.

Any plans of this nature must be clearly spelled out in the letter of agreement. Don't quote a flat fee without a cutoff date and expect to be paid extra if the job drags on.

For commercial or contract jobs, a common method of billing uses a "multiplier." When a multiplier is used, the number of hours expended is multiplied by an hourly rate times a multiplier. A typical multiplier is defined as DPE (Direct Personnel Expenses), which is explained in the following paragraphs.

Direct Personnel Expenses

This is a clause used by design firms that charge on a DPE basis:

We propose to be compensated for services on a time-card basis at a rate of 2.5 times DPE with a not-to-exceed amount of $20,000. All out-of-pocket expenses for reproductions, travel, postage, messengers, long-distance telephone calls and report typing are to be reimbursed at cost. If inflation continues at its present rate, our firm will increase staff salaries to adjust to cost-of-living increases after four months. This cost-of-living increase would increase the not-to-exceed amount to $23,000.

Direct Personnel Expenses are defined as the direct salaries for all our technical personnel engaged on the project and the portion of the cost of their mandatory and customary contributions and benefits related thereto, such as employment taxes, and other statutory employee benefits, insurance, sick leave, holidays, vacations, pensions, and similar contributions and benefits.

If, after your written approval of documents, you wish to change them for any reason, any additional services required by us for the change will be performed at a rate of 2.5 times DPE. These are addenda fees, which are in addition to the base fee.

Most smaller firms do not use the DPE method. However, you should know that it exists and how it works, as your competition may be using it. It is more fully explained in Chapter 2. However, there are some observations to be made about this example. Since charging DPE is a function of hourly time rates, some clients may be nervous about salary increases over the life of a project, especially when they are being billed on a multiple. Therefore, note that the design firm using this clause included an "upset figure" of $23,000. Although the project was not scheduled to cost that much, at least the client could be certain that design fees would not exceed that amount.

Note also that the term *Direct Personnel Expenses* is defined directly in the agreement. When charging on this multiple, or any other design multiple, be sure to fully define it in the agreement. Explaining it orally to the client is generally insufficient. In corporate situations, contracts usually must be approved by officers, directors, and other personnel. Therefore, a commercial agreement should be as self-explanatory as possible.

There is a growing movement among designers, both commercial and residential, to charge clients on an hourly basis. In the 1980s, professional design showrooms for goods and services began to be eclipsed by a plethora of retail stores where consumers made direct purchases. In these situations, residential designers accompany their clients and charge on an hourly basis for their advice.

Many large clients have their own in-house purchasing departments. For that reason, many commercial designers are retained to prepare design plans and specifications only. Their services are frequently contracted for on an hourly or flat-fee basis.

Another method of charging on a commercial basis is to use a square footage charge, often coupled with a percentage of the project budget. The following is a typical clause for a relatively small commercial project:

> You have advised us that the amount of space to be designed in your office is 10,000 net rentable square feet. Our fee for work under this agreement is as follows:
>
> $1.50 per square foot for preparation of all design plans including cabinet work, elevations, reflected ceiling plans, painting and wall covering schedule, etc., plus ten percent (10%) of the cost of all purchases of goods and design services specified by our office to implement the plans. A retainer of $7500 will be due upon signing the agreement. A second payment of $7500 is payable upon acceptance of our plans. The balance of our fees will be billed in conjunction with the issuance of our purchase orders.

Notice that the retainer is one half the cost of preparing the design plans. The balance of that cost is due upon delivery and acceptance of the plans. In commercial situations, designers are frequently required to prepare a complete set of design plans. Often, the retainer is one half of the designer's fee for preparing the plans. The balance is due upon delivery of the plans. The percentage charged by designers for purchases of goods and design services is generally lower for commercial projects than for residential clients.

The preceding example is a variation of the cost-plus basis, as discussed earlier. In fact, there are an infinite number of variations on charging procedures and their presentation in a letter of agreement.

Some of these methods may be familiar to you. Perhaps you are already using them in your letters of agreement. Most likely, you have your own variations. However, regardless of how you charge, make sure to structure a thorough and professional-looking discussion of fees in your agreement.

Disbursements

Always discuss disbursements. If they're not mentioned, many clients assume that all incidental expenses, which can be considerable, are included in the design fee. They may refuse to pay later when billed for extra charges if this obligation is not made clear. Specify all additional charges that are not included in your fee, as in the following example:

> In addition to our fee, you shall pay for actual and reasonable disbursements for this project, including the following: blueprints, reproductions (photostats), messenger service, long-distance phone calls, and

local travel expenses. If outside consultants (such as air conditioning, lighting, or structural engineers, etc.) are needed, their fees will be paid by the client. If, after your written approval of the basic plans, you wish to change them, any additional services required by us for the change will be performed at a rate of $75 per hour. All such disbursements will be billed on a monthly basis, except for outside consultants, who will be retained only upon your approval.

The first sentence of this example is self-explanatory. These expenses typcially occur on all design projects. Outside consultants, however, are an entirely different matter. After you have examined your prospective client's space, you'll have a fairly good idea of whether an outside consultant will be needed. If there is a reasonable chance that one will be required, provide for payment as an additional disbursement. If consultants are not required, leave that sentence out of the agreement; it will only confuse and mislead your client.

One of my designer clients always used the "outside consultants clause" in his "disbursements" section as standard language, whether it was necessary or not, against my advice. A prospective client consulted him for a decorating job, but when she saw that provision, her first reaction was, "What is this designer getting me into? I just want to buy furniture." After that incident, he used the clause only when necessary.

The fee for changes in basic plans after a client's written approval should be on an hourly basis. In an interior design project for a residential client, for example, a designer should not prepare design drawings for cabinets until the client approves design sketches. A complete set of drawings, prepared by draftsmen, can cost a great deal. These are then submitted to the client for his written approval. At this stage, the designer should not pay for extensive changes without being reimbursed. Clients have been known to change their minds about everything once a design has been completed. If they do, the designer should be paid for the additional drafting charges; otherwise, he'll begin losing money on the project even before he starts to implement the plans.

Some designers use renderings as a visual aid to sell their initial presentation even though they are expensive and time-consuming. Such designers often stipulate that if additional renderings are requested in the event of extensive design revisions, the client will be billed.

Additional Fees

Clients often change their minds about design plans after they've been completed and approved. For example, after a designer has completed all purchase orders for a traditional living room, a client may have a change of heart. A friend or relative may convince her to use a more modern approach. Then the client will call and cancel—it's not what she really wants. It may have taken the designer months to design the room, shop for the fabrics and furniture, prepare a floor plan, and confer with the subcontractors. If the designer is being paid on a cost-plus basis, she may have to start from scratch with little financial gain to show for all her work.

To prevent this type of situation, the following clause is used:

> If, after your written approval of purchases of goods and design services, you determine to make substitutions or changes, 30 percent additional design fee shall be payable on all these approved changes.

Obviously, this is a tough clause to negotiate. I make my clients aware of it but advise them that some customers will oppose it. When a prospective client sees this clause, she may think, "Do I have to pay double if I don't buy the first thing he shows me?" In other words, you may be creating suspicion. However, if you don't use this clause, and your client changes his mind, you may work without being paid if you're charging on a retail or cost-plus basis.

PAYMENT

If payments are not being made during the project, state that you will stop work until the account is brought up to date, as illustrated in the following example:

> If payment to our office should be withheld longer than fifteen (15) days after billing, we reserve the right to stop progress until such time as remuneration is forthcoming.

Stopping work is one of the most effective ways to make sure you get paid. It's a drastic measure, especially if you're in the middle of supervising contractors and your client advises that she is temporarily short of cash. In that case, you will have to decide whether to continue. However, warn your client about your intentions before you are retained. Then, if payments are withheld, while you are implored to continue, your answer can simply be, "I'm very sorry. It's simply office policy not to work on jobs on which payments are in arrears. That was made clear from the inception of our relationship."

Of course, this can be a very gray area, and you must consider the situation carefully. If the job is lucrative, and the client has paid you substantial fees, think twice before stopping work. If the amount of the arrears is substantial, and your client is a habitual offender, it makes it easier to walk away from the job.

PHOTOGRAPHING PRIVILEGE

A designer's stock-in-trade is his portfolio and the publicity from his published work. Reserve the right, if possible, to photograph your completed work, as illustrated in the following clause:

> We reserve the right exclusively to photograph our design work after it is completed and to give permission for use of the photographs in any publication, although your name will not be used without your consent.

Some clients shun publicity and refuse to permit their interiors to be photographed even when their names are not used. The overwhelming majority, however, will be more than delighted to see their names and environments in print. In fact, the presence of this clause is often impressive. Some clients will be thrilled to think that you can take their space and make it "magazine worthy."

ARBITRATION

Most businesspeople, including interior designers, at least once during their careers, are faced with the prospect of being sued or having to sue someone. An arbitration clause in a letter of agreement can usually prevent a lawsuit between designer and client. The advantages and disadvantages of arbitration are discussed in Chapter 11. Keep in mind for now that the following clause compels any disputes between you and your client to be settled in an informal, administrative hearing instead of in a courtroom:

> Any dispute or disagreement between parties arising out of or relating to this agreement shall be settled by arbitration in (your state) under the rules then obtaining of the American Arbitration Association, and judgment upon the award may be entered in any court having jurisdiction.

PAYMENT SCHEDULE

As discussed in the section entitled "Fees," your client may pay you pursuant to a fixed schedule of payments, depending on how you charge and the way the agreement is structured. That section includes a sample payment schedule, which is incorporated into the body of the letter of agreement. Usually, however, payment schedules are provided in an appendix that requires the client's signature and the date, just as in the agreement itself. The following is an abbreviated schedule:

Schedule of Payments

Upon Signing	$1500
February 1st	$2000
March 1st	$2000
April 1st	$2000

_____

Client's Signature   Dated: January 1st

_____

Designer's Signature   Dated: January 1st

The amount requested "upon signing" is the retainer, which should have been requested earlier in the letter of agreement. The amount does not necessarily have to bear any relationship to the payments themselves. Generally, the remaining payments are the same, although they can be varied, depending on the situation.

As I have emphasized, once a payment has been made, make certain that you don't have to refund the money. Your letter should state that each payment, including the retainer, is nonrefundable. On the Schedule of Payments, however, do not insert the word *nonrefundable*. That word appears so glaringly obvious there that I prefer to slip it into the letter during, for example, the discussion of fees.

CLOSING

The final paragraph is of the standard type used to conclude a letter of agreement for most purposes. It can vary in style but should contain certain elements, as shown in this example:

If the above meets with your approval, your signature below will indicate your acceptance of the terms of the agreement and will indicate your authorization to proceed with work. Kindly return the duplicate copy to us. Of course, if you have any questions, please don't hesitate to call.

We are looking forward to working with you.

Sincerely,
Designer's Name
Design Firm, Inc.

Designer's Signature   Dated: January 1st

Send the client two signed copies of the agreement. Although you do not specify in the closing that you won't start the project until you receive the first payment (the retainer) don't begin work until you have it. If your new client sends back the agreement without the check and then starts calling to make appointments and ask questions, advise him, pleasantly, that you never start projects prior to the receipt of a retainer. Even if you know the check will be sent later, it is important to set a precedent for prompt payment, particularly at the outset of your relationship.

CONCLUSION

The letter of agreement is the cornerstone of the designer-client relationship. As the job progresses and difficulties occur, you and your client will refer to it to clarify responsibilities and obligations. Of course, you want to avoid statements that will come back to haunt you, but don't leave gaps or create ambiguities out of fear of putting things in writing. Unfortunately, only personal experience can guide you, but these suggestions will help you along.

As your business evolves and your techniques become more sophisticated, your letter of agreement will change. Even a neophyte, however, should be certain that it is professional.

2

CHARGING A CLIENT

Alternative methods of charging a client were introduced in Chapter 1. Their manner of presentation was also discussed, in the event the designer had already selected a method to use. Chapter 2 discusses *how* to choose a method, the most important issue.

How a designer charges very frequently determines whether or not a client retains him. Most design firms develop a standard method of charging. However, the circumstances of prospective jobs can vary so markedly that one standard can rarely cover all situations. Many prospective clients, especially for large projects, consult with several designers before making a choice. For that reason, your fee must be competitive and your method of charging responsive to the demands of the job.

VARIABLES INVOLVED

An almost infinite number of variables can influence your decision about which method to use, either as a general policy or in specific situations. The following list, by no means exhaustive, presents a number of these variables:

1. **General type of work.** Does your firm do more decorating than designing? Do you specify furnishings essentially, or plan designs with architectural drawings? Designers who perform decorative work, for example, often charge "retail." Designers who perform architecturally oriented work frequently charge on a cost-plus basis.

2. **Type of job.** Some specific jobs require more decorating than designing. The same designer may charge retail for a project that involves only purchasing furniture but may charge cost-plus for a project using a lot of built-ins, requiring contractors and cabinetmakers.

3. **Size of job.** On very large jobs or commercial jobs, some clients will pay only:

   a. A preset flat fee;

   b. By the hour; or

   c. Cost-plus, with a low percentage for the purchases of goods and design services.

   On smaller projects, especially residential jobs, the percentage can be higher if cost-plus is used. Charging retail may be selected so that the designer will be paid on an item-by-item basis. Many large commercial firms bill only on an hourly rate.

4. **Size of design staff.** Designers with large offices often charge on a time-card or hourly basis, increased by a multiple to ensure that they can meet their expenses. Smaller offices sometimes gamble on a larger return, basing their charges on the size of the purchases made by their clients by using the retail or cost-plus method.

5. **Credibility of client.** Occasionally, a designer may want to undertake a project even if he is unsure as to whether the client will really pay the fee. In that case, he should charge a flat design fee, with a considerable retainer to be collected before starting work. Some designers, on infrequent occasions, have requested the total fee in advance.

6. **Residential or commercial project.** A decision often relies on this factor alone. Some designers charge retail for residential projects and cost-plus for commercial projects. There has been an increasing tendency to charge cost-plus for residential work today as well. As mentioned previously, many commercial firms have abandoned the cost-plus method and charge only by the hour.

7. **Project and client variance.** Projects and clients can vary so markedly that some designers will not specify how they charge until they receive all the necessary input. The most important factor in a large commercial project may be the party selected to make the purchases. In a hotel project, for example, if the client uses a purchasing agent instead of the designer, the designer may charge a flat fee, a monthly fixed fee, or by the hour, particularly if he has no way to keep track of purchasing costs.

8. **Consistency.** Some designers always charge the same way regardless of the type or size of project. Using one method, they feel, lends credibility and consistency to their image. A uniform

method can be easier to operate with and assures prospective clients that they will be offered a standard, fair price. Consistency does help, but no rule requires following one procedure all the time.

9. **Combination of methods.** Depending on the situation, designers often combine methods. Some residential designers charge cost-plus on all design services and retail on all purchases of goods. Other designers experiment for years with different combinations until they find those that are right for specific types of projects.

METHODS OF CHARGING DESIGN FEES

The following paragraphs describe the methods of charging design fees that are used most frequently and that have worked successfully for my own designer clients.

Charging Retail

Residential interior decorators have traditionally favored charging retail, and this method remains extremely popular. Charging retail can encourage clients to use designer services. Clients will feel that money is spent only on goods, because the designer's percentage, which typically ranges from 20 percent to 50 percent, is built in. In fact, the client is often right. If the merchandise is purchased in a showroom servicing mainly design professionals, clients pay retail, with or without the advice of a designer. Such showrooms, available to the trade, quote only retail prices to consumers and refuse to reveal wholesale costs. This prevents clients from discovering the amount of the designer's markup.

In the past 10 years there has been a tremendous shift away from this method for a number of reasons. Designers are no longer reluctant to quote a separate design fee, because our society is now accustomed to paying fees for an endless array of new services. A designer is now viewed by the vast upper-middle class as necessary in the creation of a home, and, accordingly, design fees have become an accepted expense.

Designers have naturally jumped at the opportunity to charge a separate design fee so that they can discuss wholesale or "net" prices with clients. This removes an element of secrecy from the designer-client relationship. Many clients paying retail always wanted to find out what something really costs. Now they can know.

Today's residential designers have become more "installation oriented." Budgets are being allocated for cabinetwork, sophisticated lighting, mirror work, and other construction. Designers can more easily discuss competitive pricing between vendors and contractors with clients when they can talk in "net" terms.

Retail is frequently charged under several sets of circumstances. The first is included in a traditional residential project. It usually involves purchases of antiques, accessories, lamps, draperies, and fabrics but not much cabinetwork, removal of walls and so forth. The "retail designer" largely deals with decorator showrooms and craftsmen, rather than with architects and contractors. The second set of circumstances occurs when the designer uses a combination method of charging. Cost-plus may be charged for all interior design services—custom painting and cabinetwork—and retail may be charged for purchasing furniture, fabrics, and accessories.

A third set of circumstances arises when a designer and client shop at a commercial furniture store, "open to the public." In recent years, many trendy furniture stores, selling an entire range of home furnishings and accessories, have opened to the public and provide in-house design services for free. Some offer discounts on retail prices to interior designers who shop with their clients. Although it is usually more profitable for designers to purchase through "trade" sources, many clients resist. If clients are budget minded, designers have no choice other than to accompany them. Generally, the discounts for designers are minimal, and designers attempt to purchase as little as possible from these establishments.

Charging Cost-Plus

Charging on the basis of a percentage of the wholesale cost of goods and design services (hence "cost-*plus*") was originally favored by architects. As the interior designer's approach has become more architectural, this, in a sense, has become a "modern" method of charging.

The question is, What percentage? The range is anywhere from 10 percent to 40 percent. The "10-percenters" are usually amateurs who shop for their friends and neighbors, adding a 10 percent surchage to all purchases. On commercial jobs, with budgets exceeding a million dollars, percentages sometimes deescalate to as low as 5 percent.

Most interior designers charge a minimum of 25 percent, at least on the first $50,000 of purchases. Even an office with a relatively low fixed overhead finds this to be the minimum percentage to make a job profitable. In commercial situations, the percentage frequently drops to between 10 percent and 15 percent, depending on budget size.

When residential designers become fairly successful and can afford to risk losing new business by raising fees, they often increase their percentage to 30 percent. Thirty percent will no longer raise eyebrows among clients who want well-established residential designers with good reputations. Many famous designers are now charging from 35 percent to 40 percent. This league of designers generally uses a project supervisor (i.e., a junior designer) for each client project, although the actual design work is done by the firm's principals. These firms often have very high operating overheads because of the many in-house personnel—draftsmen, senior and junior designers, architects, and so forth.

Percentages deescalate quickly for commercial jobs. Here, interior designers are competing with architects, who traditionally charge lower percentages. Then, too, jobs for corporate clients progress much faster. These clients tend to be much more business oriented and unemotional about selections and execution; design decisions move briskly. (Residential clients often take weeks to make up their minds.)

Sometimes designers charge two percentages for a single commercial job. A typical situation is a job involving several floors of office space. Fifteen percent may be charged for the design of all general office space, including drafting charges. Twenty-five percent may be charged for heavily designed spaces such as main reception areas, the corporate board room, and executive offices. In general, a high percentage for corporate jobs is 20 percent. Higher commercial fees are usually charged only when the client wants the space treated in a very customized, residential format.

If using a percentage is your sole method of charging, its size should depend on the competition, your experience and reputation, office overhead, and the amount of work on hand. Once you set a specific figure, don't vary it from one client to the next for jobs in the same category. Designers who have been known to do this lose credibility. If a large initial design fee is charged for a presentation, the percentage is often less.

An advantage of this method is the option of using the "direct payment technique" for purchases. The designer prepares all the purchase orders with specifications, but it is the client's obligation to pay for the goods and services directly. (See "Purchases" in Chapter 1). This usually cannot be done in charging retail, because the client pays the designer in full as the retail vendor.

Many designers insist that their clients purchase directly (making certain, of course, that they receive wholesale prices) for a number of reasons. First, because the designer does not make the purchases as an agent, his clerical work and bookkeeping will be much less involved. Second, if the client cancels a purchase after making the down payment or deposit, the designer will not be caught in the middle, as the agent, to obtain the payment balance or reclaim the deposit. Third, if defects are discovered in merchandise or design services, the client will look to the vendor or con-tractor, instead of to the designer, to make amends.

Some designers find the direct payment method unprofessional. They believe that if they don't make the purchases themselves, they will lose control of the job. Moreover, because commissions are earned on purchases, they feel a responsibility to maintain their middleman's role in the event of order cancellation or faulty workmanship or materials. However, a designer can still maintain the same supervisory role even if the client makes purchases directly. Legally, he will avoid certain liabili-ties (discussed in Chapter 4), which makes the use of this technique worth considering.

Charging cost-plus has its obvious advantages. The designer receives uniform compensation for all expenditures. With retail, the percentage varies. Further, a client paying retail may hesitate to make purchases rec-ommended by his designer for fear of an ulterior financial motive. Cost-plus eliminates the mystery through full disclosure about all fees.

Charging a Flat Fee

Stipulating a prearranged fixed fee for creative and supervisory services is the easiest method of charging. When cost-plus or retail is used, the designer is cast in the role of a merchant. A client realizes that the fee depends on how much is spent, so she may sometimes suspect his designer of excessive profit taking. When clients are so suspicious of their designer and wonder "how much he's going to make off me," the rela-tionship is often doomed.

A flat fee also guarantees the design fee regardless of budget cuts. Occasionally, a client plans to design an entire residence and later decides that she can't afford it. If a flat fee is specified, the designer must be paid even if the client backs out after all the groundwork and conceptual stages have been completed. This approach minimizes risk.

Conversely, this method can also work to the designer's disadvan-tage. If a client *doubles* a budget in the middle of a project, the designer will lose windfall profits that he would have made with retail or cost-plus charges. For this reason, I usually advise against fixed fees unless there are special circumstances. Most clients usually end up spending more than they intended to, not less. That's how designers make more money.

Designers can lose profits on a flat fee if they have to design, redesign, and redesign again. A difficult client who uses up too much design time can cause a real problem. It is generally difficult to renegotiate flat fees once they have been established, so be cautious about quoting a price.

Generally, fixed fees work best when a designer knows the client and her behavior pattern. Then again, you can't really predict how a client is going to act, especially in a residential job, even if you have worked with her previously.

There is one safety valve applicable to flat fees, as mentioned in **"Fees,"** in Chapter 1. A final cutoff date should be stipulated for rendering services at the specified fee. After that date, an additional fee can be imposed on a time basis, usually monthly. If, for example, a project is not completed in six months, regardless of the reason, and services were to be provided for that period for $15,000 ($2500 per month), an additional monthly fee of $1500 might be charged until the designer's work is finished.

A cutoff date also helps to bring a job to an end. It urges the client to encourage completion instead of prolonging the project with changes, delays, and indecisiveness. Clients are generally so anxious to avoid paying design fees that they will act expeditiously in order to finish as soon as possible. Of course, if, at the end of the six-month period, a designer needs only to supervise late deliveries and other odds and ends, he won't charge any extra.

The imposition of additional charges after the cutoff date requires careful consideration. In the example cited previously, six months was enough to complete the project. The designer was very careful not to shortchange the client for the flat fee. As the period was generous, the additional monthly charge ($1500) was only 60 percent as much as the initial monthly charge ($2500). As a rule of thumb, additional monthly charges are approximately 50 percent of the initial monthly charges when the initial fee is large enough and prorated monthly. Of course, the easiest way to impose an additional monthly charge is to charge by the hour.

It's difficult to tell a designer how to set a flat fee, and the whole process generally makes designers insecure. A figure too high may scare the client away, but a figure too low will not be profitable. One intangible, of course, is the client. If the job looks smooth and the client amiable, the designer doesn't have to worry as much about getting rid of the project for a specified number of dollars.

There are two basic methods for setting flat fees. The first is to estimate the size of the budget once the scope of the project is clear, then determine the amount of the design fee if cost-plus were being charged. The second method is to estimate the amount of time the project will require and put a price on the value of the services.

Try using both methods on the same project when setting your own flat fee, and see how closely the figures coincide. Comparisons of this sort can act as a system of checks and balances.

Surprisingly, some of my most successful clients never use specific methods when deliberating on the size of a flat fee. They have the experience to assess a project and say, "This is the amount the job is worth, and that's how much I want for doing it." These designers have worked on analogous projects before, and they can come to rapid conclusions. I always advise designers with less experience to avoid using flat fees unless there is some compelling reason to do so.

Charging by the Hour

Compensation for a residential design on a straight hourly basis has never appealed to many of my designer clients. Interior design for individual residences is not a mechanical process, and, accordingly, charging mechanically by the hour rarely provides sufficient compensation.

In the 1990s, however, many residential designers have had to resort to charging by the hour. If a budget is large and the client approves design plans and makes purchasing decisions quickly, charging cost-plus is profitable. Yet many design clients have slashed their budgets in the recession-torn 1990s, purchasing some items from new retail outlets. Therefore, if a residential designer is willing to take small-budget jobs, in many cases she is compelled to charge by the hour in order to make money.

Most designers are more flexible about charging by the hour for commercial work. Commercial design generally has a different point of view, and clients approach it from a more practical perspective. However, a straight hourly fee is sometimes increased by a multiple (See "Fees" in Chapter 1), such as DPE, which is frequently 2.5. Large interior design firms can justify a multiple more easily than smaller companies. They hire considerable personnel and pay a substantial overhead. Smaller firms have a more difficult time justifying a multiple and persuading their clients to go along with this procedure. These firms have to charge a straight hourly amount, which frequently ranges from $60 to $250.

Most residential designers who charge by the hour use a straight hourly rate, which generally approximates $100 per hour. However, the total design fee usually ends up as substantially less than the amount that could be realized had another method been selected.

Charging an Initial Design Fee

An initial design fee, payable upon signature of the letter of agreement, can be used when charging retail or, more frequently, cost-plus. Don't confuse this fee with a retainer, which can also be used with the cost-plus method. A retainer is an initial payment as well, but serves as an advance against future commissions. It is credited after design commissions have accrued.

A design fee is an amount in *addition* to commissions charged using cost-plus or markups received when charging retail. It is not credited against any subsequent fees.

The following are typical examples of when an initial design fee might be used:

1. *Charging retail when designing an eight-room house.* A design fee of $750 per room (i.e., $6000) is requested upon signature of the letter of agreement. If the designer completes floor plans and furniture layouts, but the client decides not to continue with the project or make any purchases, the design fee will be some compensation for the initial design work.

2. *Charging cost-plus when designing an eight-room house.* The initial budget is projected at $80,000. A design fee of $6000 is requested upon signature of the letter of agreement. The percentage on purchases of goods and design services is 30 percent. Again, the design fee acts as compensatory protection if the client doesn't follow through on the project. If the project is completed, the designer's fee will be $30,000, nearly 38 percent of the overall budget.

   Many clients entice a designer to prepare a complete set of a design plans, promising to make all purchases through the designer. Once plans have been completed, some clients make a substantial number of purchases themselves, short-circuiting the designer. For this reason, designers should always be certain to charge a design fee for preparing plans that will be sufficient compensation for the amount of time expended.

3. *Charging cost-plus when designing the interior of a large residence or commercial structure and collaborating with architects and builders.* On a project of this nature, a design fee works best when the job is divided into phases.

A three-phase structure, as illustrated by the following sample letter of agreement, shows how an initial design fee can be divided into payments and used with the cost-plus method.

> Our services to design your residence will be divided into three phases as follows:

PHASE ONE: CONSULTANT TO THE ARCHITECTS, BUILDERS, LANDSCAPE ARCHITECT, AND EXTERIOR LIGHTING EXPERTS

For all the design areas, we will supply the architect and general contractor with design concept drawings for the following:

1. Siting of house and terraces
2. Facades and roof
3. Exterior stonework
4. Entrance doors and hardware
5. Plumbing, including fixtures and appliance selections
6. Reflected ceiling plan
7. Exterior painting schedule
8. Other necessary specifications with respect to exterior decor

As compensation for these services, our fee of $60,000 shall be payable as follows:

$20,000   Upon signing this Letter of Agreement
$20,000   Upon completion and acceptance of plans, drawings, and specifications
$20,000   Upon completion of Phase I

Upon completion of our services for Phase I, we will commence the second phase.

PHASE TWO: INTERIOR FINISHES AND BUILT-INS

We will supply specifications and prepare purchase orders, where necessary, for the following:

1. Decorative hard surface floor coverings
2. Boiseries
3. Decorative plasterwork
4. Interior painting
5. Marble work
6. Fireplaces
7. Mirror and metal work
8. Decorative hardware
9. Tile and millwork

As compensation for our services, we will submit estimates based on our cost plus 20 percent.

As the second phase progresses, we shall undertake the third phase as it becomes appropriate.

PHASE THREE: FURNISHINGS AND DECORATIVE ITEMS
We will supply specifications and prepare purchase orders, where necessary, for the following:

1. Wallcoverings
2. Rugs and carpeting
3. Window treatments
4. Custom-made fixtures
5. Lighting fixtures
6. Accessories
7. Outdoor furniture
8. All other items to complete furnishings

As compensation for our services, we will submit estimates based on our cost plus 30 percent.

If you request that we select antiques, works of art, and objets d'art, you will be charged a 10 percent commission above our cost.

We will be happy to assist you to advise on the selection of china, glassware, flatware, linens, etc., through our own sources and request a 10 percent commission above our cost.

This example illustrates the use of an initial design fee with three other percentages for charging cost-plus. The initial design fee of $60,000 was based on a construction cost estimate between $750,000 and $1,000,000. This is less than 10 percent. Although the designer was not preparing architectural construction drawings, she prepared all design concepts, leaving the technical work to the architect. Because the designer was renowned, the fee was reasonable.

Inasmuch as the percentages on finishes and furnishings were 20 percent and 30 percent, respectively, the initial design fee of $60,000 was acceptable to the designer. This initial fee did not compensate her office for the time expended on the initial plans. However, because purchases of furniture and furnishings were so substantial, the job was tremendously profitable.

Of course, the designer took the risk that the client would execute her plans herself; however, since this particular designer's style was unique, she knew her client would probably never attempt to interpret her design plans. As it happens, the designer was correct, and she was able to finish the entire job.

Initial design fees are tremendously valuable in large projects, such as the one in this example, when they are well thought out. They should cover a large portion of the initial design services but should not be too high, especially if the percentage for making all interior purchases is 25 percent or more.

This discussion on how to charge is not meant as an exhaustive treatment. Designers continue to tell me about different methods they have devised that work for their own businesses. There should be no hard and fixed rules about how to charge; however, the methods discussed here are those that, in my experience, operate most efficiently and have been accepted by the public.

OWNERSHIP OF DESIGN PLANS

In this chapter, there has been substantial discussion about charging clients for creating design plans. Interior designers often ask, "Who owns the designs that we create for clients—the designer or the client? If the client pays me a fee for designing his interior, does it entitle him to ownership of the plans?"

My answer to this question has always been as follows: If a designer prepares plans, he owns them as the creator. However, based on his particular contractual relationship with his client, he may engage in certain written or verbal behavior which may relinquish his right of ownership. *Therefore, designers who want to retain ownership should specifically include language in their letters of agreement which states that the designer shall be the owner of all design plans.* Definite language will put an end to any ownership controversy, which should be resolved before the plans are created.

The next question is, "How relevant is the issue of retaining ownership of design plans?" The answer depends on the type of design work involved. For example, in my opinion, retaining ownership of design plans for residential work is of very limited value. Once plans have been submitted to the client, they can be easily duplicated. If the designer has a falling out with a client before the project is finished, it will almost be impossible for the designer to prevent the client from using the plans.

There is one precaution designers may use. Regardless of their fee structures, most designers charge an initial flat design fee or by the hour to create design plans. Once your plans are completed, show them to your client. However, don't release them until all fees are paid for preparation of the plans. When designers submit finished plans to clients, there is always the risk that the client will take them and disappear. Nonetheless, at least be paid for your efforts before releasing key information.

Ownership of design plans for commercial work, depending on the type of project, can be very important. Suppose, for example, a design firm is retained by a large corporation to create plans for a hotel. Since many hotel chains use standardized designs for all their hotels, the issue of design ownership may affect the structure of a design firm's fee. Will the plans and specifications be used for one hotel, or will they be used as a model for other hotels owned by the corporation?

Hotels offer only one example. Retail stores, restaurants, and fast-food chains also belong in this category. Designing for retail store chains requires collaboration to create a product image. The image is frequently kept uniform for each store location. Therefore, creating plans for a chain of stores is far more valuable than merely designing one store. Many designers believe, then, that their design fees should be gauged accordingly.

How do designers vary their fees to reflect the value of creating plans that will be used repeatedly? Financial success among interior designers does not necessarily relate directly to creative ability. It also relates to the ability to function as an entrepreneur. In other words, some designers are good business people who know how to make good deals with their clients; others are not.

Accordingly, some designers who design for stores and hotels charge by the hour for creating plans without retaining ownership. Once the plans are complete and the site is finished, the client retains ownership of the plans for no additional charge. These designers don't care, so long as they are paid for the amount of time they devote. If the project is successful, they hope to be retained to modify these plans for the next site. If not, they will go on to design for different clients. The most important thing, they believe, is to keep productive and go on to various projects.

Other designers have a different outlook. For example, I know a large interior design firm that designed a chain of health food restaurants. The design encompassed all aspects of the restaurant, including signage and logos, menu design, even tableware and cutlery. In exchange for the preparation of all plans and providing supervision for design services at each restaurant locale, the design firm received 5 percent of the net income. In this situation, the firm became a part of the business in exchange for its fee. This case is most unusual, but it illustrates the entrepreneurial ability of some designers.

However, there are other deals designers make that are more subtle. For example, some designers, when preparing model plans for hotels or restaurants, obtain long-term service contracts as consultants. Accordingly, when new restaurants or hotels are created using input from original plans, the designers may control the projects, or at least are employed as consultants.

When designing for companies in which your plans will be reused, there is obviously one important caveat: *Never repeat those designs in any recognizable fashion for any other client.* Although this rule should be implicit, it is shocking to see how some interior designers repeat their designs, in visible projects, for different clients. Residential projects are not highly visible, and, therefore, guarding against repetition of designs or specifications is not as important. In commercial projects, particularly for restaurants, stores, or hotels, be careful. If you sell your design plans, the sale of similar design plans to different companies may make you a target for litigation and be damaging to your firm's design credibility.

To summarize: If you are going to be designing projects that will be used as models, try to get some kind of premium for creating the initial plans. The premium will vary according to the type of project; for example, it may be a larger design fee, a contract to design additional units, or a special consultancy fee. To protect against liability, make certain never to duplicate any important aspect of a model design for another visible design project. If you are a talented designer whose services are in demand to create model plans, obtain the right guidance to use your ability as an entrepreneur.

3

PREPARING A LETTER OF AGREEMENT FOR COMMERCIAL PROJECTS

The general analysis of the letter of agreement provided in Chapter 1 is relevant and pertinent to nearly any interior design contract, regardless of the size or type of project. Design contracts for corporate clients, however, use a special language, which, like most languages, has many "dialects." Obviously, all variations of corporate contracts (their dialects) cannot be presented here. This chapter shows you how to prepare a letter of agreement for corporate clients with an architectural format. Frequent references are made to the discussion in Chapter 1.

THE AREA TO BE DESIGNED

The style of corporate contracts is succinct but thorough, as the following example illustrates:

Mr. Eugene Smith
Secretary and Director
Real Estate Facilities
Corporate Real Estate Department
The XYZ Corporation
7000 Madison Avenue
New York, New York

Dear Mr. Smith:
    The following is our letter of agreement describing our interior design services for the following project:
The Acme Building
5555 Park Avenue
New York, New York 10000

> Executive and Finance Group (approximately 300 persons)
> Floors 8,9, and 10
> 20,000 Square Feet per Floor
> Total: 60,000 Square Feet
> Occupancy Date: January 1st

Note the specificity of the title of the corporate officer in charge of the project. This is to ensure that you are dealing with the properly authorized party. The number of persons who are to occupy the space is provided to advise the client from the inception that the designers recognize needs and requirements.

SERVICES PROVIDED—INTRODUCTION

After the opening paragraph, corporate contracts frequently preface the description of services to be provided as follows:

> The services that we will provide will be outlined as follows. It is our understanding that the construction for all three floors will be building standard and that the furniture and furnishings will be new. You have advised us that your corporation has prepared standards for furniture and furnishings that will serve as the guide for outfitting the spaces. The building owner will provide both mechanical and electrical engineering services and architectural and contract documents.

Corporate designers usually present a client with all the given facts in this area. In the example, "building standard" construction is delineated, a crucial factor in preparing construction drawings. Any services to be provided by the client—for example, mechanical and electrical engineering services—should be mentioned even if there has been an oral understanding to that effect. Both services are so costly that the designer should state in writing that he will have no responsibility for their provision.

SERVICES PROVIDED—PHASE DEVELOPMENT

One of the major differences between architecturally oriented corporate contracts and general interior design contracts is that the description of services is organized into phases. The following is a typical example of phase development.

> (Design Corporation) will provide the following required services in four (4) phases:

    I. Programming/Building Analysis
   II. Schematics/Design Development
  III. Construction Documents and Fixtures/Furnishings Contract
      Documents
  IV. Construction Coordination

(Design Corporation's) work will be organized into these four phases, which will be undertaken in sequence. All phases of these services will include the following project management.

PROJECT MANAGEMENT

Prior to the detailed description of the work undertaken in each phase, project management as provided by the designer is briefly outlined. The most common types of project management described at this stage of the agreement are budget control and schedule maintenance, as the following example illustrates.

> *Budget Control.* Early in the project (Design Corporation) will prepare a comprehensive cost estimate of the project work for the corporation's review and approval. This preliminary figure will serve to establish a target for cost control of the project. As the project progresses, (Design Corporation) will continually update estimates and submit them for the corporation's review and approval. Project Budgets will be submitted at the end of each phase.
> *Schedule Maintenance.* All schedules in chart form and reports necessary for the orderly administration of this project shall be prepared by (Design Corporation) for the corporation's review and approval. All schedules in chart form and reports will be reviewed at weekly project meetings and will be included as attachments to each meeting report. Any deviations from these documents will be brought to the corporation's attention by (Design Corporation) for the corporation's review and approval.
>
> All production and construction schedules will be coordinated with any corresponding dates agreed to in the corporation's Lease Documents. Any deviation from these completion dates for whatever cause will be incorporated into the schedules and presented to the corporation for review and approval. When requested, (Design Corporation) will assist the corporation in any negotiations with the Building Owners or Contractors when their concurrence of any schedule is required.

At first glance, many of these provisions may appear unnecessary. For example, of course interior designers will devise a system of cost control and prepare the schedules for the execution of design plans. I must emphasize, however, especially for corporate jobs, how important it is to stress, during initial client interviews and in the letter of agreement, your vigilance in respect to budget adherence and scheduling compliance.

Recall the comments of the successful architect in Chapter 1 who advised that corporations are mainly concerned with having their buildings finished at budget and on time. Corporate executives have to answer to stockholders and boards of directors. Frequently, fine quality and innovative design are not as important as relevance and usefulness.

Note, as indicated in the preceding example, that you should volunteer your aid to the client in working with any third parties, such as building owners and contractors, who are in some way crucial to the operation of the project. It not only makes sense to make these affirmations in writing at the outset of your relationship, it's also the professional way to do business.

PHASE DEVELOPMENT—DESCRIPTION

The core of most corporate design contracts is the description of the phases of the project. A comprehensive description of a four-phase project is set forth next. These phases and descriptions represent a pattern of description typically used by many large corporate design firms. However, keep in mind that these phases can be consolidated or expanded, depending on the scope of the job. The titles of the phases can also be modified or substituted according to the job. The important point is that there is no law or dogma to dictate their titles or descriptions. The titles of the phases and their development need only be clearly written and easily understood. One of the worst mistakes is to prepare a contract with such complex and obtuse language that the client is unable to decipher it. In that case, the designer sometimes loses the job, as the client feels she will not know how to work with him.

PHASE I: PROGRAMMING/BUILDING ANALYSIS
Interior Programming
Working with the corporation's representatives, (Design Corporation) will conduct personal interviews as needed to verify information provided by the corporation. From the information provided by XYZ, (Design Corporation) will develop an interior space utilization program including interpretation of management objectives, space requirements, personnel requirements, furnishings, files, special equipment, storage, and departmental adjacency requirements. Summaries of space requirements by departments and subdepartment units, along with adjacency require-

ments (Functional Relationships Diagram), will be submitted to the corporation for approval.

Working with these surveys, (Design Corporation) will develop the stacking and block layout for the corporation's approval.

From the approved program, (Design Corporation) will outline special facilities and/or programs such as food service, acoustics, building security systems, life support systems, etc., that may require special consultants and will assist the corporation's representatives in securing these qualified consultants.

Scope Summary

1. Programming/Space Requirements and Functional Relationships Diagram
2. Corporate Review and Approval
3. Stacking and Blocking Diagrams
4. Client Presentation and Report
5. Corporate Review and Approval
6. Consultant Recommendations
7. Preliminary Budget

For the purposes of the example in this chapter, the corporate design project required the preparation of a functional relationships diagram and stacking and blocking diagrams. These diagrams can be omitted for a simpler project.

There are two important points to note in regard to the Phase I description. First, the client's input and approval are required for all aspects of the development of the interior space utilization program. Always insist on this input and approval, and don't proceed without it. If the client is unhappy toward the end of the project, it is important to be able to show her earlier plans that she approved. Second, a "scope summary" should be provided after the description of each phase. It's obviously much easier to refer to a list so that a potential client can see, step by step, item by item, what she is actually paying for.

PHASE II: SCHEMATICS/DESIGN DEVELOPMENT

Upon receipt of Phase 1 approval by the client, (Design Corporation) will undertake Phase II.

Space Planning

Working with the corporation's representatives and with the approved block layouts and stacking plans, (Design Corporation) will investigate various planning concepts and combinations of concepts for the development of space utilization plans.

Working with the approved stacking and block plans, work space requirements, and the corporation's furniture standard, (Design Corporation) will prepare layouts of departments, executive areas, public spaces, etc., showing interior walls and locations of personnel and equipment for the corporation's review and approval. In addition, (Design Corporation) will prepare lighting and power and telephone layout drawings for the corporation's approval.

The corporation will provide for (Designer Corporation) detailed standards of workstations.

Scope Summary
1. Receipt of phase approval from corporation
2. Layout drawings
3. Lighting and power and telephone drawings
4. Budget review
5. Presentation
6. Corporation approval

Design Development
Working with the approved concept documents, (Design Corporation) will prepare the following design development drawings to be issued to the architect after approval. From these drawings, the building's architect will develop construction documents and specifications for the building's interiors:

1. Architectural Floor Plans
2. Architectural Reflected Ceiling and Light Fixture Switching Plan
3. Power and Telephone Plans

(Design Corporation) will prepare decorative criteria for all interior spaces. Decorative criteria, furniture, and accessories selections will be submitted to the corporation for approval.

Budgets will be updated to reflect any changes or adjustments in the cost of furniture and equipment. Accessories will be included in the budget.

Scope Summary
1. Design Development Drawings for Building's Architect
2. Decorative Criteria, Furniture, and Accessories Schedule and Plans
3. Budget Update
4. Presentation
5. Corporation Approval

Note that prior to the description of the first aspect of Phase II, "Space Planning," it is indicated that Phase II will not commence until the client approves Phase I. There is always some phase overlap in every design project; however, avoid proceeding to the next phase until the prior phase has been approved by your client. Each phase acts as a foundation for the next. If the initial phases are weak, the whole project can collapse.

In the description of space planning, it is stated that the designer will "investigate various planning concepts and combinations of concepts for the development of space utilization plans. "It is important to use this language in your space planning section to reassure your client that you will consider his ideas, too, until an optimal plan is reached. Although designers usually consider such flexibility an inherent part of the design process, it is important to tell this to a potential client. Corporate clients are usually easier to work for than residential clients because a work space, as opposed to a living space, is less emotionally charged for the client. However, corporate clients usually make their decisions on a team basis, and your work will usually have to be approved by several executives. It is important to inform the executive in charge of the project in writing that you will consider any and all alternatives that the team members might suggest.

The architect's responsibilities for the project are generally specified in the description of design development. Many interior design projects that involve creating or rebuilding an interior require an architect. In these situations, specify the responsibilities of the architect in the letter of agreement. If the architect fails to provide the requisite services later in the project, the designer can at least show her client the contract and request, or even demand, that the architect fulfill his responsibilities.

PHASE III:-CONSTRUCTION DOCUMENTS AND FIXTURES/ FURNISHINGS CONTRACT DOCUMENTS

Upon client approval of Phase II, (Design Corporation) will proceed with Phase III.

Construction Documents

(Design Corporation) will finalize and specify through appropriate and detailed schedules all architectural finishes, including wall coverings, floor coverings, and paint colors, etc., for the corporation's review and approval. Upon approval, the corporation will incorporate these finishes into the construction documents.

(Design Corporation) will prepare carpet plans for issue to the carpet supplier.

(Design Corporation) will provide architectural millwork drawings as required for miscellaneous built-in cabinetry. Minimum cabinetry is expected by the corporation.

(Design Corporation) will review and cross-check necessary engineering and special consultant's drawings or specifications encompassing structural, electrical, mechanical, and special facilities requirements with the architectural drawings for adherence to the design development drawings prepared by (Design Corporation.) (Design Corporation) will review the architectural contract documents provided by the building's architect for adherence to the design development drawings prepared by (Design Corporation).

Scope Summary

1. Receipt of Phase II Approval from Client
2. Finish Schedule Drawings
3. Carpet Plans
4. Millwork Drawings and Specifications
5. Coordination of Architectural Mechanical and Electrical and Special Consultants' Drawings

Fixture and Furnishings Contract Documents

In addition to the construction drawings described in Phase III, (Design Corporation) will prepare required specifications documents for interior fixtures and furnishings. Based on approved furniture and furnishings selections developed under Phase II, (Design Corporation) will complete location drawings showing all fixtures and furnishings along with specifications describing all new items in sufficient detail for competitive bidding or negotiation on the particular pieces selected. (Design Corporation) does not purchase and/or handle furniture on a resale basis but will assist in evaluating and reviewing the bids or in negotiations. All purchasing will be in accordance and in conjunction with the corporation's purchasing procedures.

All submittals from furniture manufacturers or dealers will be reviewed by (Design Corporation) for conformance to plans and specifications. Copies of reviewed documents with appropriate stamps and notations will be forwarded to the corporation for its records.

Scope Summary

1. Plans and Specifications for Fixtures/Furnishings
2. Bid Review
3. Bid Item Review and Approvals

Note the careful itemization of the interior designer's duties under "Construction Documents." This is important for several reasons. First, if you want a client to sign the contract, it's best to enumerate all the things you're going to do for him. Undoubtedly, all these items will be mentioned during your initial consultations. But how many of them will your prospective client actually remember? Second, many corporate clients aren't really aware of the vast amount of work involved in a substantial project. The executive in charge of the project may understand how designers operate, but the other executives who must approve his decision probably won't be as knowledgable. Spelling out your duties thoroughly can impress a board of directors when they confer to examine your contract. Third, your contract will state specifically what you will not do. As indicated in the preceding section of the sample letter of agreement, the interior designer will not purchase any furniture directly for this project. An unsophisticated client might not understand the rationale of this condition. Therefore, after you have explained it to him, show him how thorough you will be in all areas. If you can project a seasoned, professional image, you can persuade a client to accept one of your operating conditions that he might not like.

There are some very cogent reasons for an interior designer not to purchase furniture for a client or to handle furniture on a resale basis, as indicated under "Fixture and Furnishings Documents." First, the client may not want the designer to make purchases. Many large corporations have their own purchasing agents or use free-lance agents who are paid a commission; if either is the case, find out before the letter of agreement is prepared so you will be able to account for that fact in your contract. Second, some interior designers want to eliminate the bookkeeping problems that purchasing entails. If a corporate client has its own purchasing department, the designer should prepare the purchase orders and submit them to the purchasing agent or department rather than handle all aspects of purchase transactions including payment, sales tax, shipping, and so forth. Third, if the client makes all purchases directly, certain risks of liability are eliminated for the designer. For example, if deliveries are late or merchandise arrives damaged, the client will look directly to the vendor for replacement or refund. Naturally, a designer will assist her client in all possible ways, but this method keeps her from being caught in the middle of a quarrel or a lawsuit.

PHASE IV: CONSTRUCTION COORDINATION

During construction, (Design Corporation) will provide the necessary design coordination and approvals and make periodic visits to the site to familiarize itself generally with the progress and quality of the work and to determine whether the work is progressing in compliance with the contract documents and construction schedules.

All site visits will be documented in field reports to keep the corporation apprised of the progress of the construction. (Design Corporation) will review shop drawings for millwork and carpet seaming plans.

Working with the corporation's representatives, (Design Corporation) will assist in the fixtures and furnishings installation phase of construction by making periodic site inspections to assure that the installation is in accordance with drawings and specifications.

(Design Corporation) will review and inspect the completed project after move-in to assist the corporation's representatives with any miscellaneous revisions or additions. Revisions and additions are addenda to the base contract.

Scope Summary
1. Construction coordination
2. Furnishing installation inspection
3. Additional purchase items

You have advised us that you will provide (Design Corporation) with plans and specifications that fully describe the buildings in detail.

Follow-through and follow-up are two of the most frequently used terms in corporate language. When complimented on the design of their offices, corporate executives have been known to comment, "Yes, I suppose the designer designed the space well, but she sure didn't follow up on the project." Your letter must reassure your client that you will do so.

Avoid, however, stating specifically the frequency of your site inspections. Different stages of construction will require varying degrees of supervision, and, for this reason, visits should be specified as "periodic." To protect yourself against subsequent criticism for inadequate inspection, indicate that visits will be documented in field reports. Send copies to your client. Obviously, inspection visit reports can become quite tedious to prepare in the midst of all the ordinary confusion of construction. Yet most experienced designers agree that the extra effort is worthwhile, particularly if the client complains that he wasn't provided with enough site inspections.

The general contractor, not the interior designer, is responsible for the quality and the supervision of the work. Many designers, however, don't want to present a potential client with that fact in their letter of agreement. They think that such information will make the client feel that the designer is attempting to avoid responsibility. The sample letter of agreement implies the absence of designer responsibility for construction by describing the nature of the designer's activities to be that of *inspection*. If possible, however, I prefer to insert disclaiming language in regard to the quality and supervision of construction in all design contracts.

FEES

Fees are discussed in Chapter 2, and fee structures are compared and analyzed in Chapter 1. However, as this chapter traces a commercial contract from start to finish, fees are discussed at this point too.

For this particular contract, the design firm chose to avoid its corporate client's internal affairs as much as possible. In this connection (see Phase III), the design firm refused to purchase any merchandise or, in fact, to assume any responsibility for hiring a general contractor directly. Many corporate designers concur with this philosophy. Even though they may sacrifice large profits by not charging clients on a cost-plus basis, they feel that avoiding responsibility for purchases of goods and construction enables them to be more objective and finish each job faster. In the long run, these designers believe, they earn more by charging on an hourly basis, using a multiple of direct personnel expense (DPE), as follows:

PROFESSIONAL FEES

We propose to be compensated for services on a time-card basis at a rate of 2.5 times DPE with a not-to-be-exceeded amount of (for example, $200,000). All out-of-pocket expenses for reproductions, travel, postage, messengers, long-distance telephone calls, faxes, and report typing are to be reimbursed at cost. If inflation continues at its present 15 percent to 20 percent annual rate, (Design Corporation) will increase staff salaries to adjust to cost-of-living increases at the appropriate time. This cost-of-living increase would increase the not-to-be-exceeded amount to $240,000.

Direct personnel expense is defined as the direct salaries of all our technical personnel engaged on the project and the portion of the cost of their mandatory and customary contributions and benefits related thereto, such as employment taxes, and other statutory employee benefits, insurance, sick leave, holidays, vacations, pensions, and similar contributions and benefits.

If, after your written approval of documents submitted in Phases I, II, and III, you wish to change them for any reason, any additional services for the change will be performed at a rate of 2.5 times DPE. These are addenda fees that are in addition to the base fee.

As charging DPE is a function of hourly time rates, some clients may be very reticent about salary increases over the life of a project, especially when they are being billed on a multiple. Therefore, note that the design firm used an upset figure of $240,000. Although the project was not intended to be that expensive, the client at least understood that his design fees would not exceed this amount.

Charging by the hour has other advantages. When being paid hourly, designers are compensated for every second they devote to the project. When charging cost-plus, designers have to worry about what is included in their budget for commission purposes. Moreover, under a cost-plus system, clients occasionally make some purchases directly to avoid paying the design commission. When a designer charges by the hour, it simply doesn't matter what the client buys or when he buys it as far as the designer's compensation is concerned.

Any additions or changes to the documents are billed as "addenda fees." Why use such a term when the hourly rate is the same? The reason is that the upset figure of $240,000 should not be used to strangle the designer financially if the client decides to make endless changes. Therefore, if the $240,000 amount is exceeded because of design additions or changes after the documents have been approved, the designer will no longer be limited to the upset figure.

PHOTOGRAPHING PRIVILEGE

As most of you will agree, a designer's stock-in-trade is his portfolio and the publicity he receives from being published. Reserve the right, if possible, to photograph completed projects by using the following clause:

> (Designer Corporation) reserves the right to exclusively photograph our design work after it is completed and to give permission for its use in any publication, although the corporate name will not be used without your consent.

Before you insert this clause in a letter of agreement, sound out the corporate executive in charge of the project.

There are two common corporate objections to the clause. First, some companies don't want their stockholders to see expensively decorated offices. Your promise to withhold the client's identity will usually not be sufficient to allay the fears of corporate executives who are concerned about such exposure. Second, most corporate executives who do want the space photographed will generally not give the designer an "exclusive." For example, executives will want free rein to photograph all their spaces for brochures and other public relations material. They certainly won't permit themselves to be hamstrung by their designer.

If you encounter any resistance when discussing this aspect of your agreement during initial client interviews, omit the clause. If the job is completed to the client's satisfaction, about 50 percent of all clients will permit the designer to allow his own photographer to photograph the space.

My rationale for urging designers to relinquish this privilege with corporate clients is based on a number of factors. Corporate clients are usually much easier to deal with than residential clients. Jobs seem to get finished faster, are less troublesome and more profitable. In addition, corporate clients are frequently repeat customers. I have several designer clients who maintain very profitable and secure businesses with only two or three corporate clients. I would not jeopardize losing a valuable commercial client over a photographing privilege.

ARBITRATON

Most business people, including interior designers, are either sued or have sued someone at least once during their careers. An arbitration clause in a letter of agreement can usually prevent a lawsuit between designer and client. The advantages of arbitration are discussed in Chapter 11. I want only to remind you that the use of the following clause can ensure that any disputes between you and your client are settled in an informal, administrative hearing instead of in a courtroom:

> Any dispute or disagreement between parties arising out of or relating to this agreement shall be settled by arbitration in (any state where you designate jurisdiction) under the rules then obtaining of the American Arbitration Association, and judgment upon the award may be entered in any court having jurisdiction.

Although many of my designer clients have been subjected to lawsuits with residential clients, I have never been involved in either a lawsuit or an arbitration proceeding between a designer and a corporate client. This is, of course, not to say that these actions don't occur, but corporate clients really aren't interested in fighting. They're less emotional than residential clients and are basically concerned with having the job completed to specification as scheduled. However, once a corporate client feels that he has been misled by a designer, regardless of the quality of the design and finished product, he will never hire him again.

CLOSING

The final paragraph is the same that is used to conclude most letters of agreement. It can be varied according to your style but should contain the following elements.

> If the above meets with your approval, your signature below will indicate your acceptance of the terms of the agreement and will indicate your authorization to proceed with work. Kindly return the duplicate copy to us. Of course, if you have any questions, please don't hesitate to call.

> We are looking forward to collaborating with you.

Sincerely,

(Design Corporation)
By: (Name of Firm President)
    President
Dated:
Agreed & Accepted:

The XYZ Corporation
By: Eugene Smith,
Secretary and Director,
Corporate Real Estate Facilities,
Real Estate Department
Dated:
Agreed & Accepted:

Send the client two signed copies of the agreement. I usually recommend that designers don't begin work until the contract is returned with a signature and some sort of payment. However, with a well-established corporate client, some designers use a different approach. Sometimes they submit preliminary design plans before a contract is prepared. If the client is solid enough, some designers feel that it is a good business risk. This, of course, is a subjective decision to be made on a case-by-case basis.

CONCLUSION

Corporate clients are different from other design clients generally. Nonetheless, the basic rules and concepts for charging and preparing letters of agreement must be absorbed and understood prior to embarking on any variations. Many different ideas and details can be "plugged into" a corporate letter of agreement as relevant to different client needs. You will define these needs according to each project.

As stated earlier, a designer's letter of agreement is a cornerstone of the client relationship. However, it is important in corporate or commercial situations for a different reason. Residential contracts must be prepared with a somewhat defensive attitude. That is generally not the case in working with corporate clients. It is usually more important to convince the corporate client of your competence *now*, than to be preoccupied about protecting yourself from a conflict that might develop in the future. In any case, before sending out a corporate letter of agreement, make certain that it is concise, well organized, and professional. It might be the marketing tool that lands you the job.

4

DESIGNER RESPONSIBILITY AND CLIENT BUDGET

DESIGNER DIVORCE AND CLIENT CONTINUITY

Designers have various responsibilities to their clients, depending on the roles they assume in the course of their projects. However, regardless of these obligations, external factors may sometimes limit the amount of power or influence they are able to exercise.

To illustrate how power can affect responsibility, I have selected two topics. The first is *designer responsibility and client budget*. Usually, the designer can be quite instrumental in influencing a client about how much she should spend on a project. However, as discussed in this chapter, many other factors beyond the designer's control can limit this influence.

Conversely, when design partnerships split up, designers often feel powerless to control their destiny. Most design alliances between partners are like marriages. When they dissolve, emotional trauma affects all the partners. However, in exploring the second topic, *Designer Divorce*, various approaches are discussed, which designers can utilize to mobilize their power to reorganize their careers and satisfy their responsibilities.

Designer responsibility and client budget and *designer divorce and client continuity* are separate and distinct subjects unto themselves. However, since both topics relate to a designer's relationship with his client, they draw interesting parallels when discussed in the same context. Although each topic is treated separately, both discussions will draw striking similarities between the issue of a designer's power and control over clients and other aspects of his business.

DESIGNER RESPONSIBILITY AND CLIENT BUDGET

One of the thorniest issues confronting designers involves a designer's responsibility and the client's budget. Simply discussing budget with clients has always been a sticky issue. Designers often ignore the budget or tread lightly when meeting with potential clients. Instead of discussing the budget during initial meetings, designers frequently handle the issue as if it were a skeleton in the closet. They keep it hidden until the contract is signed and they start specifying purchases.

In fact, few clients are firm with figures when they meet their designers. Although they may express concern about a budget, they are often reluctant to confess how much they'll spend. Designers, on the other hand, are reticent about providing "hard figures" until they're hired and advance into the project. They're afraid that if they tell their clients the truth, they'll scare them off.

An exception to this rule is the large corporate client. In most cases, this client immediately discloses the amount the company plans to spend. Smaller companies often provide a budget, but the initial figure is not always realistic, based on their design needs and requirements.

Today there is no question that designers have to be more careful with budgets than ever before. Inflation is rampant. Prices change daily. And clients are certainly more cost conscious in the recessionary economy that has periodically plagued our country in the last decade.

The most frequent budget dilemma involves dollar-oriented clients. They won't hire a designer if they don't think he's "money conscious." On the other hand, most clients also have no idea of how much things cost. They don't realize how expensive things are. Of course, the most unenlightened clients are usually those who have never worked with a designer. From their friends or business associates, they have heard it's expensive to design an interior. However, when designers present a budget with their choices, they recoil in horror.

A designer once told me a story about one of his clients, a cut-rate druggist who owned a chain of 40 stores. The druggist's wife selected custom-upholstered dining chairs from the designer's upholsterer. Her husband asked for an estimate, and when the quote was $1500 per chair without the fabric, he complained that the price was outrageous. The designer was absolutely shocked. His client, he knew, was worth at least $100 million. Financially, the price of the chairs was unimportant. His wife had insisted on a very finely crafted product, tufted and hand made. The cost was reasonable.

Then the designer asked his client, "Tell me, what kind of a car do you drive?" The husband replied, "Oh, I have a BMW and a Mercedes." "How much did they cost?" the designer asked.

The man didn't reply. He was still suspicious of the designer. The husband felt he was being extravagant, but at least he said nothing further. Besides, his wife wanted the chairs.

The point is that you must deal with the budget issue from the moment you become involved with a client. Be prepared to defend your choices and to explain the prices.

There are a variety of ways to approach these issues. Some clients are easier to handle than others. For example, when a client is sophisticated and understands interiors, it's easy to talk about prices right from the beginning. The client has had experience in the design world. Since she's already been indoctrinated with the design process, it's no problem to discuss costs immediately.

Another example involves the client who doesn't care about the budget. She's not a wild spender, but she knows what she wants and can afford to pay for it. So if she selects a silk damask fabric that costs $220 a yard net, she will buy it. She may not be worth a fortune, but she's got enough money to satisfy her expensive tastes. This does not mean every client can afford a $200,000 oriental rug; however, some clients know what they want as basics and are willing to spend the money.

Another common situation occurs when a client has a flat amount to spend, regardless of her needs. The amount cannot vary. Then it's up to the designer and the client to weigh alternatives and to cut corners when necessary. This situation is typical in dealing with corporate clients, who tend to be less emotional. In a residential situation, a client may tell you that she has a fixed amount of money to spend. However, if her choices exceed her price range, your client may become unhappy. She really wants to buy everything she likes but at a price she can afford. In short, your client wants you to be a magician.

Corporate clients tend to be far more clinical. They're also more realistic and, therefore, pragmatic about the budget.

These are some simple cases. Those that follow involve more difficult situations.

Some clients have sufficient funds to adequately fund their budgets but are uncertain about committing themselves. This is frequently the case when clients are new to the design world. Some are afraid to spend because of a lack of confidence in their designer's judgment. It's not only the design fee that concerns them. Owing to their unfamiliarity with interior design, some clients lack the confidence to commit themselves to their designer's choices. Unless a client believes in her designer, the budget issue may remain a stumbling block throughout an entire project.

Another familiar scenario arises when a client is willing to spend enough money and has confidence in her designer. However, the client doesn't have enough cash to complete the project after the presentation has been accepted. She hopes she'll get it as the job progresses. This situation has been typical during the last four or five years when the economy has been so mercurial.

During the 1980s, when clients from the financial markets were getting rich from leveraged buyouts, many were earning huge bonuses. Some figured that as their design projects progressed, they would earn enough money to pay expenses. However, planning on future earnings to pay current bills places a great strain on designers. It makes it very difficult to plan if funds arrive late.

Of course, the worst instance is when a client tells her designer, "I've got $50,000 now, and I'll have $50,000 by Christmas. Start the project." The designer then advises his client to sign a contract with a general contractor and orders furniture and furnishings. When the time arrives to make the final payments, the client doesn't have the money. She can pay neither the contractors nor the balance of the custom-ordered goods. The client's lack of cash flow also jeopardizes her deposits.

When a client loses her ability to meet expenses, her designer can be forced into a very precarious position. If the designer is warned in advance that cash flow may be a problem, he may advise his client to take a different approach. He may recommend dividing the job into separate phases, progressing gradually as the budget becomes secure. However, when a client insists that she has the ability to spend and later comes up short, the designer may be forced into a dilemma. As a result of the client's financial instability, the designer's own credit may be placed at risk.

Another difficult situation arises when a client doesn't want her designer to know her real budget. She figures that if she tells the designer the actual figure, for example, $50,000, the designer will spend $100,000; if she tells him that it's $100,000, the designer will spend $200,000. The client wants the designer to use his expertise to deliver the budget for less. She believes that by withholding the truth, she'll get more ingenuity. In fact, the client's friends may have warned her, "Don't tell your designer you'll spend $50,000. Tell him that you'll spend $25,000, and you'll spend $50,000 anyway."

What can designers do to resolve these problems?

A designer must learn to be a detective. You must use your best instincts to figure out how much your client really wants to spend. However, prior to discussing budget in detail, you must know how much your client *needs* to spend based on current prices. Consider rampant inflation as an ongoing problem. Before you prepare a budget for a client, you must check current price lists. Sometimes prices rise 10 percent a year. If goods are imported, new duties may be imposed that had not been assessed the last time you checked prices. It's crucial to keep abreast of price changes.

It occasionally happens that a designer prepares a purchase order for goods, and after the order has been received, the vendor calls the designer. "Unfortunately," the vendor advises, "there's been another price increase of 10 percent." It's very embarrassing for the designer to have quoted the wrong price to the client. Sometimes this can't be avoided. Prices occasionally change between the time the order is placed and the time it is received. However, you must use your best efforts to keep as current as possible.

Remember, when it comes to the budget, you must learn to be a detective. Find out what your client's capabilities are during initial interviews. Try to determine your client's attitude about spending money on design.

Once you can "get a take" on your client's mentality, you'll know how to deal with him. For example, many designers show clients portfolios of their photographed interiors. Some designers use slides with a prepared narrative. Still others take serious clients to visit finished projects. If you do this, you may discover what kind of ambience your client wants. You may even tell your client, "This living room cost $75,000 to design" or "The lobby that I designed for that building cost $350,000." Give the client a rough ballpark estimate.

When you're conducting interviews with a prospective client, it's important to find out what the client is going to retain from his former office or residence. Does he want to keep everything? Half of it? Or none of it? Make a list. Tell him it's important, because it all relates to cost. That makes sense even to an amateur. Your client will respect you for using this approach.

During interviews, when possible, try to define a client's desires. For example, if you get the client to admit that he wants a brand new living room, from top to bottom, throw out a general figure, for instance, $15,000, $50,000, or whatever your own "guesstimate" is. Orally, you can estimate general figures for carpentry, upholstery, floor coverings, and so forth. If a client is overwhelmed by the amount, advise him realistically what can be done for a fixed amount he is willing to spend.

When a client establishes a budget, outline the type of design you can provide for that amount. If the budget is inadequate to significantly improve the space, ask him to consider an alternative approach. For example, designers often create interiors by designing backgrounds initially. When the client is able to spend more, furniture and furnishings are purchased.

Your approach may hinge upon the physical requirements of your design plans. For example, if you're creating an interior with a great deal of built-in cabinets and furniture, construction can't be postponed. Platforms and built-in banquettes should be built simultaneously. However, if you're designing an interior where everything is free-standing, you can fill in the basic floor plan after the backgrounds have been completed, depending on the client's financial capabilities.

Should you put a ballpark budget figure in your letter of agreement? Some designers always do. They feel it establishes reality from the inception. It presents a client with a minimum budget for the project immediately. Accordingly, a client will not become disillusioned about his expenses after he pays the designer a retainer.

Some designers never give a ballpark amount. They think that discussing the budget in a letter of agreement can scare off even a good spender. These designers believe a client must be led into spending. They like to inspire their clients with the project. Some designers feel that if they emphasize the budget initially, they risk losing a client.

The designer has to use her own judgment to make this decision. There is a trend today to discuss costs as soon as possible. Some designers provide written estimates or financial proposals. This is particularly important in corporate situations, where a board of directors must approve all decisions.

If you establish a preliminary budget in your letter of agreement, is it your responsibility to complete the job for that amount? That depends on your terminology. After all, an estimate is only an estimate. Don't make any absolute commitments. Even if you include a budget in your agreement, you will probably revise it after your presentation is approved. Your client should approve any revised budget.

Once a preliminary budget is approved, you're no longer bound by an estimate in your agreement. Would it matter if your estimate is much lower than the budget? Not necessarily. However, unless your client has changed the scope of the project, the difference shouldn't vary more than 20 percent.

Once a client has made her furniture and material selections, suppose your preliminary budget is much larger than the initial estimate. Your client may be shocked by the budget even though you had discussed prices in detail while offering alternatives. The client may become so upset that she even considers cancelling the project.

There are two ways to approach this crisis. You might say, "If you want this design concept, this is what it's going to cost. Before changing your mind, I suggest thinking about it carefully. Otherwise, you won't have the interior you want. You will have to compromise."

A second approach is to be casual saying, "You can still have a very beautiful interior, but we're going to have to eliminate certain things. Let's cut out the leather for the sofas, and eliminate the wet bar." It is most important to remain flexibile.showing your client that you're willing to make changes. If you do, she may spend the money anyway. When the job is finished, you will be a hero.

Some designers take a misleading approach when dealing with their clients and budget issues. I'm going to advise you about what *not* to do. Don't intentionally mislead clients about the budget in order to make larger commissions. The following story is a typical example.

One of my former clients, a designer, included a preliminary estimate in a letter of agreement with a new client. He stipulated $60,000 to design a one-bedroom apartment. During the design process, the client kept adding custom items. For example, he added special cabinetry, a custom master bath with steam shower, and other options never contemplated for the original budget. The designer deliberately didn't warn his client about the increasing costs. The designer charged cost-plus, so he anticipated larger commissions. He was thrilled that the budget had expanded.

Of course, this is true for most designers: The more their clients spend, the more money they make. Eventually the day of reckoning arrived. The designer presented the client with a revised budget for $140,000. The client became incensed; he fired the designer and sued him for the return of his retainer in an arbitration proceeding. The arbitrator awarded the client $5000 of the initial $10,000 retainer.

This was a case in which a designer led his client down the garden path and got caught. Obviously, he enticed his client to ignore the budget, hoping that he would fall in love with the design. Instead of earning more commissions, the designer ended up losing substantially. He had invested nearly $15,000 of design time, billed on an hourly basis, plus legal fees for the arbitration proceeding.

Sometimes encouraging a client to ignore the budget works. However, it can also backfire, as in the preceding example. There are other devious techniques that some designers use to increase their clients' budgets.

Some designers encourage their clients to buy one or two expensive items at the beginning of a project. For example, I know a designer who encourages his new clients to purchase a very expensive oriental rug even before he prepares the floor plan. He tells his clients to buy the rug initially in order to create a color scheme and select harmonizing fabrics. He takes clients shopping at selected dealers, who pay him a kickback, or secret commission, after a sale is consummated. Of course, the client pays the designer a commission on the rug as a design fee, the kickback remaining a secret between the designer and the dealer.

From a financial standpoint, here's how the designer works. Presume the budget is $200,000. The designer encourages a client to spend $50,000 to $60,000 on a rug. Obviously, this is a disproportionate expense, which throws the budget way out of scale. When the designer presents a preliminary budget, the client usually protests and tells the designer to trim the costs. So the designer replies, "Well, we can always return the oriental rug and put you back on budget."

This designer banks on the fact that the client loves the rug, the foundation for the color scheme. Obviously, the designer employs a devious psychological strategy in an attempt to inflate the budget and his commissions. In many cases, this game plan has worked.

I believe that this is a treacherous way to do business. It places the credibility of the designer severely in question. If you use a strategy like his, it will most likely work from time to time. However, I think designers who take kickbacks and inflate budgets eventually pay a high price for their lack of integrity. Clients aren't stupid; they realize when they've been taken. Client referrals and repeat business, which are the backbone of a designer's reputation, will be undermined by chicanery.

Analyze all project limitations before presenting the budget. Here's an example of why this is so important.

A client gave his designer a budget to design a commercial space, a brokerage firm dealing in commodities. The designer reviewed the budget carefully before determining that the job could be completed for the budgeted amount. Then he agreed to undertake the project.

The design plans were complex. They accommodated computers, audiovisual equipment, and other electronic equipment necessary to operate the client's business. The cabinet designs were involved, but the designer produced a beautiful and functional result. The plans were ultimately completed and approved by the client.

The designer presented the client with a list of general contractors to submit the plans for bid. The client approved the list but remarked, casually, "Of course, you realize that all the construction has to be done after three o'clock, so I can run my office without any interruptions."

The designer was shocked. He assumed that the client had planned to move elsewhere during construction because of the magnitude of his plans. It never occurred to him that his client planned to work on site, because his other commercial clients had never made that demand. Of course, the designer should have explored that issue prior to submitting a budget. Unfortunately, he simply overlooked it. To accommodate his client, the on-site construction and installations were estimated on union overtime scale. This caused the budget to inflate more than 50 percent.

When the client reviewed the revised budget, he had a tantrum. He blamed the designer for the increase and demanded new plans for no extra fee. In retrospect, he was right. The designer should have never presented his client with a dramatically increased budget. The budget had been the client's main concern from the beginning. When it became clear that construction would be billed at an overtime rate, the designer should have scaled down the plans to comply with the original budget. Then, if the client wasn't satisfied, the designer could have proven that increased labor costs necessitated downscaling the design.

The moral of the story is that a designer should never shock a client with an excessive budget. If it becomes apparent that a budget must be larger than anticipated to satisfy a client's needs, clue him in gradually. If a client expects a budget to fall within a certain financial framework, he may react badly if it's substantially larger. The designer will lose credibility and may even be fired.

Sometimes your client will decide he wants all the extras and will go way over budget. He will undoubtedly enjoy his sumptuous interior, and your fees will increase proportionately. However, he still may resent you for spending too much. On a subconscious level, he contends, he didn't spend the money. *You* spent it.

Therefore, when a client decides to spend much more than initially anticipated, make sure his decision was carefully made. Don't pursue more expensive design plans until you are convinced that your client wants to take that route. Some designers actually try to persuade their clients to spend less, arguing that a less expensive interior can be just as effective. Their clients actually order them to increase the budget. This reverse psychology sometimes works well. Regardless of the amount the client spends, the designer is not blamed for overselling or high-pressure tactics.

On occasion, a client will be sorry that he didn't spend more and may blame his designer. A typical lament is, "I wish I had purchased brass hardware instead of chrome. My designer told me it wasn't worth the extra money, but now I wish I had spent it." Of course, this shows how designers can never win. However, at least under these circumstances, the client can't blame the designer for trying to push him into extravagant spending.

As far as the legal liability of the designer for the budget is concerned, is the designer responsible if the budget exceeds his initial "guesstimate"? In most cases, I think the answer is no. If the designer has acted in good faith, I don't believe that he is responsible if purchasing quotes and contractors' estimates exceed the designer's initial "guesstimates." As long as the client hasn't relied on prices to his financial detriment, a designer should not be held responsible if confirmed prices are greater than anticipated.

However, although a designer may not be liable for guesstimates, a court or arbitration board may insist that he return part or all of his design fee. Recall the designer mentioned previously, who added extras to his client's design plans without warning him about increasing costs. The arbitration board ordered him to return half of the design retainer.

It's my conclusion that if a designer blatantly exceeds his initial guesstimate, he may be legally liable to return his design fee. However, legal actions for this offense rarely occur. Most likely, such a designer will lose credibility with his client. Even though the designer won't have to defend himself in court, he'll be judged on a different level.

My recommendations are as follows. Discuss the budget with your client thoroughly before preparing design plans. Don't design your client's fantasy, only to discover that he can't afford it.

If you provide a guesstimate in writing, base it on realistic prices. Make sure your price lists are current. Once the preliminary budget is completed, obtain your client's written approval. Ideally, don't prepare purchase orders until a budget is signed by the client.

If the budget exceeds your initial guesstimate, make sure all additions are approved in writing.

Many designers take a very simple approach to determine a client's budget. They show clients different options before preparing design plans. These designers take their clients to visit showrooms and completed projects. Once the designer gets a feel for her client's taste level, she can be more astute in her "guesstimates" and preliminary budget. Once the project is finished, the client will still recommend the designer and send her repeat business. The designer will make more money.

In this discussion, many examples have been presented to demonstrate how a designer can cope with an unhappy client. Various psychological approaches have been suggested.

The following section discusses how a designer can cope with another designer—an unhappy partner. Although the mechanics are different in dealing with a colleague rather than a client, many of the psychological approaches are similar.

DESIGNER DIVORCE AND CLIENT CONTINUITY

Creative businesses in the fields of arts and science are characteristically hotbeds of entrepreneurial talent. A substantial percentage of interior designers operate as solo practitioners or are in partnerships with fewer than 10 members. Furthermore, many solo practitioners frequently joint-venture with other designers and architects for specific projects. It is not unusual for designers to change their type of business organization and format of operation several times during the span of their careers.

This type of flexibility usually has a positive effect for the creative mentality. When the concept of change is built into the designer's thought process, new ideas flourish. However, the process of change has its own price, which can be very high, depending on the circumstances. For example, the dissolution of a design partnership of two members, a common experience in the career of many designers, can cause the same type of unpleasant side effects, financial and psychological, as the dissolution of a marriage. Consequently, in the event of a "design divorce," various therapeutic measures can be taken to reduce the trauma of the separation process.

The following situation is typical of many design divorces. An anatomy of the designers' background and business problems can be helpful in determining how to deal with similar cases. Accordingly, some of the details of a partnership are analyzed for illustration.

━━━━━━━━

A partnership of two designers is in the process of splitting up after successfully operating for more than four years. One partner is a decorator in her late forties who has worked in the design business for more than 20 years. She has worked for a fabric showroom and for two well-known decorators in their own businesses, acting as a business manager, decorator, and public relations spokeswoman. She had always wanted her own business and, several years ago, decided to take the plunge and go on her own. Clients always liked her. She had numerous contacts with vendors at showrooms. Many clients of former employers had asked her to decorate for them in the event she started her own business. In short, she was well plugged into the "designer scene" in the New York area.

Since she had no formal design education, she felt the need to have a partner. She picked a younger man, in his early thirties, a graduate of an excellent design school. His family had been in the design business in the West. The partners had become acquainted when they were employed by the same design firm. They knew each other extremely well before deciding to work together. In spite of their differences, they wanted to remain close personal friends. It was a marriage, many other designers thought, that was made to order.

During the first year and a half, when both partners were looking for new business, they got along very well. It was success that ruined them. Their early work became published in major design periodicals. Within three years, they had 25 clients, more than half with budgets exceeding $100,000. There was a healthy mix of residential work, which the woman favored, and commercial work, which her partner liked. The culmination of their relationship was to work on a showcase house. Although neither one of them liked the way their assigned room looked, as it was a "design compromise," it was well received by the public and the press. Then, all the "past" resentments in their relationship surfaced, and they decided to separate before their relationship deteriorated further.

Atlhough the male partner was ambivalent about the divorce, the female partner was adamant about it. She had brought in most of the business. However, she had certain questions about the separation, specifically, as well as how to proceed once she was operating alone.

First, the partners had formed a corporation. Should they buy each other out? They each owned 50 percent of the stock.

Second, how do they handle their existing projects? They have nine active clients at the moment, with their interiors in various stages of completion. How do they decide which partner completes each project? Should they finish all of them together? When do they tell their clients that they are getting a "divorce" ?

Third, what do they do about new referrals from now on? How do they decide how to split up new business?

Fourth, their office was set up in the woman's apartment, located in the midtown area near the design showrooms. The business always paid half the rent. How should it be allocated now, and for how long?

Fifth, there are a number of details that require special attention. They have assembled a sample room, well-stocked with catalogs. For each of their projects there is a complete presentation, with sketches and samples, useful to both of them. How are they to be divided? After the separation, who gets to keep the business phone number? They both want it.

Sixth, they have a lawyer and an accountant. Should they each find a separate lawyer and accountant to help divide their business?

An interior design business can be compared to an expert bobsled run. In many cases, it may take very little effort to get moving, but, once on course and gaining momentum, only an expert can retain balance and complete the run without sustaining severe injuries.

Before analyzing this situation and addressing the issues raised, one should consider the foremost point. Fortunately, both partners have maintained a certain amount of equanimity about each other and their situation. In design divorces, it is important for the divorcing partners to keep calm, to maintain a sense of fairness, and to remember their regard for each other. If these feelings remain mutual, they will sustain the partners during their period of crisis.

The issue of representation is discussed first, because it has certain ramifications that affect the success or failure of a dissolution. In any business of substantial size, various partners frequently retain separate counsel and accountants in the event of a dissolution. Partnership agreements or shareholders agreements for corporations frequently provide mechanisms for the division of assets and liabilities should a dissolution become inevitable.

In a small service business, however, regardless of high profitability, such steps may not be necessary, because expensive assets, such as inventories of goods, real estate holdings, and manufacturing machinery, aren't involved. A reputation for creativity, responsibility, and reliability is a designer's most important asset. It behooves partners to maintain an operable relationship throughout a dissolution to avoid squandering what they have both endeavored to create during their years together.

It is the business of lawyers and accountants to represent their clients by obtaining what is most favorable on their behalf. Despite good intentions, obtaining separate representation at a premature stage can cause more problems than it may solve. These partners are savvy adults with experience and maturity. Before consulting others, the partners should reason together to decide what makes sense.

Usually, not all negotiations between dissolving partners can be completed in one conversation. Both partners must be willing to bend so that many problems can be resolved during the "windup process." Of course, if after serious negotiation all settlement attempts fail, outside professionals must be consulted for guidance and advice. Initially, however, it can be useful for the partners to work together, alone.

Second, I do not recommend either partner's acquiring each other's stock. Once all the affairs have been "wound up," the corporation should be dissolved by an attorney. In some states, if corporate franchise taxes aren't paid for a certain period, the secretary of state may dissolve the corporation as a matter of course. Technically, the shareholders can be held liable for these unpaid taxes; however, in many states, no serious efforts are made to collect them.

In certain cases, partners buy each other out. Usually, such a purchase relates only to the company's tangible assets, not the shares themselves. There are a variety of reasons for this practice, but common sense provides a simple explanation.

Corporations insure "limited liability" for shareholders in most states. Theoretically, a corporation is solely liable for any damages sustained during the period of its ongoing business operations. The shareholders cannot be personally held responsible, except in very limited situations.

Forming a new corporation for a private practice is a fairly simple and affordable process. For the future, why risk having skeletons from an old business haunt a new one? At some later time, a former client may institute a lawsuit for damages, although the business may have no inkling of that now. Why take that risk? Unless there are compelling financial reasons for either partner to operate in the future under their existing corporate structure, I encourage dissolution once all business has been completed. However, since this is to some extent a technical legal question, I always advise dissolving partners to discuss the matter with an attorney once all other loose ends have been tied up.

Third, upon deciding to divorce, the partnership had nine active clients with budgets exceeding $100,000. There are a number of important questions in this regard: When should clients be told about the divorce? Are the partners required to finish all projects jointly? If not, how should the jobs be split between the partners?

Of course, without being familiar with the partners and the details of each project, attempting to answer these questions conclusively is difficult. Instead of formulating a hypothetical solution, I offer some guidelines to present a clearer picture.

First, at what stage of completion is each project at the time of dissolution? The answer is more definable if the project is in the initial stages (i.e., project planning and formulation of design decisions) or in the final stages (i.e., final supervision of implementation of design plans).

Once the decision has been made to divorce, it's probably best to wind up the relationship quickly, dividing all projects, if possible. It makes little sense to prolong a relationship that is destined for termination. It's better for both partners to develop their new careers individually without being bogged down by old problems. Therefore, if a project has recently begun, the partners should confer with the client immediately. After being advised of the divorce, the client must make the decision. She may not want either partner individually. If she selects one, the chosen partner should continue only if he is capable of performing alone. If outside assistance is necessary, this must be disclosed and sanctioned by the client in writing.

If the project is in the wind-up stage, occasionally, it's preferable not to advise the client of the impending dissolution until the project is fully complete. Supervision of design implementation, including visits to the job site, is usually allocated to an individual partner anyway. Accordingly, if the partners are able to divide their duties, it may be wise not to risk creating apprehension in a client so long as the divorce will not affect job supervision.

Obviously, the most difficult determinations are for projects in the middle stages of development. Prior to taking a course of action, a sound rationale should be calculated. Any hostility between "design spouses" should be put on hold. It should always be remembered that the partner-ship has been entrusted with important financial and emotional commit-ments by their clients. Their welfare should be considered paramount.

Sometimes the problem isn't serious. A client may become accus-tomed to working with one partner very early in the design process, and, therefore, a divorce may not be a big issue. However, if the client is a "multiple," such as a group of doctors, lawyers, officers in a corporation, or even a husband and a wife, a choice may not be easy if the husband, for example, relates well to one partner and the wife relates to the other partner. What then?

Again, a decision based on subjective factors must prevail. However, some designers won't disclose their divorce until all major design deci-sions have been made and construction and design implementation are well under way. Prompt disclosure, some designers believe, is not timely if it will cause their clients undue trauma.

If a client finds out about the divorce through a third party, the designers must be prepared to offer an explanation. For example, one partnership in the throes of dissolution told its clients that the divorce was due to differences in career objectives, not personal difficulties, and that continued collaboration on specific projects was intended. The part-ners promised, "We are aware of our duties and responsibilities and are fully able and eager to fulfill them. Our separation as a formal business entity is not due to personal reasons. Your project will progress uninter-rupted, as if our business were to continue on an indefinite basis."

Of course, to keep such a promise isn't possible. Clients are always affected by a design divorce. However, the damage can be minimized if the designers make a major effort.

Splitting up new business that appears during the dissolution period may create a bone of contention between the partners. Nonetheless, I don't believe it has to be a serious problem. Frequently, when a new client approaches a design partnership in the midst of a divorce, one of the part-ners doesn't want the job. If each partner does want to be retained, the client should be advised of the split and offered a choice of partners as an option. Usually, when new business originates from a referral, the refer-ring party has a preference for one of the design partners. This will undoubtedly have an important effect on a prospective client's judgment. In any event, if a new client insists that the designers continue to operate as a team, the project should be turned away for all the reasons discussed previously.

The details of dissolution are important but shouldn't be afforded undue signficance. In the example, "marital property" included a well-stocked sample room, including catalogs, and client presentation boards accompanied by sketches and samples for all completed projects. If both partners want the inventory, it shouldn't be divided. It should be duplicated. Granted, it's an expensive and time-consuming process. Nonetheless, partners should use their best efforts to supply each other with the tools of their trade gathered during the tenure of their relationship.

Further, in the example, the partnership office had been located in one partner's apartment. Prior to the separation, the business had paid half the rent. Questions arose about a new percentage allocation of the rent and the duration of such payment during the wind-up process. It's my feeling that so long as a partnership continues to operate in any meaningful fashion, the business should continue to pay half the rent. Clearly, the "design spouse" living with the business must endure a severe intrusion until the wind-up process is complete and is entitled to reasonable compensation.

Finally, both partners wanted to retain the business telephone number. There's no question that a telephone number can be a valuable asset, particularly if the partnership has been in existence for a substantial length of time and has invested in public relations to create an identity.

Any active partnership, however, takes a fair amount of time to wind up if handled properly. Some projects may even extend for up to two years after the decision to divorce has been made.

During that interval, both designers may have grown in such different directions that at the close of the wind-up period, the phone number issue may become moot, no longer relevant because of a change of circumstances. For example, one partner may make a geographic change or become a partner in an existing design firm with an entirely different clientele.

This is an important point, because it illustrates how other issues of the dissolution may ultimately be resolved. When the initial decision to divorce is made, both partners are usually in a very sensitive, emotional state of mind. Everything seems to loom with overpowering significance. As time progresses, however, many details seem to resolve themselves, especially after the impact of the separation has been absorbed by both partners.

In summation, although I have dealt with all these issues rather simplistically, I do not minimize the difficulty of design divorce. Although the process may be painful, solutions can be found to make each partner whole. If both partners make a sincere effort to protect their clients, instead of trying to outsmart each other, their divorce will be much simpler. A peaceful ending will enable each partner to retain a positive frame of reference when approaching a new beginning.

CONCLUSION

In regard to *designer responsibility and client budget*, the designer is obligated to his client for structuring the budget carefully, based upon the client's needs and requirements. In regard to *designer divorce and client continuity*, the designer is responsible for discharging his professional responsibilities to his client regardless of his firm's internal problems.

In both situations, the designer must use his ability to navigate around obstacles that may interfere with his fulfilling his responsibilities. However, by using similar analytical problem-solving techniques, the designer will be able to surmount these hurdles. The end result will produce an optimal solution for both the client and the designer.

5

PROFESSIONAL ANALYSIS FOR CHARGING CLIENTS

Chapter 2, "Charging a Client," offers a set of ground rules for charging clients. Chapters 1 and 3 establish guidelines for the preparation of letters of agreement. Various methods of charging, to be integrated within the context of a structured contract, are explored.

In this chapter, two hypothetical clients present the facts relating to their complex projects. One is in the residential category, and the other commercial. Then an analysis of how to charge for each project is provided. Although you may disagree with my analysis, it will raise many thorny issues, including designer responsibility in relation to other professionals.

CLIENT 1: THE COUNTESS

We begin with a residential client. While sipping cappuccino in your terraced, elegant office one morning, your secretary tells you that Countess Ursula von Clutter is on the phone. The countess and her husband, Count Klaus, live at 901 Park Avenue in Manhattan, a building for which you have recently completed the lobby. The countess tells you that she likes your sense of color and, for that reason, is consulting you.

She advises that she is selling her eight-room apartment because she has recently bought the apartment formerly owned by her aunt, the Baroness Marlene von Clutter, in the same building. The baroness left New York permanently for Buenos Aires after some recent unfortunate publicity about her German affiliations during World War II.

The countess's new apartment is the crown jewel of the building, a magnificent 14-room penthouse with four baths, servants' quarters, and a restaurant-sized kitchen and pantry. The kitchen and baths have recently been updated.

The baroness left town in a hurry and sold the apartment furnished. It contains many pieces of valuable antique furniture and art deco treasures that compliment the countess's own furniture collection.

Upon inspection, you find that the baroness had decorated her apartment in rich, heavy colors, while the countess prefers a light, airy feeling. A lot of clever editing to integrate the furniture from both collections will be necessary, as well as some restoration and reupholstering.

Most rooms need painting or wall coverings. The countess mentioned that she likes glazed walls and other decorative painted finishes. The wood parquet floors need refinishing, and some rooms will be carpeted. There is a large collection of oriental rugs which requires editing and restoration.

The wraparound penthouse terrace, nearly 2000 square feet, has been neglected badly. Many terra-cotta tiles need replacement. A new outdoor lighting system is required, and complete relandscaping is a must. Although the apartment is basically traditional, some interior cabinet-work and recessed lighting will be used in strategic areas.

The countess uses her New York residence as a pied-à-terre, since she maintains houses and apartments in other parts of the world. Owing to her busy social schedule, she hasn't much time to shop with a designer. However, she insists on perfection. She will allow you to photograph the apartment upon completion, which will undoubtedly be pursued by many prestigous shelter magazines.

The countess has asked "how you work." Accordingly, you must provide her with information on how much you charge and how your office will manage her project. Prior to preparing a proposal, you must think about the project and outline your thoughts.

Identify the most important issues that may influence your decisions. Review various methods of charging to determine how they would integrate with the dynamics of the project. Ideally, dissect each issue and prepare an answer. Once you have completed your analysis, review mine to determine whether you agree or disagree.

One factor to consider is your interest in the project as a whole. If you recall, I mentioned that the client is a countess who lives at 901 Park Avenue in Manhattan, a formidable address. She called because she liked your design work in the recently completed lobby. You might view this as an opportunity to work with a wealthy, influential individual with international connections.

Obviously, this is a very grand client, whom I created for a purpose. Clients often try to impress their designers with their status to intimidate them into taking a job on their own terms. Many designers have told me that they submitted to unreasonable demands because a certain project seemed like such a plum. That is the reason I portray the client as a wealthy, titled society woman living in a grand Park Avenue apartment.

What could sound more perfect? My point is never to be fooled by a pedigree. Don't become mesmerized by the superficial glamour of a client's appearance. It's more important to analyze a client's character and personality to determine how well you can work together.

Let's return to some of the fundamentals of the job. Your potential client is moving from a smaller space to a much larger one. Ordinarily, in that situation, a client would require purchasing more furniture and furnishings. However, this is not the case here. Since your client is combining her existing furniture with furniture from her aunt's apartment, she won't need to buy much.

The amount of purchases is a most important issue in determining how to charge. When designers know they will make large purchases, many like to charge cost- plus in order to earn hefty commissions.

However, this project mainly requires the use of extensive decorating services. The rooms need painting and wall covering, and the parquet wood floors need refinishing. Carpeting will be installed in certain rooms. Construction is required for the terrace, and builts-ins and recessed lighting must be designed and installed.

The bottom line is this: There is a lot of work to be done in this apartment. However, most of it involves construction and decorating services. And because the client is an "absentee owner" for the most part, your extensive supervision is required.

You might think that because the budget will be considerable, perhaps you should hire all the contractors yourself. Then you can charge for your services on a cost-plus basis. That way, your commissions will be substantial.

However, that may be a big mistake in regard to liability. The countess's apartment is in a very opulent building, which obviously has strict rules for construction. We're not talking about painting a bedroom or two or building a few bookshelves; this project involves major decorating, and your client wants you to assume complete control.

I would advise the countess as follows. She should hire a general contractor to organize and supervise all construction, including painting, wall covering, lighting, cabinetwork, and tilework. I recommend consulting three different general contractors. I would also ask the building manager for the name of a contractor who has worked in the building on prior occasions.

If you supervise the project yourself, you could be violating a number of laws. Unless you are licensed, you may be working as an unlicensed home improvement contractor. Moreover, since you would supervise several contractors, you may be working as an unlicensed general contractor. Finally, depending on the construction involved, you may also be working as an unlicensed architect.

Urge your client to hire a general contractor. If architectural drawings are required, let the contractor hire an architect and obtain any necessary permits. If problems arise with the construction, let them be resolved by the general contractor.

What should your role be? It is your job to design the space and prepare a complete set of schematic drawings, including a color scheme. For that aspect of the project you can charge a flat fee or an hourly fee. Generally, well-established designers would charge a large flat fee for preparing design plans. For a project of this scope, the fee would most likely start at $10,000, depending on the caliber of the designer.

Most of the purchases involve architectural materials, and, accordingly, the contractors and general contractor will make them. However, you could charge the countess cost-plus for any purchases you make on her behalf. For example, you can specify all window treatments, custom hardware, custom lighting, and wall coverings. You can also attempt to specify the carpeting as well.

Other than making those particular purchases, most of your work will be of a consulting and supervisory nature. You will be constantly meeting with the general contractor, architect, and subcontractors. Most likely, you will be the design liaison between them and the countess, who, for the most part, won't be available. Therefore, all your consultation time should be billed by the hour.

Send the countess monthly statements to avoid an accumulation of a large balance. The countess may not realize or comprehend the amount of time that must be devoted by you and your staff to adequately supervise the job. If you wait too long to submit bills, she may be appalled by the number of hours.

Suppose the countess tells you that she doesn't want to be billed by the hour. She wants to pay you a flat fee—the first payment when you start the project, and the balance when you finish. Should you consider that option?

Of course, the job is very tempting. You have a most prestigious client who may be in a position to refer you to her friends. Moreover, your client will be "in absentia" for the most part. You are thrilled to avoid dealing with your client on a daily basis. Clients sometimes interfere with a designer's job, but in this case, that won't be a problem.

Further, the countess has agreed to your photographing the apartment upon completion. Since the project will look spectacular, obviously, you will get it published in an important shelter magazine, which can be invaluable for public relations.

The problem with charging a flat fee is the difficulty in determining its size. Some designers would begin by estimating the countess's budget for all construction and decorating services. Assume the guesstimate is $400,000. Then they would decide to charge 20 percent of the budget for all their consultation and supervision. Accordingly, the flat fee would be $80,000.

In any event, with a flat fee, I would not provide the client the option to withhold 50 percent until the job is completed. If the client is unhappy, she could refuse to make the final payment. By allowing such an option, you would place half your design fee at risk—not a smart financial decision. I wouldn't allow a client to withhold any more than 20 percent until the end of a job.

However, a large flat fee might scare a client away. If you bill by the hour, you may ultimately earn more. Yet, since the bills will be submitted on a monthly basis, the client isn't faced with a large fixed obligation at the inception of a project. If the countess insists on a flat fee, however, don't undercharge.

If a flat fee is charged, place an "outside date" in the letter of agreement for your services. For example, if the job should take nine months to complete, be generous. Allow a year for your services to be rendered. After a year has expired, if the job still isn't finished, bill on a monthly basis, or by the hour, until your services are no longer required. In any case, don't allow your services on a flat fee to be open-ended. Otherwise, a client could keep you working indefinitely for one fixed amount and you would lose considerable money on the job.

CLIENT 2: SIR CLEM CASINO

Now let's discuss your commercial or "contract" client. Sir Clem Casino is the chairman of the board of a large foreign company, a prestigious importer and distributor of fish products. He plans to open corporate offices in New York City, and announces that he has just leased 8000 square feet in the commercial section of Fifth Avenue Tower. He wants to retain your services to revise an existing design plan prepared by his architect, retain a general contractor, and act as liaison with the skyscraper's engineers.

Sir Clem employs an English architect, who designed the space. He plans to have a maze of aquariums constructed in the executive office suite to complement his art collection with a nautical motif. He already owns most of the furniture for the executive offices that, in turn, complements this collection. He will require new furniture for the secretarial areas.

You are aware that Sir Clem is interviewing several interior design firms. He wants to find the most interesting, creative, and economically viable solutions. Sir Clem asks you how your firm would manage the project and how you would charge design fees. What will you tell him?

Prior to preparing a proposal, think about the project and outline your thoughts. Identify the most important issues that may influence your decision. Review different methods of charging to determine how they would integrate with the dynamics of the project.

As far as the competition is concerned, if Sir Clem approaches a "contract" firm that services only commercial clients, it will probably undertake this project on an hourly basis. Frequently, contract firms submit a list to their clients with hourly rates for their employees. Usually, the rates are itemized (i.e., partner, senior designer, junior designer, draftsman, etc.). Sometimes, these rates are multiplied by a "multiplier," which may range from 2.5 to 3.25. These firms frequently ask for a retainer. Some bill on a monthly basis.

For your purposes, I would not suggest proposing a multiplier. Larger firms have more leverage in persuading clients to accept a multiplier, but it is usually more difficult for smaller firms.

Charging by the hour is an excellent method in this instance. Make certain that your hourly rates are high enough to cover the cost of your overhead. Then, you won't need a multiplier. A thorough discussion of the multiplier can be reviewed in Chapter 1, "Preparing a Letter of Agreement."

Assume that you have devised a schedule of hourly rates that are approved by Sir Clem. Yet, he may respond, "I will agree to your rates. However, I don't have an open-ended design budget and would like an upset fee. What is your maximum design fee?"

An upset fee, as you may recall, is an absolute ceiling on the amount of your design fee. When a client demands an upset fee, consider the matter carefully before providing one.

An upset fee transforms your remuneration into a flat fee that is charged on an hourly basis. If you charge a client a flat fee, you risk the profitability of the job. In this situation, you have reasons for concern.

First, you have no prior working history with Sir Clem. You have no idea how reasonable he will be. Second, Sir Clem has an English architect who will undoubtedly supervise your design services. If the architect is not satisfied with your plans or supervision, he may create extensive additional work for your office. These two factors raise a red flag in regard to the request for an upset fee.

I would recommend the following course: Charge for all purchases on a cost-plus basis and for preparation of your design plans and supervision on an hourly basis. I would present Sir Clem with a very reasonable list of hourly rates but would not agree to an upset figure.

Here is my rationale. The project involves dealing with many people. This client is a foreigner. He and his English architect may be coming and going from the project site without coordinating their supervision. You will also be dealing with the building engineers of Fifth Avenue Tower. Since Sir Clem wants an extensive aquarium, you will have to consult an aquarium designer. That designer will consult with a lighting designer and a plumber. Of course, this will all be under the direction of the general contractor, but you must be involved in those meetings. It's your responsibility to coordinate the project from a design perspective. Consequently, the amount of time you may need to devote could be open-ended.

The commissions earned in charging cost-plus will probably not be significant since your purchases will be limited. Although the size of the space is 8000 square feet, Sir Clem has advised you that he has a collection of furniture and art. Essentially, your design work is to create an interior to showcase these items.

Your purchases will be for the secretarial and utilitarian spaces. This is a small part of the job and represents a minor expense in relation to the entire scope of the project.

Don't forget to charge for disbursements in your letter of agreement. Since your client is foreign and the architect is English, you will continually be involved with various forms of international communications. There will be numerous telephone calls, faxes, and shipments of documents from one locale to another.

Assume you have ruled out Sir Clem's request for an upset fee. Suppose he asks you to reduce your hourly rates or your cost-plus percentage on purchases? Would you be interested?

You might consider providing a discount for the following reasons. The client is international, and the project is in a very visible building. It will be seen by everyone. Furthermore, it will undoubtedly be photographed, which would provide excellent public relations. Considering these two factors, the project might be a perfect vehicle to promote your business.

On the other hand, there are good reasons not to discount reasonable rates. The project is located in a major New York building. In a building of this nature, there are always complications. Your installations, involving an aquarium, will probably be difficult. Further, you have to contend with a foreign architect in addition to the general contractor and subcontractors. There is no question that this will be a very stressful project, for which you should be fairly compensated.

Consider this compromise. You may refuse to provide Sir Clem with an upset rate and insist on charging your normal hourly rates. However, you could reduce the percentage for cost-plus purchases. If you lower it, Sir Clem may think he's getting a bargain. It may create a sufficient impetus for you to be awarded the job. On the other hand, since purchases won't be substantial, you won't sacrifice a great deal of income.

The purpose of analyzing both hypothetical projects here is to make a point. Regardless of whether a project is residential or commercial, it is important to analyze the dynamics of each job prior to preparing a proposal or quoting a fee. From a business standpoint, determine the value of working on each project. Make a list of the pluses and minuses. Then, evaluate the importance of all the factors as weighed against each other. Using this approach, you will be in a far better position to decide how to charge and to make more money.

These two hypothetical clients bring into focus several issues confronting the designers:

1. The role of the designer and the general contractor
2. Competitive bidding for design fees
3. Defining specific needs of a client in the letter of agreement

THE ROLE OF THE DESIGNER WITH CLIENTS AND A GENERAL CONTRACTOR

Chapter 6, "Contracts, Contractors, and Liability," discusess how designers should deal with general contractors, subcontractors, and outside consultants. However, since both hypothetical projects in this chapter involve general contractors, a discussion of the role of the designer vis à vis the general contractor, specifically, is in order at this point.

Under optimal circumstances, a competent general contractor can simplify the designer's supervisory role during the construction process. Many designers agree that one of their most difficult jobs is construction supervision from a logistical standpoint. Because busy designers have a number of projects in progress at any given time, it is impossible to be at all job sites to supervise every facet of construction.

Theoretically, a general contractor should be the solution to this problem. He should be an expert in the construction business and be thoroughly familiar with the designer's plans. It is his responsibility to interpret the drawings, schedules, and specifications to the subcontractors who rely on him to supervise their installations. He, not the interior designer, should be responsible for the quality and supervision of the work. The designer must, naturally, make periodic inspections, spot-check field dimensions, and make decisions about changes due to varying field conditions if necessary. In a sense, once a client approves the design plans, which are accepted by a general contractor, the designer's role shifts from being a planner and creator to being an adviser. Or does it?

The key to this analysis is the qualifying phrase "under optimal circumstances." As most seasoned designers will relate, a large percentage of their jobs don't operate under optimal circumstances. Either financial considerations, the site itself, or particular idiosyncrasies of the client may create a condition that can cause a marked deviation in the designer's normal functions.A common result is a change in the designer's traditional relationship with the general contractor. The number of role permutations can be almost infinite.

To illustrate, I present two situations that caused a designer severe hardship. One was the result of the presence of a negligent general contractor. The other was due to the absence of a general contractor, when one should have been retained. Because either of these particular circumstances may occur during one of your own jobs, note the analysis and logic used in both situations. This may help you to develop an approach if faced with a similar conflict.

Since the following cases actually occurred, they are presented in a question-and-answer format.

QUESTION: *I am the head of a small but extremely successful commercial design firm in New York City. In the last 10 years, we have had a substantial number of foreign clientele who have hired us to design their New York headquarters. These clients don't live here, but generally inspect their projects only two or three times while they are under construction. Their personnel arrive to occupy the space only after completion.*

Since our reputation has become well established, our policy has been to retain general contractors directly. All client contact is solely with our office, and we assume responsibility for everything. Our clients are liberal with their budgets. In exchange, they don't want to be involved with any problems that might arise. Once the plans and purchases are approved, we complete the job and present a key to a finished interior. This method has always worked for our firm— until the last project.

We began the construction phase of a $2,000,000 office suite, using a general contractor who had successfully finished several projects for us in the past.

Unknown to us, he had encountered serious financial difficulties. As a result, he had to cut corners by using second-class materials and subcontractors. For example, all the plasterwork has to be redone. Major electrical rewiring will be necessary, even though he had used a good electrical contractor.

Our inspection last week revealed the construction phase to be in a chaotic state. When we met with the general contractor, he refused to acknowledge the reality of the situation. He claimed that everything could easily be resolved. In addition, he has demanded a $50,000 payment. He refuses to continue until he receives the money to pay his subcontractors.

Our client called from London, advising that an employee would be arriving from New York next week to visit the site. I'm afraid that when he sees the project in its present condition, we'll be discharged. Is there a way to resolve this situation?

ANSWER: The case of the "absentee client" has become more common in the past several years. In the two hypothetical examples in this chapter, both the countess and Sir Clem were absentee clients. For that reason, I discuss this designer's problem here.

For both economic and political reasons, foreign corporations have been opening stores and offices and purchasing residences with increasing regularity in key American regions. They often retain design firms based on the recommendations of their trusted friends and associates. They need to feel comfortable in delegating all authority to their designer. Many foreign clients have no domestic locations to enable them to supervise.

The designer is then placed in a precarious position. In one sense, he is free to use his own discretion and work without the handicap of a troublesome client. On the other hand, he also assumes certain responsibilities, including hiring key personnel, such as the general contractor. He remains answerable to his client if something goes wrong.

Here, the design firm was faced with an urgent situation that could have resulted in instant dismissal. Drastic measures had to be taken immediately. When faced with a general contractor who has cut corners and used inferior subcontractors, I think the best course of action is to adopt the plan of seasoned investors. When confronted with a hopelessly declining market, they cut their losses.

This general contractor destroyed his credibility with shoddy workmanship. I would not trust him with the responsibility of making necessary changes when a client relationship is at stake.

Consequently, I advised the removal of the general contractor immediately, but without recriminations. If dismissed with rancor, he may have become vindictive, placing a mechanic's lien on the building for unpaid improvements by subcontractors. Legally, he could file liens whether or not such claims were justified. That would have immediately alerted the designer's client to the trouble.

The general contractor, then, was ultimately told that the client himself had inspected the premises and ordered his termination. This shifted the blame from the design firm. During settlement negotiations, it was intimated that the contractor might be retained at some future date if settlement for outstanding bills was reached on an amicable basis.

The next step was to contain the damage. A new general contractor examined the site with the designer, the existing qualified subcontractors, and any new subcontractors. They estimated the cost to bring the project up to specifications.

Substituted general contractors are frequently reluctant to estimate the cost of redoing work. Here, the new contractor had no choice. The design firm required a detailed estimate to repair existing conditions in order to award him the job.

Subsequently, it was determined that the original general contractor's demand for $50,000 was totally without foundation. In fact, considering the damages he had caused, he was entitled only to $10,000. A meeting revealed that although this contractor was desparate for money, he was also very stubborn. He realized that he held a threat over the design firm, being able to file a mechanic's lien. However, he was also anxious to resolve the situation and to obtain quickly as much money as possible to satisfy his other creditors.

Although the design firm owed him $10,000 at most, a settlement was soon entered into for $25,000. Prior to making payment, all subcontractors submitted "completion certificates," notarized statements indicating balances due to complete their contracts to specification. It was essential for the design firm to ascertain its financial position prior to entering into a settlement. A lien search was conducted. It indicated that no liens had been filed against the client's building by subcontractors, the general contractor, or any third parties.

Before making the settlement offer, the design firm's principal made some thoughtful evaluations. He knew he could sue the general contractor, possibly avoiding payment of any damages. However, that may have resulted in serious consequences. It may have caused delaying project completion, losing the client, or paying considerable legal costs for litigation.

The paramount concern of the design firm was to satisfy the client by finishing the project. A design fee of $300,000 was at stake, not including future business from referrals. Ultimately, the new general contractor was substituted, and the job proceeded. Fortunately, the inspection by the client's employee was delayed. By the time he arrived at the site, progress looked normal.

The circumstances of this case may seem a bit unusual at first glance. But given some thought, some general guidelines might be extracted for use on many jobs.

First, should a design firm work for an absentee client by assuming all responsibility? A thoughtful value judgment should be made in each case. If the project is a good one, with a large fee and guaranteed payments, (e.g., a letter of credit), it might be good business for the design firm to take over the job. In that case, the designer must hire the general contractor and supervise every detail.

If the client appears to be difficult, or if the fee is not especially rewarding, the design firm should insist that the client retain his own general contractor. The client must enter into his own contracts and make all payments directly. The client could object, remain "absentee," and hire a different designer. However, taking all things into consideration, in this situation, it's worth risking the loss of a client rather than assuming all potential liability.

Second, how should a design firm deal with a general contractor who has hired inferior subcontractors and failed to supervise properly? As indicated previously, my feeling is that once a general contractor is guilty of sins of omission or commission, he should be discharged immediately.

Two major functions of a general contractor are to ensure that the job is completed at budget and that it is finished on time. If the contractor's work appears inadequate while the job is in progress, don't wait until something else goes wrong. Fire the contractor.

Dismissal may not be easy if it was the client who hired the general contractor. If that's the case, the designer must use his best efforts to convince the client to fire the contractor. Negligent general contractors often make glaring errors, so this isn't difficult. Moreover, if the client retained the general contractor, damages aren't the designer's responsibility. Nonetheless, the project must still be finished, which leaves the design firm to resolve the situation.

Third, even if you have faith in your general contractor, don't have blind faith. Check out each subcontractor prior to signing any contracts. Tell the general contractor about your favorite subcontractors and see how he reacts. If he objects strenuously, ask yourself whether he may have a vested interest in hiring his own subcontractors.

A general contractor should be a blessing, not a burden. Use as much care to select one as you would to create design plans for a new environment. It can make the difference between losing a project and satisfying a client.

The preceding example emphasizes the importance of the general contractor's performance level during the construction phase of the design process. General contractors are usually a necessary element for a project of any consequence. They supervise subcontractors during all facets of construction, interpret design plans, and act as a liaison with the designer. This is crucial for the designer who is usually unable to be present at every job site with the same degree of consistency because of other client demands.

As stated earlier, the general contractor should be an expert at the construction business and thoroughly familiar with the designer's plans. The quality and supervision of the work is his responsibility. The designer should, naturally, make periodic inspections, spot-check field dimensions, and make any necessary changes due to varying field conditions, if any. Once a designer's plans are approved by the client and accepted by the general contractor, his role, in a sense, becomes that of adviser, rather than that of planner and creator. At that juncture, it is the role of the general contractor to create.

It has been customary practice for many general contractors to charge a percentage of the construction budget as compensation for their services. Fifteen percent to 20 percent is a common going rate, but there are no rules. Although well-heeled clients sometimes balk at paying for a general contractor, they realize that the designer cannot be expected to oversee construction for the design fee. Ultimately, as designers often testify, a good general contractor is worth his weight in gold. Proper supervision is the key to quality workmanship, adherence to schedules, and project completion at budget.

These financial times, however, have proved to be most extraordinary. Due to the worldwide recessionary economy of the past several years, the design and construction industries have taken a brutal beating. Corporations and consumers have tightened plans for expansion and construction, and many design projects are undertaken only by necessity.

Many clients insist that budgets be kept minimal and slice expenses to reduce costs. In some cases, clients eliminate hiring a general contractor to save money. The following example illustrates what happened when a designer assumed the role of general contractor without being paid for the extra supervision. The results, unfortunately, were disastrous.

This case emphasizes the reasons for hiring a general contractor for both hypothetical clients described earlier in this chapter.

QUESTION: *My partner and I operate a small interior design firm, employing one part-time assistant on a regular basis. We have been in business for two years and have kept our staff to a minimum, hiring draftsmen and assistants temporarily as the jobs require.*

About six months ago, a client retained us to design a small office suite. As part of his leasing arrangements with his landlord, he was provided with the labor for a complete paint job, at no extra charge, by his landlord's painting contractor. Our client was required only to supply the paint.

Since partitioning of the space was necessary, the landlord also provided his cabinetmaker, who supposedly charged less than the market rate for quality work. Electrical and phone installations were required, but no plumbing was necessary.

My partner and I recommended hiring a general contractor even though it was a small job. We charged a flat fee, advising the client that we could not intensively supervise the project. We would not assume responsibility for the quality and supervision of the work.

Nonetheless, the client refused to hire a general contractor. He said he couldn't afford it and suggested that he would supervise the job closely himself. He encouraged us to inspect the project whenever we could, although our fee did not include supervisory services. Unfortunately, we did not specify the scope of our duties in our letter of agreement.

The first set of problems occurred with the paint job. We specified the color in an oil-based, high-gloss finish. We issued a purchase order and received an acknowledgment from the paint supplier. We arrived at the job site while the painter was putting on a primer coat. The walls appeared to be in good condition, so we left the job to visit another project.

When our client telephoned us the following day, we were faced with an unexpected problem. The paint supplier had shipped the right color but had delivered a water-based, semigloss instead of a high-gloss oil. Two finished coats had been applied over the primer, and the painter had left the premises. The client insisted that he wanted the oil-based finish. New paint was purchased, the painter returned, and a primer coat and two additional coats were applied. The painter disclaimed all liability. He said he only used what had been provided. The paint supplier also disclaimed liability and even refused to supply the correct order without additional charge.

A second set of problems arose over the cabinetwork. A number of the cabinet details were improperly executed, although our plans were very specific. Some of the finishing work was also very sloppy. The cabinetmaker refused to make any corrections when we pointed out the flaws. The outcome has been a lawsuit instituted by our client, naming the paint supplier, cabinetmaker, and our firm as defendants, with a cause of action for $10,000. Are we liable at all? Should we offer to settle?

ANSWER: The dilemmas in this situation were caused by an underlying problem: What does a designer do when a general contractor's services are required, but the client refuses to hire one?

The first option is to pass up the job. Let the client hire another designer. Yet, in this economic climate, this is not always feasible. Many designers have reported to me that their business is off as much as 40 percent. They can't afford to turn clients away. However, each case should be examined carefully.

If the scope of the project is large, the designer will lose money if she functions as the designer and general contractor for a standard design fee. On the other hand, if the designer assumes responsibility for supervising the contractors, she must use constant vigilance. If not, she will pay the inevitable consequence of being involved in crises arising from inadequate supervision.

Many states require general contractors to be licensed. If a designer assumes that role and is unlicensed, she may be acting illegally. Some states require designers to have a home improvement contractor's license to supervise contractors. Others make it illegal for a designer to design or supervise any architectural changes. Find out what your state requires.

If you charge by the hour, it can be to your advantage to confer with contractors and supervise a project, especially if your business is slow. In that case, a client may ultimately spend the same amount he would if he had hired a general contractor. However, psychologically, a client may believe that there is a savings because he is paying only one company.

A second option is to take the job to prepare design plans only. If you feel that you will be pushed into acting as a general contractor without being paid, charge a flat design fee for the design plans. Tell your client that you can't be involved in construction supervision. This approach can work well in cases where the client decides to be his own general contractor.

It never ceases to surprise me how frequently clients with no prior experience decide to act as their own general contractor. Of course, these clients plague their designers with phone calls, asking for advice. The designers, however, aren't responsible for any supervision. A disclaimer for supervision should be spelled out in your letter of agreement. Consequently, if something goes wrong, you can't be liable for any damages later on.

It is not uncommon for clients to change their mind about acting as their own general contractor. On several occasions, designers have told me that once construction actually began, the client couldn't cope with the project. At that point a general contractor was hired. Yet, although this can happen, don't plan on it.

A third option, as described earlier, is for the designer to assume the role of general contractor and to be paid for her work. This assumes that the designer is legally qualified to assume the role. It also depends, naturally, on whether the designer wants the business. Some designers refuse to do any general contracting, regardless of circumstances. Others are more flexible, depending on their business, and are licensed general contractors.

Some designers become licensed general contractors because they believe that there are fringe benefits to acting in a dual capacity. First, they insist it is easier to coordinate a project when they create and supervise the execution of design plans. Second, they like the freedom of being able to select their own subcontractors. For example, if a designer thinks that a certain project, such as a restoration, requires unique craftsmen, acting as general contractor will enable her to hire whomever she wants. Third, they feel it is important to be understand all technical aspects of construction, which most designers don't know.

The most important point to remember is this: If a client wants you to act as both designer and general contractor, don't assume both roles unless you want them and will be paid for them.

The design firm in this example was conned into the role of general contractor by its client and worked in this capacity for nothing. After attempts at settlement with the client failed, it was sued and lost. The court ordered the designers to pay for half the cost of the paint job. The paint supplier was instructed to pay the other half, in addition to the cost of the paint. The judge reasoned that if a general contractor had ordered the paint, he would have been liable. However, since the designers had ordered the paint, they were partly responsible.

As far as the cabinetwork was concerned, the judge held the design firm liable for one third of the repair costs. The judge stated that the cabinetmaker was primarily responsible for damages, since he had been supplied with an adequate set of design plans. However, the court felt some liability should be imputed to the designers for failure to provide adequate supervision.

In my opinion, the design firm made its fatal mistake when it failed to limit its liability in its letter of agreement. The client's mentality was to try to get as much as possible for nothing. The designers should have understood that prior to entering into the agreement.

The client had exhibited certain danger signals. He had managed to connive a free paint job, as well as to get a special rate for construction. Moreover, he refused to spend the money to hire a general contractor. The designers should have understood that their client would stop at nothing. Then they should have placed a disclaimer clause for supervision in their contract to avoid liability.

Further, if the client had agreed to pay the designers for supervision, they may have supervised more carefully, possibly preventing the damage. However, since the designers charged only a flat fee for plans, they didn't provide professional supervision.

I believe these designers handled their client like amateurs. Seasoned designers would have been more astute. They know when a client is trying to pressure them, but submit only if its to their own advantage. This firm, however, was obviously afraid to risk losing a client. It apparently didn't have enough confidence to insist on being paid for supervision, or to disclaim liability and refuse to perform it.

An experienced designer would have warned the client of the need to pay for professional supervision. If the client had refused, the designer would have prepared the design plans and withdrawn completely from supervision. If the client had tried to pressure the designer to supervise for free, the designer would have passed on the project.

Thus far, the discussion has been geared to larger projects. But what happens on small projects? Obviously, in those cases, a general contractor won't be hired. Are you liable for inadquate supervision if a subcontractor does something wrong?

Unfortunately, I can't provide a generalization. Each case has its own special facts that dictate the answer. However, I make the following recommendation: If a general contractor isn't being hired, don't assume responsibility for supervision of any contractors. Limit your liability in your letter of agreement.

Further, even if little supervision is required, it is still important to use the best quality and most reliable contractors. Any additional cost is worth the extra expense. In any event, do not ignore the issue of liability for supervision. Especially in today's economy, weigh each potential client's demands carefully and proceed with caution.

Chapter 6, "Contracts, Contractors, and Liability," continues the discussion of general contractors.

If you recall, in the second hypothetical case, Sir Clem Casino was interviewing several firms to design his office space at Fifth Avenue Tower. He told prospective designers that the amount of their fee could be a decisive factor in their being hired.

Designers are often faced with competitive bidding for design fees. The issue is, should you beat the competition?

It's common practice for clients to consult a number of interior designers before making a hiring decision. They may shop around for any number of reasons. Large corporations must be convinced that a designer is technically competent and capable of finishing the job on time, at budget. Smaller businesses may be extremely cost conscious but have requirements that must be satisfied within their financial limitations. Residential clients may place greater emphasis on style and design.

Frequently, a designer can sense a client's major concerns during initial interviews. Then it becomes his challenge to meet those needs.

In some cases, the design fee may be a focal point. The following is a typical situation in which a designer knows his fee must be competitive; however, he doesn't want to take the job at the risk of sacrificing profits. Although this project may differ from those in your own office, the logic used in competing against other designers is essentially the same.

QUESTION: *My partner and I have a small but successful firm, employing 10 people (i.e., assistant designers, draftsmen, and clerical help). Our client mix is approximately 60 percent commercial and 40 percent residential. We would like to expand commercial work and limit residential services, but have been unable to make that transition so far.*

We have been approached by a hotel chain to design a resort hotel in Florida. In the past, the company has hired large design firms with standardized corporate approaches. However, it wants a special design concept for this hotel. Other designers have also been interviewed, who emphasize the "design story."

During initial interviews, hotel executives seemed impressed with our ideas. We have been asked, in addition to four other firms, to submit a detailed proposal outlining our method of operation and fee structure. The client has its own architect and purchasing department. We will only be preparing design plans and inspecting installations of our custom fabrications.

We want the job but still need to make a profit. Since we haven't worked for the company before, we don't know whether it's an "easy client." The other four firms are good ones and are anxious to be hired. If the client feels that our designs are the best, we think the only major issue will be the fee. We don't know how the other firms plan to charge. We are unsure how to structure our own fee, making it competitve but profitable. Can you advise?

ANSWER: Do you want to bid the lowest fee to try to get the job? That's the main issue. Sometimes it's impossible to guess what your competitors are doing. However, in thinking about fees, there are certain factors to consider.

The first is how much you want the job. It sounds as if you need this client. You indicate that you want to expand your commercial business. Frequently, in working with a chain, one hotel can lead to another. Client desirability is usually a very important factor when competing against other designers for jobs. I have seen astute, business-oriented designers make substantial allowances to lure clients that have potential repeat business. Naturally, you don't want to lose money on any project; however, underbidding can be considered a business investment if future projects loom on the horizon. Even if you decide to bid low, structure your bid to avoid setting a bad precedent for other projects with the same client in the future.

I think it is a good idea to delay quoting a fee until submitting your proposal. In uncertain situations, it's always wise to take enough time to make an intelligent decision.

The second factor is how much your competitors are charging. Can you discover how their fees are structured? Sometimes it's possible to find out, but, generally, it's difficult. They're also concerned about being underbid. Even if a competitor is underbidding, it doesn't necessarily mean that you will lose the client. Make sure your fee is well within reason even if you underbid.

The third factor is who your competitors are. In this case, it appears the competition is stiff. Sometimes, second-rate firms charge less. You really can't compete against that. If a client is concerned only with price, he can always find someone cheaper. That's not the issue here, as the client is searching for a creative approach.

Are you competing against architects as well as designers? When charging cost-plus, architects frequently charge less than interior designers, particulary if they're designing an exterior as well. Don't be concerned about that. Frequently, an architect's approach to an interior is much diffcrent than an interior designer's. Sophisticated clients are aware of how these approaches vary. Assessing the variables is one of their objectives for having preliminary meetings and requesting proposals. If design is the issue, as opposed to budget or scheduling, the client will pay more because good design costs more to produce.

The fourth factor is the scope of your responsibility on the project. Here it appears minimal. Since the client has its own purchasing department, you will only prepare the specifications. A tremendous amount of detail has been eliminated for your office

Further, since the client is purchasing goods and services directly, liability for any defects or late deliveries has been removed from your concern. That doesn't mean you won't make inspections and attempt to expedite deliveries. However, from a financial and legal standpoint, your role has been eased considerably. This should make it more affordable for your fee to be competitive.

The fifth factor is how much you like the work. Have you designed a hotel before? Do you like designing hotels? Do you need a completed project for your portfolio to interest other prospective clients? It's not unusual for designers to make financial allowances to acquire special design opportunities.

Once you have weighed these factors, and I'm sure you can add others, estimate the amount of time required, conservatively, to complete the job. If you're unsure, discuss it with other designers familiar with this type of assignment. Then, estimate the cost of overhead, including salaries. Add on a certain percentage, for example, 15 percent, as a safety factor. The result is your "break-even cost."

If you're anxious to be hired, your fee won't exceed that amount. If you really want the job, and are willing to sacrifice some of your operating profit, then it's a question of judgment. First, eliminate the 15 percent safety factor. Then reduce your fee, reflecting your desire to design the hotel.

Once you make your decision, you probably won't be able to increase the fee later. If you have a history with the client, it might be possible to renegotiate a fee. For example, you could discuss the "going rate" and the value of your services. But that isn't possible in this case. Because your fee is being submitted like a sealed bid, pricing must be based on your costs.

The method of charging probably isn't crucial, as long as a bottom-line figure is presented. For example, some commercial designers charge hotels on an hourly or monthly basis. Others use a fixed fee. Cost-plus pricing isn't appropriate here, because the designer isn't purchasing goods or services and has no cost control. It would probably be difficult to monitor the purchasing department to know the true costs. Since your design drawings won't relate to basic interior construction, it doesn't sound feasible to charge on a per-square-foot basis.

Assume you decide to charge on a time basis. Then, you may have to provide an upset figure (as mentioned in the hypothetical commercial example). The upset figure is a not-to-exceed amount, which may be divided into payments as the job progresses. In any event, be certain your retainer is at least 20 percent of the whole fee and is nonrefundable. This is usually a nonnegotiable point.

Now the question is, are you willing to bid below your break-even cost, and if so, how much? That's a truly subjective determination. The largest reduction I have seen a designer use is one third, which is most unusual. Generally, most firms cannot afford to go below 20 percent.

As a matter of sound business practice, many financial advisers never advocate making a bid of less than operating costs. I understand that point of view but don't agree. There is sometimes an "opportunity cost" in a situation where foregoing a profit in the short run can later result in far greater rewards.

How far should you go to beat the competition? That decision should be made with precision and with much deliberation.

For both hypothetical clients discussed earlier in this chapter, the designers were confronted with special needs. The residential client's needs were the less complicated. That challenge was to integrate two collections of art and furniture into one environment for an absentee client.

The commercial or "contract" client had more intricate needs. The project required a special environment to house a collection of art and furniture for corporate offices as well as the design and construction of a complex aquarium.

In both situations, an architect and a general contractor were required. Therefore, it is most important that the designers' letters of agreement define their clients' needs and designers' responsibility to fulfill them.

I have always encouraged designers to outline precisely their project responsibilities in letters of agreement. Chapters 1 and 3 deal with letters of agreement, and Chapters 7 and 8 cover design proposals. In these four chapters, the importance of framing the scope of a potential client's design project is discussed and analyzed.

There appears to be an increasing tendency for clients to hold designers responsible for problems arising due to factors beyond their control. When designers tell me about these unfortunate situations, my first question is, "Did you define your responsibilities in your letter of agreement to limit your liability?" In nine out of ten cases, the answer is no.

Basically, there are two reasons to map out your duties and responsibilities in your letter of agreement. The first is apparent. Describing your role in the design process reinforces your image as a seasoned professional. Most clients don't stop to think about how much a designer really has to do. When you submit a letter of agreement, you must quote a fee and ask for a retainer. It's logical, when asking for money, to emphasize the amount of work that needs to be done and your approach to the project.

The second reason is to outline your responsibilities and limit your liability in areas where your own involvement may be uncertain. In other words, you must explain, in effect, "I will do this, but I won't do that." Theoretically, this appears to be a simple process, and in many cases, it is. Nonetheless, client conflicts that develop into lawsuits seem to persist. Why?

TAKING PRECAUTIONS AGAINST REDUCED DESIGN FEES

There are many cases in which a designer becomes trapped when he hasn't thoughtfully limited his liability because of his eagerness to sign the client, be paid a retainer, and start working.

The following question reflects a typical situation in which a client unjustly blames a design firm for a problem. Although advice is provided to help resolve the problem, the important point is that you take steps to avoid a similar predicament with your own clients.

QUESTION: *My partner and I own a small design firm. We were contacted by a brokerage firm to design a suite of offices approximating 3000 square feet. The firm had two partners who rarely met with us together or agreed with each other. After several consultations, we submitted our standard letter of agreement. The clients eventually signed the agreement and sent us a retainer. Unfortunately, they delayed too long, leaving only three weeks for construction before move-in once our plans had been completed.*

Predictably, an inadequate amount of lead time prevented completion of the project prior to occupancy. During initial interviews, the brokers stipulated their intention to retain their existing computers. Consequently, we designed the cabinets to accommodate that equipment. At the last minute, that is, when construction was substantially complete, the partners decided to buy all new equipment. The cabinet details and the electrical plan had to be redone. A newly built ceiling was ripped out to rewire for increased electrical requirements, and this involved some handholding. My partner and I met with the electrical contractor daily until he finished the work so the firm could move in and conduct business.

It worked out until we submitted our final bill for design fees. After several weeks without payment, I called one partner. He told me that he didn't intend to pay, blaming us for the extra expense for the new ceiling and cabinet changes. I corrected him, explaining that those changes were due to their last-minute decision to buy new computers. His reply was that our plans weren't flexible enough to adopt to simple changes. Was he entitled to reduce our fee, and what should we do?

ANSWER: In my opinion, your client didn't have the right to make this arbitrary deduction, and I recommend pursuing this matter until you collect the original balance. Before discussing the strategy for collection, examine the precautions that may have been used to avoid a misunderstanding.

Was there a clause in your agreement relating to the status of the client's electronic equipment? Based on your question, I don't think so. In your contract, the area to be designed must be described. Certainly, you listed the address and the square footage of the space. At that point, you should have mentioned any existing conditions affecting the scope of your design duties. Here, you could have used the following language:

> You have advised us that you intend to use all of your existing electronic office equipment, computers, and other related equipment. Accordingly, you will provide us with all relevant specifications so that we can design appropriate electrical and custom cabinet facilities to meet those needs.

If this had been clearly stated, I think there would be no question about your absence of liability. In fact, you could have charged the client an extra hourly drafting charge for changes, since your initial fee provided designing to accommodate only existing equipment.

Before proceeding further, I note that you have fallen into the same trap as many other designers. Most likely, you prepared the agreement yourself, using language from old contracts, perhaps even taking advice offered by your colleagues. You neglected to think carefully. How do you gain the necessary insight? It's not that difficult. Before preparing a letter of agreement, meet with your partner or members of your staff and take an inventory of what a prospective job is going to involve.

Start with the premise that you will design the entire space, without outside consultants (e. g., architects or engineers) and that you will be specifying all new equipment, furniture, and furnishings. As you know, designers rarely have the opporunity to create an entire project without collaborating with other design professionals or without being encumbered by a client's furniture, fixtures or equipment. Delineate in your letter of agreement all significant aspects of the project. Clearly indicate a comprehensive understanding of the provisions of your job.

Use simple examples of these provisions, some of which are alluded to earlier. For example, if an architect or engineer will be retained, mention your role in assisting him. If he's already been hired, include his name. Indicate the salient factors of your collaboration.

If a client plans to use furniture and furnishings from a former office or residence, ask him to list these items in writing. Attach the list, with notations regarding modifications, to the letter of agreement, or send the list in separate correspondence. If your supervision is needed for refurbishing, make it clear that you intend to charge.

If there are partners in a firm whose approval is required prior to making major decisions, indicate to whom you are responsible. Prevent any possible subsequent accusations about working without proper authorization.

Generally, analyze each job before submitting a contract. It's unfortunate to find designers, many of whom consider themselves to be business experts, talking about using "standard letters of agreement" exclusively. Do you have standard clients, and is your job to create standard interiors? It's foolish to presume that a standard formula can be applied to prepare all letters of agreement or to set design fees. Generally, I find that designers who use a "standard" approach are afraid to think.

If you don't approach each contract individually, you may find yourself in difficult situations, such as the one you described in your question. Generalizations may cost design fees and incur legal fees. Designers must handle each client as a separate package. Obviously, some cases are easier than others; however, always ask basic threshold questions before preparing a contract. If you use a lawyer, discuss any pertinent factors. Don't rely on her to explore the details.

In regard to collecting the balance of your fee, I suggest moving slowly. Don't apply pressure until it becomes clear that your client simply won't pay. Once clients occupy a space, it may take a while to recover from the impact of dealing with initial expenses. You've already rendered the majority of your services, so you may as well finish the job.

First, try dealing through correspondence. Send a statement with a brief letter of clarification. Indicate that your initial plans were based on requirements that your client changed. Wait a month, then send another statement. During this interim period, oversee any details on the job and continue to act as a professional. After three months, send a polite but firm letter requesting final payment. Fifteen days later, advise that legal action will be taken to collect the unpaid balance. After that, institute litigation or arbitration proceedings, depending on the terms of your letter of agreement.

You haven't indicated any other legal grounds for your client to avoid payment. Therefore, unless your client's a chiseler, his lawyer will advise him to pay. There's no reason to compromise your fee, but you may decide to reduce the balance to make a quick settlement.

Once the matter is settled, don't place yourself in jeopardy again. Use your experience when entering into client relationships. As part of your professional image, it makes sense to draw clear lines to avoid costly mistakes.

Obviously, this design firm may have been spared a client conflict if it had specifically defined its responsibilities in its letter of agreement.

Apply this logic to the two hypothetical cases at the beginning of this chapter. It is important to specify all the responsibilities of the designer and client, given the facts. Itemize them carefully. Once you are accustomed to this procedure, it will become easier for each project. You will maximize your profits and minimize your potential legal liability.

6

CONTRACTS, CONTRACTORS, AND LIABILITY

One of the most important functions of an interior designer is to recommend general contractors and subcontractors. True, it is not always easy. If you have a big job pending, certainly, it is a lot easier to find good contractors. Smaller jobs, contract and residential, can be a different story. Finding competent general contractors to work on jobs for $50,000 or less can be an impossible task. Eventually, someone will be available, but how responsible is the designer if the contractor doesn't provide what he promises?

The following is an example of what can go wrong if a designer is not careful about making a recommendation.

An experienced designer was retained to renovate and design a loft for residential use. The space was approximately 2500 square feet and the budget was $100,000—$50,000 for construction and $50,000 for furniture and furnishings.

The designer prepared floor plans and a materials presentation and received the client's approval. Subsequently, she hired an architect to prepare all necessary architectural drawings, which were also approved by the client.

While searching for a general contractor to bid on the drawings, the designer experienced problems. The contractors known by the designer were busy for months and would not bid on the job. The designer started inquiring about recommendations for other contractors. She heard through a friend of an available contractor who worked for a real estate company.

The designer met with the contractor and was impressed. Without checking other references, she recommended the contractor. The client, a young woman who traveled a great deal, also liked the contractor and signed his contract.

The project began, and at first all went well. Less than three weeks into construction, however, trouble started. Some of the work was substandard, and design changes were made by the general contractor without the designer's approval.

The designer inspected the job frequently, but each meeting with the contractor turned into a confrontation instead of collaboration. The contractor made design changes with the client directly and produced shoddy millwork.

The client didn't notice the inferior workmanship until the designer called it to her attention. Moreover, it became obvious that the client had become romantically involved with the contractor, who was married and had children.

The contractor became even more belligerent. At their final meeting he told the designer not to come to the site when he was there and to take out the trash when she left.

Ultimately, he made a physical threat against the designer, who then contacted me. I called the police and wrote the contractor, warning him against harassing the designer. The detective assigned to the case called the contractor and told him he would be arrested if he ever called the designer again.

The designer then explained all this to her client, who then fired the contractor. Their affair had by now, fortunately, come to an end. But, unfortunately, the client had paid the contractor for most of the contract price, against the designer's recommendation.

The designer then recommended another contractor, who fixed the millwork and finished the job. The client was thrilled with her loft and recommended the designer for other jobs, paying her in full for her services.

The designer was fortunate because the job ended well. She should have checked with at least three different clients of the general contractor before hiring him. If the client hadn't become involved with the contractor personally, she might have held the designer responsible for any substandard work.

How responsible is a designer for the recommendations made for general contractors or any contractors? From a legal standpoint, the designer is an independent contractor and has no direct legal relationship with the general contractor or any independent contractor.

Minimally, the designer has the duty to make recommendations based on a thorough inspection of past performance. That duty under no circumstances should be taken lightly. Don't recommend anyone's work who has not been verified. Don't try to save your client money by recommending second-rate contractors because they charge less. If the work doesn't meet a certain basic standard, your client may hold you responsible.

Are you liable for the work of the contractors you recommend? It depends completely on the facts of the situation, which are usually complex when conflicts occur. Unfortunately, I have found that judges do not have a positive image of the interior designer as a competent professional, particularly if they have had a bad design experience of their own.

Therefore, interior designers must be very careful about covering their tracks. Check out sources as carefully as possible prior to making a recommendation. Your letter of agreement should firmly state that you cannot be responsible for the work of any contractors, although you will inspect progress on the job as necessary. I have made this clear in the model agreement in Chapter 1.

Some designers are reluctant to disclaim responsibility because they are afraid prospective clients will hire someone else. Don't fall for that. Your design fees are simply not substantial enough to risk liability for any damage caused by a negligent contractor. Your best protection is to know all your contractors before recommending them.

In addition to general contractors, designers must also deal with subcontractors. Who are these other independent contractors? They are your resources, with whom you deal every day: your carpenter, upholsterer, mirror installer, tile installer, and so forth.

Frequently, clients interfere with your own relationships with independent contractors and create trouble. How responsible are you then? There are clients who supervise their own jobs, refuse to listen to their designers, and are unhappy with the results. These clients attempt to blame others and use their dissatisfaction as an excuse not to pay their bills. Sound familiar? The following situation happened to an interior designer, a client of mine.

A wealthy older woman wanted to redo her Park Avenue apartment in New York City, a job that included either reupholstering or fabricating slipcovers for 20 pieces of furniture. The client took weeks to pick out various fabrics, driving the designer nearly crazy.

Upon realizing how difficult the client was, the designer decided not to pursue any other aspects of the project. Finally, the fabrics were delivered to the upholsterer. Seven pieces were upholstered and delivered to the client without any complaints.

After the delivery of several other pieces, the designer received a hysterical phone call from her client, ordering her to her apartment immediately. When she arrived, she found four sets of newly completed slipcovers thrown on the floor of the majestic entrance hall.

"See how these fit!" the client screamed. The designer picked them off the floor, fitting them on the furniture. They weren't perfect, but fit nicely and were, after all, slipcovers.

Then the designer noticed something strange. The brown stripes, repeated in the pattern of the original fabric, were missing. The designer called her upholsterer to ask for an explanation. He responded that the client had called directly, told him she didn't like the brown stripes, and ordered him to cut them out. Without checking with the designer, the upholsterer eliminated the stripes and pieced together the material. Obviously, the fabric never hung as well once it had been resewn.

The designer told her client that if she had been consulted, she would never have permitted the alteration. The client could not be placated. She demanded a refund for the fabric, refused to pay the upholsterer, and demanded the return of her remaining furniture and fabrics being stored at the upholsterer's shop.

At this point the designer called me. She told me that she had tried to reason with her client's husband, a retired Broadway producer. The husband knew that his wife was crazy but backed her up anyway. He didn't want a lawsuit but insisted that his wife's demands be met.

The designer approximated that meeting her client's demands would cost $15,000. Of course, the upholsterer was seriously at fault. He should never have made any changes without the designer's approval. However, due to their long-standing relationship, the designer had to handle him carefully because she couldn't afford to alienate him. She used him for all her other jobs.

The solution turned out to be fairly simple. We refused to release any fabrics or furniture until the matter was resolved. The client was desperate to get her furniture back. She had owned most of it for more than 30 years and thought it was priceless.

Obviously, lawyers had to take over, but no lawsuit was actually ever started. I represented the upholsterer and the designer. I advised the lawyer representing the designer's client as follows: If they wanted to start a lawsuit, that was their option. However, such an action could easily continue for two years. Pending the outcome of the litigation, however, the furniture and fabrics would be held by the upholsterer in storage as collateral. It would not be released under any circumstances pending a court order.

That resolved the problem. The clients paid the designer and the upholsterer a settlement. Mutual releases, signed and notarized by all the parties, were exchanged simultaneously. The furniture was released to the client, and the settlement, in the form of certified checks, was tendered to the upholsterer and the designer.

There are a number of valuable messages here. Obviously, don't work for crazy clients, and if you do, end your relationship with them as soon as possible. If you are designing custom work for clients, make sure your craftsmen, independent contractors, don't deviate from your instructions without your explicit permission.

Don't purchase materials for work in progress unless the client pays on a pro forma basis, providing full payment in advance. Finally, don't deliver custom-made goods to clients without full payment unless you are holding other goods that belong to the client that can be used as collateral. Then, in the event the client refuses to pay you, you have collateral and leverage to settle the claim.

If you do reach an impasse with your client and must settle through lawyers, make sure you exchange mutual general releases that have been notarized. Don't merely accept a letter from the client or the client's lawyer. Obtain something official, signed by your adversary, to prevent the possibility of ever having to deal with him again.

From my experience and observation, it is much easier for a designer to be extricated from a problem with a general contractor than from a bad situation with an independent contractor. A general contractor is viewed as someone who has a direct legal relationship with a client with a formal, separate contract. His job is, in fact, to supervise. He is the "general." He is supposed to control everyone else and is being paid for being in charge. When something goes wrong with a subcontractor, point the finger at him, not the designer. At least, that is what we tell the courts, and that is what we believe.

Yet many of your jobs don't have general contractors. When a designer, as an independent contractor, deals with another independent contractor, such as an electrician or cabinetmaker, results can be unpredictable. The outcome can cause the designer problems.

Accordingly, as the designer, if you recommend subcontractors, it is likely that you will be asked to resolve any problems. If your client selected his own workers, such as painters or plasterers, defective workmanship is not your responsibility. As a designer, you should be paid for your consultation and your time spent in inspecting workmanship. If you did not recommend the subcontractor, you are not responsible for any failure of the workers to provide fabrications that conform to your specifications as long as you have performed necessary site inspections.

Remember, it is your recommendations that will draw you into any conflicts between a contractor and a client. A client's own sources aren't your problem.

The liability a designer may incur for work performed by general contractors or independent contractors varies, depending on the situation. However, there are measures that can be taken for protection.

One option is to incorporate. When an interior designer asks me whether to incorporate, I immediately see flashing red lights. To consider this question is an elementary rule when going into business. If an experienced designer doesn't know the answer, he usually has neglected the business side of his career and, typically, has many business problems and limited profitability.

As most business people know, the advantage of incorporation is to limit one's personal liability, to establish "limited liability." In other words, if one's business is locked up in a corporate capsule, and that capsule is attacked and drained as a result of bad business judgment, creditors, actions, lawsuits, or other misfortune, the owner of the corporation is personally off the hook. The corporate shell protects him like a bullet-proof vest, even if it bears his own name, such as "John Smith Interiors, Inc."

Suppose John Smith, the individual, designs an interior for a corporate giant. Problems develop on the job, and there is trouble with many of the subcontractors. For example, all the plasterwork must be redone, and the plasterer goes bankrupt in the middle of the project. A $20,000 leather sofa comes in the wrong shade. The corporate giant becomes angry and sues the designer for $250,000.

Although none of these problems may be the designer's fault, who knows what a jury will find in damages? Who knows what a clever lawyer can do to shift the responsibility to the designer? If you think that bad outcomes are impossible, think again. I have had a number of desiger clients who have been sued in cases in which the allegations have not been justified.

But suppose a jury finds a verdict against John Smith Interiors Inc. for $50,000, and the corporation does not have that kind of money. Does John Smith have to sell his condominium, purchased in his own name, to pay off the debt? Absolutely not. He can walk away from the corporation, leaving it to lie fallow, laden with judgments. Because the corporation has no assets, it is "judgment-proof." John Smith keeps the condo, as well as all other possessions owned in his name, and can form a new corporation with a different name.

Does incorporation have additional tax consequences? Businesses owned by large corporations pay a corporate income tax on corporate profits. Executives drawing salaries pay personal income tax. Any additional profit left for the shareholder is taxable to each shareholder personally, as income. This is referred to as "double taxation." The corporation has to pay income tax on the profits, and when the owners of the company distribute profits, they pay personal income tax on the dividends.

This tax structure does not necessarily operate the same way for small corporations. Clever accountants do their best to make sure that small corporations don't show a profit. Although IRS regulations restrict these deductions, the "business" ends up paying for as many of the shareholder's expenses as possible under the legitimate umbrellas of travel and entertainment, corporate automobiles, and other items. Some accountants elect to have small companies taxed as "Subchapter S" corporations. Using that election, the corporation (the designer) pays taxes on the profits only once, as if it were an individual.

Incorporating, in my opinion, is a *must*, but it is not foolproof protection. If a wealthy client wants to harass you, be certain that your financial books are in perfect order. To ensure corporate protection, be certain your corporate records are not mixed with your personal ones. Keep separate bank accounts. Pay yourself a salary as a corporate officer. Operate your corporation as a separate entity. If you don't, you can be subject to attack later. A client could try to "pierce the corporate veil." If you've maintained a separate identity, have no fear. However, if you've merely formed a corporation, using the name but operating like an individual proprietorship or partnership, the veil might be pierced. In that event, you could be held personally responsible.

Angry clients also use a different approach. When they sue designers, they sue their corporations as well as the designers personally. Do they get away with it? It depends. You have to hire a lawyer to defend you, and that alone can be very expensive.

The bottom line is this: In my opinion, any small business should incorporate before it transacts any business of any substance. Will incorporation protect you 100 percent from everything? No, but neither will anything else, and this is one of the easiest steps in the right direction that you can take.

Check with your lawyer and accountant to find out the financial ramifications of incorporation. In addition to the initial expense of incorporating, there may be annual corporate franchise taxes, which are charged by many states. However, if your company transacts any reasonable amount of business, incorporation is well worth the price.

Still, being incorporated isn't enough protection. When businesses are hit with a lawsuit, most owners don't walk away leaving a wasted corporate shell. Instead, they defend their claims and try to continue in the business.

Most designers don't know whether liability insurance can help them, whether they need any, or whether it's worth the cost. "Errors and omission insurance," known as malpractice insurance, is too expensive for most designers. National interior design organizations have programs for liability insurance for their members, and if you belong to one, investigate the program. If you're not certain how effective the protection is, ask your lawyer to verify the information.

Liability insurance for doctors and lawyers and architects is also very expensive, but these professionals have no practical alternative other than to carry it. The risk is simply too great.

Clients of designers are not known to be as litigious as those of doctors, lawyers, and architects, but in the past several years a trend has developed toward designers becoming targets of litigation. The following situation, which happened to a client of mine, shocked even me.

An interior designer designed a hotel in Florida. Two years after completion, a waitress slipped in the coffee shop, breaking her hip and leg. Apparently, according to the Workers' Compensation laws, she was prevented from suing the hotel, her employer, so her attorneys named the following as defendants: the general contractor for the hotel, the subcontractor who installed the tile, the tile manufacturer, and the interior designer who merely specified the tile for the coffee shop floor.

At first, my client was not at all concerned. Being farsighted, he had purchased "independent contractor liability insurance." This type of insurance protected him so long as he functioned only as an interior designer, without usurping the functions of the general contractor. In other words, he was protected from liability incurred by any other contractors involved on the job.

There was, however, one flaw. The insurance was effective only during the period of construction. Once the period of construction ended, he no longer had any protection. This was really a shame and was, in my opinion, his insurance agent's fault. If he had added a rider to his policy called "Completed Operations," he would also have been protected for incidents occurring after completion of construction.

I had to hire a litigator to represent my client, and he eventually settled out of court at a cost of $8000 for settlement and legal fees. After that episode, I began advising all designers to do the following: Call your insurance agent and purchase "independent contractor liability insurance with a completed operations feature." Some of my clients responded, stating that their insurance agent told them that these premiums would be enormous.

Upon further examination, those agents never understood the designers' needs. They provided estimates for "errors and omissions insurance," which can be very expensive, or insurance as a general contractor, which is also costly.

Remember, the two key phrases are "independent contractor" and "completed operations." Generally, a premium is based on the amount of gross billings of fees. Policies and premiums vary among insurance companies and according to the prevailing insurance laws in different states. However, regardless of your location, find an insurance agent who understands your needs and the nature of the interior design business.

I consider liability insurance to be a *must* for all interior designers. Unfortunately, many designers won't spend the money for the premiums until they have experienced a lawsuit with a client. Liability insurance is a very viable option for most designers. Investigate the cost of the premium for your own office before experiencing a loss.

There are other ways for designers to insulate against liability that cost absolutely nothing. However, most designers fail to use this basic kind of protection simply because of a desire to please the client and get the job finished as soon as possible. I suggest that you explain to your client in your letter of agreement the limitations of your liability for providing design services for his project.

Do not underestimate the value of "exculpatory language" for protection. Refer to Chapter 1, "Preparing a Letter of Agreement," for one approach. Simply using the appropriate lanuage could help save you a fortune.

I have a designer client who walked into a trap costing her $25,000 in damages. About three years ago she was hired by a wealthy residential condominium to redo the lobby, halls, and other public spaces in the building. She was thrilled by the opportunity.

The residents of the building were rich, well connected, and very visible. She anticipated with relish all the clients she would have once the job was completed. Since there were to be no structural renovations, she didn't use a general contractor but retained her own painters, cabinetmaker, glassworkers, and electricians.

The condominium board paid her directly, and she paid all the contractors from the proceeds. Her assistant prepared all the cabinet drawings, as well as the painting and finishing schedules.

Unfortunately, the contractors didn't do the best job, and none of the residents were satisfied. Instead of finding new clients, the designer was named as a codefendant in a lawsuit with every other contractor on the job. After two years, she settled out of court.

If she had been a savvy business person, notwithstanding the shoddy workmanship, she might have walked out without paying damages. She wasn't incorporated. She had no liability insurance and no disclaimer language in her letter of agreement for contractor's mistakes.

Would it all have helped? Absolutely. Having protection would have given the designer's attorney more ammunition to make a much lower settlement, or perhaps none at all.

Some designers limit their liability with contractors based on their method of charging. In contract and commercial work, many interior designers charge by the hour. For residential work, charging cost-plus or retail with a retainer for a design fee, is a common method.

Many residential designers refuse to charge on an hourly basis. However, because of to the liability factor, many designers charge hourly for certain jobs. If you charge by the hour, you can stipulate in your letter of agreement that you are acting strictly as a consultant.

When you charge by the hour, your fee isn't geared to either purchases or construction. Your client can use any contractor of his choice. If you are asked to recommend sources, of course you will accommodate your client. However, since you are acting as a consultant, your role should simply be of an advisory nature.

Unfortunately, many residential interior designers depend on commissions earned from selling their clients furniture, furnishings, antiques, and design services. They don't believe that their business would be profitable if they charged by the hour. However, not all residential designers agree with this philosophy. If charging hourly on a residential job is viable for you, it will enable you to insulate yourself somewhat from liability for contracts and contractors.

Many designers do not charge any commission for construction. They act as a purchasing agent for goods on a commission basis, and they recommend contractors and subcontractors. But they will not hire these subcontractors and contractors, nor will they pay them. They act merely as a consultant and get paid for their advice on an hourly basis. I believe this is a sound approach.

Many designers refuse to hire contractors themselves on behalf of their clients because of the resulting problems. In some states, this practice is illegal, depending on the situation. I agree with this view. And very often, clients use their own contractors anyway, especially for out-of-town jobs.

For example, if a New York designer is engaged to work on a client's house in New Jersey, how could the designer best operate? The client should be instructed to retain her own contractors, and the designer will inspect their work as the job progresses. Then, if there are problems on the job, they are not the designer's responsibility. The designer has been paid by the hour only to advise.

Occasionally, however, hourly rates work even for purchases on residential jobs. I recently had a case in which two designers, partners for 10 years, consulted me with a problem.

They lived in Connecticut and were recommended to clients by a historical society to furnish a huge eight-bedroom house. The designers had no role in the construction because their clients, a married couple, had their own architect.

Their clients advised the designers that they wanted to furnish the entire house with quality antique furniture. The designers submitted their letter of agreement, stipulating that they would charge "cost plus 33 1/3 percent" for their services. In other words, the designers agreed to work on commission, charging their clients their own cost plus 1/3 of net for their design services.

The clients signed the contract, and the designers began work. Their first assignment was to purchase furniture for a huge dining room with a fireplace, which required a banquet-sized table with twelve chairs and two large buffets.

When the designers asked their clients how much they wanted to spend, the answer was, "We don't know much about furniture"—some of their existing pieces were by Ethan Allen—"so we can't give you a budget. We don't have a Rolls-Royce budget but we do have a Mercedes budget."

The designers spent several months researching furniture. They took their clients to auctions, dealers, and antiquarians and found several appropriate selections, which cost approximately $100,000. The couple agreed to spend $100,000 and purchase certain pieces.

However, the clients never followed through and, instead, purchased nineteenth-century reproductions of the designer's choices through a different source. They didn't pay the designers any commission. Then the couple invited the designers to their house and showed them the furniture.

The husband made the following comments. "Well, ladies," he began, "you're not going to make anything on the dining room, but I promise you that you will make it up on the rugs." The designers didn't know how to proceed. They had been paid a $5000 retainer, which was inadequate compensation for all the time they had invested in the project.

However, the designers decided to continue working for the clients, believing they would earn a commission on the rest of the furniture in the house. They began shopping for rugs. The designers devoted at least six weeks to searching for a very large, unique oriental rug for the living room. Again, after a great deal of time was spent, the couple purchased a rug through a different dealer. They paid the designers a commission, but only 20 percent. Then they wrote the designers a letter. They told them that they wanted them to continue but would only pay "cost plus 20 percent."

The designers then consulted me. They had been paid 20 percent on a $35,000 rug (i.e., $7000) plus their $5000 retainer, totaling $12,000 in fees. They were, however, very dissatisfied. They couldn't decide whether to accept the 20 percent commission arrangement or to leave the job.

My suggestion was to charge by the hour. Their client spent months shopping prior to making any single purchase. Before purchasing the dining room furniture and oriental rug, the couple shopped at various dealers for four months. They always wanted the designers to accompany them to give their opinion.

Furthermore, the designers had been recommended by a prestigious historical society and wanted to maintain goodwill. Their clients liked them and valued their opinion, so it was simply a matter of renegotiating the financial aspect of their arrangement.

At my suggestion of charging by the hour, the designers settled at a $125 hourly rate. Then they provided the couple with a schedule in a letter, explaining how the hourly rate would operate. The minimum billing amount was one quarter of an hour—for example, for a telephone call.

The minimum billing amount for a personal consultation or a visit was one hour. In fact, one of the designers was almost a neighbor of the client, and the client was always inviting her to "drop by."

A minimum of two hours was specified for a local shopping trip. A minimum of four hours was specified for a trip to any local design center. A minimum of eight hours was specified for a trip to New York or any other out-of-state location.

The clients agreed to this, and the designers started working and billing. The clients paid according to the letter of agreement, which stipulated semimonthly payments. A new statement was generated every two weeks so that no big bills accumulated, and the fees started to roll in.

The designer's clients were very nervous about shopping for expensive furniture, so they were constantly calling the designers, who, fortunately, kept accurate and meticulous time records.

After the couple bought an antique secretary for $30,000, it was discovered that their "original" was, in fact, a reproduction. The dealer refused to refund the purchase, and the clients sued him. The designers, however, were not sued and were not considered liable in any way. The antiquarian was very well known. And, after all, the designers were consultants. They provided only an opinion, not a provenance, as a museum would.

If the designers had earned a commission, they may have been held liable for the provenance of the secretary, but, as consultants, they were in the clear. The designers only recommended the antiquarian as having an established reputation; they did not guarantee his integrity on any specific purchase.

This was a situation in which designers earned large fees by the hour on a residential job and avoided all liability.

I'll never forget the story that a designer told me about a client who liked to shop. She had heard about this client from another designer before she was hired. Realizing that the client had a reputation for rarely buying anything, the designer charged by the hour.

The client shopped for two years with the designer, paying fees but never buying. I asked the designer, "You shopped with this woman for two years and collected thousands of dollars in design fees, and she never made one purchase?" The designer laughed and said, "No, that's not quite true. She did buy two window shades once."

Relationships with clients and contractors are like marriages. Some are good, some are bad, some are fair, and some are better than others. Rough spots can often be worked out, but they can also lead to a divorce, which can be traumatic and expensive.

Learning how to cope with liability is a difficult challenge. Since it is so important, the subject is also explored from different angles in Chapters 10 and 14.

7

PREPARING A RESIDENTAL DESIGN PROPOSAL

When a potential client walks through your door, of course you can impress her with your creative ability. But can you convince her that you are worth your fee? Can you convince a potential client that you are able to cope with the financial aspects of her project, including budgets and scheduling?

Residential jobs in the design field today are big business. Many experienced designers won't handle clients unless the minimum budget is $50,000. Ten years ago, a project for a client with a $150,000 budget was considered a very big job. Today, it is considered a good job, but not unusual or spectacular. With the current cost of furniture, furnishings, construction, and cabinetwork, money simply doesn't go that far, as designers know so well.

Residential jobs very frequently involve a married couple, although not always, of course. The single client proportionally has been on the increase, particularly in urban areas. However, husbands and wives are a very strong segment of residential clientele and, generally, husbands are often finance oriented and wives design oriented. These roles are sometimes reversed. Nonetheless, for the sake of argument, assume this stereotype for the moment. If a married couple has never before been involved with the design process, a budget of $50,000 may sound like a lot.

Once a budget is prepared and the clients see how little that amount buys, then it may not seem like such a large sum. However, we must turn our attention to getting hired before a budget is prepared. If the husband is the stronger financial contributor and less design oriented than his wife, it is very important to convince him that you are financially responsible and competent to help him spend his hard-earned $50,000 or more.

A succinct financial proposal, outlining the parameters of the job and your functions, can be a formidable weapon to encourage green lights for signed letters of agreement and payment of healthy retainers. Large commercial interior design firms have traditionally prepared in-depth analyses for multimillion dollar projects.

In fact, some of the top-grossing firms have a special staff devoted solely to preparing proposals for potential clients. Although such an expense is considerable, it is viewed as part of the cost of operating a business. Many design executives are satisfied if three out of ten proposals result in their being hired by a client.

Because project analysis is so important in the preliminary stages, a basic financial proposal is presented here, step by step, with model clauses. The final letter of agreement contains clauses similar to those discussed in Chapter 1.

Critically important, and stressed in this discussion, are what to put in, what to leave out, and, depending on how you operate, the project at hand. The project I have conceptualized for the model is a suburban home, built in the late 1930s, which needs a great deal of renovation in areas such as the kitchen, bathrooms, porches, and other spaces.

Home owners with extensive renovation plans typically consult a number of designers before hiring one. Designers often want the chance to redo an entire house, because it is an excellent vehicle for client referral and publication.

With a sufficient budget, renovating a house presents the design challenge of making custom architectural changes as well as creating luxurious residential design. However, I don't think it's necesssary to prepare a financial proposal if a potential client has only a casual interest in hiring you.

If, after the first meeting, the client has a "We'll see, I'll call you next week," attitude, wait for him to call you next week. Make sure there is a certain amount of chemistry involved before you start drafting a proposal.

Can you be certain that writing a proposal is worth your time? That is a subjective question, and I can't always answer it easily. If the job is for a repeat client, the answer is, obviously, yes. If the budget is substantial, the client may say, after several meetings, "Now, I'd like to know how you work financially." Instead of just glibly reciting your fee structure, answer, "Why don't I get back to you with a short proposal? That way, you can see exactly how the project will work financially. If you approve of the proposal and submit a retainer, then I will submit a full letter of agreement while I am working on your initial basic design plans."

Particularly for residential projects, it is appropriate to present proposals in a letter format to avoid a highly structured approach. The following is a suggested introduction.

Dear Mr. and Mrs. Smith:

After meeting with you about the design and planning of your residence, it appears that we are ready to begin making definite plans. This proposal is to generally outline my financial requirements in regard to my design services, responsibilities, and fees. It is also to define my role relating to other design professionals while we are engaged in this collaboration.

If you approve this proposal by signing it and sending the initial payment, I will submit a comprehensive letter of agreement.

Note the flexibility of this approach. Less confident designers are often insecure about presenting any sort of written proposal until plans are finalized and a budget has been established.

Aggressive business people frequently equate a lack of business imagination with an inability to design creatively. They prefer consulting with designers who are able to express themselves in a businesslike fashion and in writing. If they are on corporate boards of directors, they are accustomed to commercial design proposals necessary to advise a corporate board about a budget appropriation.

After the introduction, the proposal letter addresses design areas, as in the following example:

DESIGN AREAS

My work shall pertain to your entire residence. While you may retain an architect and hire a general contractor, my work shall be comprehensive to provide a complete design harmonizing with architectural plans based on our consultation.

I have always stressed the importance of discussing design areas, particularly if you are going to charge an initial design fee. For example, charging a "per-room fee" for preparing floor plans and drawings is common practice.

Note also whether the client has mentioned hiring an architect on the project. Mention it in your proposal so that he will be reassured that you will welcome collaborating with another professional.

Next, the letter gives a description of your services.

DESIGN SERVICES

With respect to your entire residence, I shall perform the following services:

Initial Design Study

You have provided me with some existing floor plans that will most likely undergo revisions based on your needs and requirements. Further consultation with you will clarify the scope of these revisions prior to the preparation of preliminary interior design concepts.

As you well know, some clients have existing floor plans, and some don't. If you have to prepare floor plans, make a point of it. Obviously, if the space has already been surveyed and measured, it is easier and cheaper for your office to start work on planning the space right away. If not, it is going to cost your client more. Advise her about that expense immediately.

A basic description of your services on this specific job is the next component of your proposal letter, as in the following example:

PRELIMINARY INTERIOR DESIGN CONCEPT

A complete design presentation shall be prepared for your approval, summarized as follows:

1. Design Drawings. We shall prepare design drawings for all interior changes for your renovation, for design concepts only.
2. Preparation of Complete Floor Plans. Complete floor plans will be drawn to scale and will include a proposed furniture layout.
3. Finalization of Design Concepts. Subsequent to initial preparation, all design concept drawings will be submitted for your approval. If you request, consultation will be provided with other design professionals involved with the project. Any necessary revisions will be made, and final approval will be acknowledged by you in writing.
4. Materials Presentation. Upon approval of our layout drawings, our complete presentation shall include furniture selection, materials, fabrics, wall coverings, curtain design, floor design, color selections, lighting, etc., and other visual aids necessary to illustrate our design plans.

This section obviously offers the most comprehensive description of your services. Each client has particular requirements that will demand a special explanation or alteration of normal working procedures.

Although you may have an idea of what these deviations might be, it is usually wise not to try to provide for them in the initial proposal. Use durable, comprehensive language, as in this example. Once the proposal has been approved, that is, signed and affirmed with payment of a retainer, then you can make any changes in the final letter of agreement.

If a prospective client becomes very critical of your proposal, the best thing to do is to react as little as possible. I find that designers are very anxious to please prospective clients especially if the job looks particularly appealing. Don't make concessions without careful consideration.

Businessmen are often quite adept at playing word games. Their business is, to some extent, negotiating and drafting contracts. They are well trained to meet these challenges. Designers, on the other hand, are more service oriented. They seem to relate more comfortably to visuals than to the printed word.

Therefore, particularly early in the client relationship, don't let your client play a word game with you. Use general language that is descriptive, effective, and has impact. You don't have to defend it, and you don't have to change it.

Once you have submitted the proposal, you might get a call in a few days with the following typical response: "We have examined your proposal and would like to know how long it will be before the project could be finished. We would like to be able to move in within the next six or eight months. Will it be finished by then?"

Your answer might be: "I can't really estimate an approximate time at this point. Once I have met with your architect and the general contractor and studied their timetable and our working arrangements, I can give you a rough idea."

The point is this: Avoid giving specific answers in a vacuum when you haven't got all the information or control of the project. A miscalculation can be held against you later. Reserve making important judgments until you are hired.

If you must make certain commitments about scheduling, use caution prior to outlining them in your proposal or letter of agreement. If the project is a large one, it's smart to refer to working with an architect or other design professionals in your proposal or letter of agreement. Regardless of whether you work together at all, it reminds your client that the project is a collaborative effort and that you are used to collaborating.

The proposal letter next presents a section on purchases, as suggested here:

PURCHASES

All purchases will be made available to you at my wholesale or net cost. I will act as your purchasing agent, and all bills from vendors will be forwarded to my office for payment. I will prepare all specifications and purchase orders, outlining payment terms with which you must comply, but I will deal with the vendors on a financial basis.

Obviously, a large part of the job will be making purchases to implement the design plans. Most designers on residential projects make the purchases on the client's behalf for two reasons:

1. To obtain their professional discount
2. To control the project in order to avoid mistakes

Clients rarely understand how to acknowledge invoices with specifications for purchases of furniture, furnishings, hardware, and so forth. The procedure is simply too technical for them.

In your letter of agreement, you will specify that you will not process the order unless your client has provided the necessary payments. So, for example, if a fabric or wall covering must be paid for pro forma or in advance, the purchase order won't be processed until you have received full payment from the client upon order.

This is exactly the kind of information that you *don't* have to discuss with the client at the proposal stage. Clients hate to pay for purchases in full prior to delivery and, for the most part, are not really used to doing so. Why, then, bring it up at this point? All you have to say is that your role is to make the purchases and the client's role is to comply with the terms of the purchase orders.

Once the project starts, and you have been paid your retainer, then you can explain it all upon submission of the letter of agreement or the first purchase order. By then you will have established a working relationship with the client, who will trust you.

Basically, this approach is the underlying philosophy of these design proposals. Put something down on paper that will show clients that you know what you are doing. This gives you a great deal of credibility. But don't tell them too much too soon.

Do they really want to know now, and do you really want them to know it all? If in fact, they have renovated other residences, they will probably have experienced furniture deliveries that were six months late or fabrics that arrived damaged after a 12-week order period.

They will remember the tile contractor that went bankrupt during the job and walked off with their deposit. Unfortunately, this is part of the design business, and you can't change that. However, if new clients aren't aware of all the potential problems, don't tell them now. If they do know, don't remind them. They will want to forget and hope that such difficulties won't happen again. Of course, some are inevitable, but this is not the appropriate time to remind them.

Finally, the proposal letter discusses compensation, as in the following illustration:

COMPENSATION

My office will bill on an hourly basis for our design and planning services, as discussed in the description of my design services. Rates are scheduled as follows:

Firm principal—$100/hour
Senior designer—$75/hour
Drafting—$60/hour

Further, my fees for selecting and specifying all purchases of furniture and furnishings shall be based on certain percentages of the furniture and furnishings budget (F&F budget), which shall be as follows:

30% on the initial $150,000 of the F&F budget
25% on the F&F budget above $150,000 but less than $300,000
20% on the F&F budget above $300,000

This method of charging is basically a cost-plus method with a decreasing sliding scale. I have found this to be effective on projects with very large budgets. Using this method, you don't have to charge different percentages for different types of purchases. For example, some designers charge a different percentage for design services (e.g., custom painting) than for artwork and furniture. The decreasing sliding scale replaces that method and encourages the client to spend more money. The higher the budget, the lower percentage the designer will earn. However, the greater the budget, the larger the overall fee will be.

I have also found that a decreasing sliding scale works well when designers are competing with other design firms for large projects. Most designers who work on a cost-plus basis won't vary their percentage. This can cost them the job if there are other designers who are willing to reduce their fees.

Obviously, I wouldn't charge less than 30 percent unless the budget goes over $150,000. But once that happens, it might be worthwhile to take less if you think it might capture the client.

Notice, in this example, that there is no flat design fee for preparing design plans or working with outside architects. All designer input on this job, aside from making purchases, is billed by the hour. I find this is useful for larger projects. For example, if a potential client has a $50,000 budget, many designers would charge an initial design fee of about $2,500. If the scope of the project or budget increases, so will the initial fee.

There are, of course, many ways to charge for designing, which are discussed in Chapter 2, "Charging a Client." The example given here simply structures one way of charging a client for a large residential project.

If a client has any objections to your fee or method of operation, it is best to find out as soon as possible. Then you can decide whether you want to make changes to accommodate the client before becoming more involved.

Looking at this proposal, you might ask, "What does it really mean, and why bother?" I began preparing proposals when a designer consulted me and said, "Robert, I've got a new potential client. His project has a big budget, and I really want the job. The client has asked for a written proposal to explain my services and design fees."

At such an early stage, I felt that it was premature to prepare a comprehensive letter of agreement. Instead, I composed a brief proposal for the designer.

I was absolutely amazed at the positive response. The designer was hired for the job, and I received similar requests for proposals from other designers. In order to prepare a proposal, a designer must make an in-depth analysis of how to charge. It is important to take time to make careful decisions about a potential project. Once your analysis is complete, a client can't catch you off guard.

Many successful designers, competing with my designer clients, never bothered to assemble a plan as succinct and well organized as this little proposal. However, business people who scrutinized the work of these designers were very impressed.

Obviously, if you are redecorating a few rooms, you don't have to bother. Simply tell clients with smaller budgets how you operate. If a client is interested, then prepare a concise letter of agreement.

The proposal illustrated in this chapter is geared for:

1. Larger-budget jobs

2. New clients

3. Clients who consult with other designers

When designers ask whether a proposal is necessary, I tell them to consider the following: If the job is substantial and the potential client, unfamiliar with your work, is shopping around for other designers, a proposal should be worthwhile..

If you don't understand the significance of a proposal, ask other successful designers about its effectiveness. Create one for a project, even if you don't need it. Then, when your client asks pointed questions, particularly of a financial nature, see how easy it is to provide the right answers.

Study the proposal given here, analyze it, and decide whether it will be helpful. Using it once may convince a potential client to hire you.

8

PREPARING A CONTRACT OR COMMERCIAL DESIGN PROPOSAL

When a potential client walks through your door, of course you can impress him with your creative ability. But can you convince him that you are worth your fee? Can you convince a potential client that you are able to cope with the financial aspects of his project, including budgets and scheduling?

Presenting a succinct financial proposal, outlining the parameters of a job and your functions, can be a formidable weapon in winning the "green light" to a signed letter of agreement and payment of a healthy retainer.

Large commercial firms have traditionally prepared preliminary studies for multimillion dollar projects. In fact, some of the top-grossing firms have a special staff devoted solely to preparing proposals for potential clients.

Although such an expense is considerable, it is viewed as part of the cost of operating a business. Many design executives are satisfied if three out of ten proposals result in their being hired by the client.

Because project analysis for contract or commercial design is so important in the preliminary stages, this chapter presents a basic financial proposal, step by step, with model clauses. Each clause is discussed separately.

Critically important, and stressed in this discussion, are what to put in and what to leave out and, depending on how you operate, the project at hand. The project conceptualized for the model is a hotel. Hotel owners typically consult a number of designers before hiring one; thus, an astute proposal is a necessity to beat the competition.

This model, however, is adaptable as a proposal for other commercial spaces.

Designers often want hotel owners as clients. Hotels provide an excellent vehicle for exposure and publication. They offer the designer a challenge to respond to corporate requirements while creating luxurious hospitality-oriented interiors.

Frequently, a proposal is requested by the client or volunteered by the designer after two or three meetings. Once an initial proposal has been accepted, a final, detailed proposal may be requested before the designer is hired.

The sample proposal given in this chapter is an introductory response to initial inquiries from a prospective hotel client. For this reason, it is presented in a letter format to avoid the formality of a highly structured approach. The designer used this proposal as a vehicle to become better acquainted with the client's needs and requirements.

I recall the circumstances under which I originally prepared this hotel proposal. A well-known professional sports association was planning to build a hotel in Florida as a flagship to market its tournaments. A commerical hotel chain financed the venture and wanted this hotel to be unique.

Although the hotel chain had its own in-house staff designers, its corporate president decided to look elsewhere for creatively accomplished designers. The president's wife researched many prestige shelter magazines, noting designers whose work she found most intriguing.

She selected five designers, and her husband interviewed each one. Three of these designers contacted me to prepare proposals. I disclosed my affiliations to each designer but still prepared all three proposals. Why? Each designer worked differently; accordingly, each proposal was structured to meet their particular organizational and financial needs. Since there was no conflict of interest, I was able to represent all three designers.

Examine this model, which, of course, can be modified to meet your own organizational needs. The following is a suggested introduction.

Dear Mr. Winston:

I enjoyed meeting with you to discuss various alternatives regarding the interior design services for The De Luxe Hotel. I have received the preliminary development plans for the project, which were helpful to me in estimating the scope of my design services.

However, based on the fact that your plans are still not complete and a budget has not been established, the following is a breakdown of preliminary services that I am able to undertake now.

If you approve of my preliminary proposal, I will begin work immediately. At any time during design planning services, I will be happy to discuss the rest of my services required for completing the hotel. When it is appropriate, I shall submit a final contract outlining my fees and responsibilities.

Note the flexibility of this approach. Less entrepreneurial designers are insecure about presenting a written proposal until architectural plans are finalized and a budget has been established. However, aggressive business people frequently equate a lack of business acumen with an inability to design creatively. They prefer to consult designers who are eager to express themselves in writing. Design proposals are often necessary, for example, to advise a corporate board of directors about budget appropriation.

After the introduction, the preliminary aspects are presented as follows:

The following will confirm our agreement relating to the preliminary services to be performed by me and members of my staff with respect to the interior design of The De Luxe Hotel, Palm Beach, Florida.

All references to the hotel premises are understood to be in accordance with your plans. You represent that the hotel premises are owned by you and shall remain your property during the design period described in this agreement.

DESIGN AREAS

Our design work shall pertain to the entire interior of the hotel. At this time, we do not have a complete list of the design areas and would appreciate your submitting an itemized list as soon as possible.

You have advised us that the areas for our design encompass approximately 400,000 covered square feet, excluding terraces, plazas, and other outdoor areas. The number of sleeping rooms, according to the submitted plans, approximates 400.

We anticipate presenting a total concept that includes and relates to all adjacent areas to the hotel interior as well.

I have raised the issue of the ownership of the hotel premises during the designer's employment period for a very compelling reason. If the hotel's ownership changes while the designer is engaged for the project, the contract should provide a hidden option for the designer to terminate his agreement. This is a very significant point in this era of leveraged buyouts and corporate takeovers.

Although the proposal shouldn't be too explicit about the issue at this juncture, at least some foundation should be laid. If the ownership of the hotel changes, the designer may not want to continue working for new management. If the designer does not reserve the right to resign under these circumstances, he risks being sued for breach of contract.

In reference to the "Design Areas" section, I have always stressed the importance of listing each design area in the letter of agreement. Unfortunately, in this example, the architectural plans are incomplete, making it impossible to specify each design area. This language makes it clear that a final commitment can't be made until all design areas have been itemized by the client.

The following description of design services is truly the essence of your proposal.

DESIGN SERVICES

In respect to all design areas approved by you, we shall perform the following specific interior design services.

Phase I: Initial Design Study

We shall prepare an initial design study after consultation with you about your needs, criteria, design treatment, and your budget requirements.

Phase II: Preliminary Design Concept and Presentation.

Upon your written approval of the initial design study, we shall prepare a design presentation for your written approval consisting of the following:

Design concept plans, space studies, floor plans and layouts, elevations, decor and color schemes, reflected ceiling plans indicating light fixture placement, concepts for custom-designed items indicating finished appearance and function, data descriptive of standard furniture items, and initial sketches of custom-designed units.

Presentation sketches, renderings, and other drawings and documents will be supplied to describe the size and character of the design areas accommodating the furniture and furnishings. All documents, including a preliminary budget, will be prepared to estimate costs for the execution of the design presentation.

Phase III: Final Design and Project Planning

When the design concept has been completed and approved by you, we shall prepare a final presentation. This will consist of complete plans and specifications required for the execution of the design presentation, all for your approval.

These plans and specifications shall set forth in detail the requirements for all our interior design work.

Phase IV: Design Implementation

After you have approved all our plans, we shall inspect all design services. We will confer with suppliers of merchandise and materials to be utilized in executing the design presentation. This shall include all installations of furniture and furnishings at the site to guarantee conformance with plans and specifications.

All details with respect to the services we will perform in Phases III and IV will be itemized in a subsequent contract to be prepared by mutual agreement during Phases I and II.

This section is obviously the most comprehensive concerning the description of your services. Each client has particular requirements that will demand a special explanation or alteration of normal working procedures.

Although you may have an idea as to what these deviations might be, it is usually wise not to try to provide for them in the initial proposal. Use durable, comprehensive language, as in this example. Once you have met with the client several times and it becomes clear that you will be hired, then make changes for your final proposal.

Why wait? I find that designers are very anxious to please prospective clients, particularly if the job looks appealing. Consequently, they sometimes make business or legal concessions that they regret later on. Corporations, however, are adept at playing word games. Their business is, to some extent, negotiating and drafting contracts. Their personnel are well educated and trained to meet those challenges. Quite often, large, expensive law firms are hired to examine all contracts.

Designers, on the other hand, are more service oriented. They seem to relate more comfortably to visuals than to the printed word. Therefore, particularly early in the client relationship, don't try to second-guess the client with words. Use general language that is specific and has impact.

Once a proposal has been submitted, undoubtedly, you will have meetings about the project with key corporate personnel. A frequent response is as follows: "We've examined your proposal and would like to know how long it will be before the preliminary concept could be finished. We would like our hotel to open in 48 months. Can you specify time frames in your proposal?"

Your answer might be: "I can't really estimate an approximate time at this point. Once I have met with your architect and general contractor and studied their timetable, as well as our working arrangements, I can give you a rough idea."

Avoid giving specific answers in a vacuum when sufficient information hasn't been provided. A miscalculation can be held against you later. Reserve making important judgments until you are hired. If you must make certain commitments about scheduling, for example, try not to make them in writing.

You may expand on a proposal, orally, at meetings with corporate personnel. Use the proposal as a framework, as a platform to demonstrate your professionalism. If a client insists on specific deadline commitments, offer to make them in a final contract after you have been paid a retainer. If you have to go out on a limb, make your client hire you first.

When designers work on large projects involving massive renovation or new construction, they usually collaborate with other professionals in formulating plans and inspecting the design site. The "Consultation Services" clause demonstrates an awareness that the project is a collaborative effort.

CONSULTATION SERVICES

We shall consult with your principals, architects, and other specialists retained by you at your request. We shall provide design direction in respect to floor plans, reflected ceiling plans, and elevations as they relate to our design plans.

Direction will be provided to facilitate installation of our decorative and built-in light fixtures, as well as all special-effect light fixtures.

We shall also act as consultants in respect to signage for the interior and exterior, development of graphics for logos, and selection of uniform items for the hotel staff.

Although it is understood, use this opportunity to remind your corporate client that you are fully equipped to deal with the project, the architect, and any others retained to create this hotel. Although discussing consultation for graphics and logos may be superfluous at this stage, it is effective in indicating your attention to detail.

The next section, "Working Arrangements," is a general description of how you will follow through once design plans are approved.

WORKING ARRANGEMENTS

As discussed, our work will be undertaken in phases for the design areas once you finalize your plans. All items of merchandise, materials, and selected third-party services to be utilized in executing our design concept plans shall be specified and purchased by our office in accordance with purchase specifications approved by you.

The details of our purchasing procedures and your payments are also included in Phases III and IV and will be set forth in our subsequent contract.

Although precise working arrangements with a prospective client don't have to be explicit in the initial proposal, it is important to clarify how your firm will operate generally. The selected operational method frequently ties in with fees, as discussed subsequently under "Compensation."

For example, in this situation the design firm will act as the purchasing agent for the client. The method of charging will be on a cost-plus basis. Since the design firm will be processing all orders, it is easy to monitor the cost of purchases made by the client. This is essential knowledge for billing purposes.

I have also counselled many design firms about commercial projects in which clients have made their own purchases through independent or in-house purchasing agents. In some cases, the purchasing agents have resisted forwarding copies of purchase orders to the design firms.

Of course, without actual knowledge of expenditures, it becomes impossible to bill on a cost-plus basis. If you are unable to determine the cost of purchases, don't charge cost-plus.

Frequently, large corporations, including hotels, don't want designers to process purchases. In such cases, it is usually wiser to charge a flat fee or on an hourly basis. Hourly methods typically assign various rates to different personnel, for example, senior designers, draftsmen, and so forth. Sometimes these rates are subject to a multiplier, which is more fully discussed in Chapter 2.

To summarize, remember to outline "Working Arrangements," including "Purchases," in a proposal to complement the subsequent section, "Compensation." Settle these issues before your final contract is submitted.

The next section, "Compensation," discusses fees.

COMPENSATION
Design Services
We shall receive a fee in the amount of $100,000 for the completion of Phase I, Initial Design Study, and Phase II, Preliminary Design Concept and Presentation. This shall be payable as specified by the Schedule of Payments enclosed herein.

If we are retained to undertake performing Phase III, Final Design and Project Planning, and Phase IV, Design Implementation, we shall receive a fee as follows:

10% of the cost for all merchandise, materials, and third-party services specified by us and approved by you for the implementation and execution of our design presentation for all guest rooms;

15% of the cost for all merchandise, materials, and third-party services specified by us and approved by you for all the implementation and execution of our design presentation for all public spaces;

All purchases and third-party services specified by us will be made available to you at our wholesale cost.

In this discussion of compensation, note the difference in percentages for purchases for hotel guest rooms as opposed to public spaces. Purchases for the guest rooms, large-volume items, will be somewhat repetitious and easier to specify.

Accordingly, the cost-plus percentage is lowered to reflect the reduced amount of time required. This logic also applies to specifications for clerical offices, which also tend to be repetitious.

Public spaces, however, are more distinctive and design intensive. Each area tends to be unique, requiring greater detail. For that reason, the cost-plus percentage is frequently higher. This also applies to corporate board rooms and executive offices. These areas demand considerably more design effort than those allocated for general administrative staff.

A second segment of "Compensation" relates to disbursements, discussed as follows:

Disbursements

You shall reimburse us for any out-of-pocket expenditures we incur in order to perform our obligations under the agreement, including, without limitation:

1. The cost of blueprints, toll calls, long-distance communications and faxes, postage, packing, trucking, handling, shipping, insurance, warehousing, and customs charges;
2. Travel expenses will be billed as follows:
   For firm principals, $400 per day, and for associates, $300 per day, plus travel expenses;
3. $3000 for each full-color rendering that you request and $60 per hour for drafting expenses. We shall bill you for our out-of-pocket expenditures monthly and shall submit appropriate documentation at your request.

Although the disbursements that have been itemized here may differ from yours, note that drafting expenses should always be listed.

Regardless of whether your client wants to purchase full-color renderings, the cost should be mentioned. Renderings are often utilized for many large-budget jobs, particularly hotels, and your awareness of that fact makes you appear professional.

The next section, "Schedule of Payments," guarantees the designer's compensation.

SCHEDULE OF PAYMENTS

Upon Contract Execution	$25,000
30 Days from Contract Execution	$25,000
60 Days from Contract Execution	$25,000
Upon Presentation	$25,000

The final item should be the payment schedule for Phases I and II. Note that the payments are based on a schedule of events rather than finite dates. Because of the indefinite schedule of the project, it is impossible to prepare a schedule of specific dates.

Also note that any payments made to the designer are nonrefundable, as indicated in the following clause:

> Each payment, when tendered, shall be nonrefundable. If you desire to terminate our services, all payments made up to date of termination shall be considered for services rendered and shall be nonrefundable.

This is a very innocent way of adding a termination clause. Clients often want a termination clause in design agreements. Although it should be provided, always make certain that you will not be liable to return any payments for fees.

The following are the concluding paragraphs of the proposal:

> If you approve our proposal, we would appreciate your signing the enclosed copies of this letter and returning one copy with payment for $25,000.
>
> We are looking forward to collaborating with you.
> Sincerely,
>
> Corporate Interiors, Inc.
>
> By_____
> Accepted and Agreed:
> The De Luxe Hotel Corporation
> By: John Winston III, President
> Dated:

In the concluding paragraph, always request the signed proposal with your initial check. Be certain the corporate officer designated has authority to bind the company, so as to ensure that your contract will be binding.

The examples given in this chapter constitute the basic outline I use to prepare financial proposals for my own clients. Obviously, variations are necessary for each designer, particular client, and components of a specific project.

Nonetheless, I have found that this basic format seems to work well in most cases. Try using it for your next large project as an organizational tool, and observe whether your prospective client is impressed with your financial acumen. I think you will be pleasantly surprised.

9

FINANCIAL MANAGEMENT AND PROTECTION FOR RESIDENTIAL DESIGNERS

For residential interior designers, with both large and small offices, financial management is an area of great concern. Collecting money from clients and allocating funds to pay operating expenses and suppliers can often be a tedious and difficult daily task.

During the course of my career, I observed that most of my clients who were successful residential designers followed a similar pattern. The designer would spend an expensive weekend at his country house. He undoubtedly entertained clients and, of course, purchased furniture, art, or accessories unearthed while browsing through shops owned by local antique dealers.

The financial paranoia, of course, asserted itself each Monday morning and escalated to a major panic throughout the week. Wall Street had one Black Monday; my clients experienced Black Monday every week.

This is when the designer would storm into his office. He always looked a little green around the edges and would blurt out, "Are there any checks? Who paid? Did the Smiths send a $6000 deposit on the Chippendale chair? Oh, no, you mean they still haven't decided? I was counting on that to pay for my American Express bill. Hurry, get on the phone, start calling for money, and, whatever you do, leave my name out of it. Just say you're the bookkeeper and that it's your idea to call."

Although each designer expressed his fears differently, the message about money was always delivered with anxiety and, sometimes, terror. The pattern was usually the same, but, of course, there were certain exceptions. Some designers got upset on Friday instead of Monday, *before* they went away for the weekend.

To be able to plan effectively for financial management and cash flow, you must review basic accounting procedures involved in the designer-client relationship. Cash flow will be affected by various aspects of the working procedure with your client; these include client meetings, shopping, and selection of furnishings. The timing of these factors affects the collection of design fees and commissions. Obviously, this is the crux of your cash flow.

Cash flow problems vary from one design office to another. Frequently, liquidity shortages vary within the same office from one time period to another. The quality of your active list of clients will directly influence your financial plans.

The following are a few examples of factors affecting cash flow.

First, assume you are running a busy office and have a few good projects in progress. Some jobs are in fairly advanced stages and commissions are being collected regularly.

A new client walks into your office. You like the project and the client. It is your policy to charge a fixed design fee initially for preparing design plans and to charge additionally for purchasing goods and supervising installations. The question is, how large should the design fee be for preparing a design presentation?

1. Should you charge what you're worth, i.e., a substantial fee, based on your reputation, yielding a healthy profit in addition to your operating expenses?
2. Should you charge a fee based on an estimate of the amount of time enabling you to break even on your overhead cost for creating these design plans?
3. Should you charge less than your overhead cost to prepare these plans, to act as financial enticement to your prospective client?

Of course, there are many factors that will influence your decision, but in my experience the number one issue in making your determination is *cash flow*. When you are successful financially, you may decide that your priority is to earn money on each phase of a potential project.

Perhaps a potential client will make a lot of purchases, generating large commisions; perhaps he won't. Employing this approach, you will request a substantial fee for the design plans. If your client ultimately doesn't make many purchases, you will have made a profit on the presentation. Using this rationale, you may refuse a potential project if you can't earn a substantial fee for preparing the design plans. In this situation, cash flow was given an immediate priority.

Consider the second alternative. You are thinking of charging a reasonable design fee that will cover your overhead cost to prepare the presentation, allowing you to break even. Is that the most desirable route? Taking this "middle of the road" approach is considered to be safe. You can't be criticized for keeping costs as low as possible to lure a client, so long as you don't lose money.

You may decide that although your office is operating profitably at present, you want to use every possible strategy to attract future business without losing money. If a potential client doesn't proceed after the presentation has been completed, all is not lost. At least you have broken even.

This is a predictable approach, and many designers—and business people, for that matter—would tend to use such a strategy.

There is still a third alternative. Assume your office is still operating profitably. You become intrigued by a particular project and potential client. You believe that you will earn large commissions if your client accepts your presentation.

Under these circumstances, you may decide to charge a minimal design fee. It won't offset your overhead costs for preparing the plans, but will, you hope, beat your competition in attracting this plum client.

You may take this approach if you are more interested in attracting the client instead of making a profit on the design plans. If you don't get the job, at least you won't feel that you weren't competitive in your business strategy.

Regardless of your decision, there is a certain logic to be considered in selecting one of the three approaches. Even if your office is operating profitably, the concept of cash flow must always be considered prior to making any decision.

Years ago, I had a young designer client who was struggling to make a reputation as an important New York decorator. One day, he received a phone call from a wealthy woman, a grande dame in New York society.

She summoned him to redesign her huge living and dining rooms in one of Fifth Avenue's premier buildings. Her original decorator had completed her apartment the year before. Now she had decided to give a large cocktail party and dinner to show it off to her rich and influential guests.

Two months earlier, her former designer had completed the redesign of a famous hotel on Central Park South. It was a gorgeous restoration. All of New York had gone to see it, including the wealthy client from Fifth Avenue.

To the socialite's shock and horror, she saw that the designer had selected the same wallpaper for the hotel lobby as for her living and dining rooms. She had already scheduled her dinner party and realized that she had to redecorate before her guests discovered that her living room resembled a hotel lobby.

She was furious, and started calling her friends to research names of popular decorators. She was referred to my client, among other designers. During the initial interview, she told the designer that she refused to pay an initial design fee and would pay only a small commission on any purchases.

My client saw the opportunity as his big chance. He realized that he would meet many well-heeled guests with social connections at his client's party. If he played his cards well, he knew he might attract some of the "right people" as new clients.

Instead of worrying about cash flow, he visited the socialite at her Fifth Avenue apartment the same afternoon of her call. He merely inquired, "How can I help you?" He redecorated the living and dining rooms, charging retail.

The client was in such a bind for time that she was unable to prolong the redecoration process; she had no time to interview many other designers, making it easier for the designer to get the job. Since the designer's cash flow was good, he was able to afford preparing the design plans for free. He never charged a design fee but earned substantial commissions on all the purchases. Ultimately, he earned a healthy profit from the job and a nucleus of referral clients that made his career.

. Now *he* writes books on decorating.

This story has an important message. At crucial times during your career, you have to ignore the concept of cash flow. However, that shouldn't be too often.

One of the favorite topics of designers is how to set design fees. This subject is discussed in Chapter 2, "Charging Design Fees." The point I want to emphasize here is that it is wise to avoid becoming fixated on the same method of charging for every single job.

Fee structures may vary, depending on the scope of the project. Alternative methods of charging fees for design plans, using various financial strategies have been discussed. You can also use these alternatives in selecting a percentage to charge for purchasing goods and services.

The percentage a designer charges for purchasing goods and design services, using the cost-plus method, doesn't always have to be the same. There are two important factors to consider: the magnitude of the project and the likelihood of being paid for all your specifications. Of course, flexibility can sometimes be carried to the extreme.

Years ago I worked for a well-known decorator in New York City who designed a Manhattan apartment for an unnamed client. The job was so hush-hush that the bills were sent to a lawyer to protect the client's identity.

The client had purchased the apartment for his mistress and wanted to remain anonymous so his wife wouldn't know. He had instructed the designer to deliver the apartment in turnkey condition, including "his and hers" toothbrushes.

The decorator had no trouble cooperating since he was an expert in accommodating his wealthy clientele. At first, I thought, "Why do all that? Decorating is hard enough." But the designer was an expert at public relations and, as I also found out, at business as well.

When his bookkeeper examined the purchase orders, she told me that even the toilet paper had been marked up 25 percent. The decorator hadn't missed one item. Although that particular markup couldn't have amounted to much, it was an example I remembered. Designers should always be paid for everything they specify.

Design offices often have difficulty collecting payment for estimates. Most purchases require a 50 percent deposit to initiate production. Very often, designers send out estimates to their clients with a list of items. A total amount is posted at the end of the list. A deposit, usually 50 percent of the total, is requested to process the purchases.

After the client receives this estimate, too often she returns it with changes, without reviewing them with the designer. Usually, the changes increase the amount of the estimate, and the deposit as well. For some reason, however, the client's check for the deposit is usually less than the requested 50 percent. Ultimately, when the bookkeeper bills the client for the final balance prior to making all deliveries, it becomes very confusing.

It is important for the designer to be responsive to any changes initiated by a client. If changes are made, a final revised estimate should be submitted with corrected figures and deposit amounts.

A simple example can illustrate. Suppose a client is making purchases for $20,000, that is, a table for $10,000, four chairs for $8000 and two candlesticks for $2000. The estimate requires a deposit of $10,000—50 percent of the total cost.

Now suppose the client changes her mind about the tabletop, deciding to buy granite instead of marble, thus increasing the price another $1000. Assume the client ignores the designer's revised estimate and still sends the initially requested $10,000 deposit. This reduces the designer's cash flow, since the he must pay 50 percent to the supplier. Unfortunately, the designer winds up financing the additional deposit, $500 in this situation.

When the client receives the final invoice and the merchandise is ready for delivery, she typically expects to spend another $10,000—50 percent of the original estimate. Instead, she is billed for $11,000 by the designer. When the client complains, she insists she owes only a balance of 50 percent and acts confused, refusing to listen to the explanation for the additional $1000 billed.

The bookkeeper must now resolve the bill, reviewing each item, which sometimes creates ill will between the designer and his client.

At first glance, this example may seem a bit absurd. Obviously, the client owes an additional $1000, and there is no rational reason for her to be upset. However, you must realize that I used a very basic example to prove a point. Usually, on an estimate, there are 40 items instead of 4. These changes are often very subtle but frequently very expensive. A statement with 40 items is fairly complex and often confuses clients.

For example, changing a finish on a chair frame may seem like a minor detail to a client, but when the change is from lacquer to gold leaf, the financial difference isn't minor at all. Clients have a convenient way of forgetting the cost of upgrading their choices. However, when the invoice comes, the shock and anger begin.

The proper preparation of designer's estimates is crucial to earning fees. When charging retail, the designer's commission is included in the sales price listed on the estimate. Therefore, only one estimate is necessary for each item purchased, since fees aren't billed separately. However, it is not recommended to include 50 percent of the sales tax on retail estimates that require a deposit of 50 percent of the purchase price. The reason for this is that, in most states, sales tax shouldn't be billed until the merchandise is physically delivered. Several accountants have advised me of that fact. However, when billing on a percentage or *cost-plus*, the designer's commission is *not* built into the sales price on the estimates. In this situation, request a separate deposit for your commission.

Dealing with sales tax is a crucial issue. Do not attempt to deal with paying sales tax without consulting a certified public accountant (CPA) in your state. Explain to the CPA how your office handles purchases of goods and design services. The accountant will advise you accordingly on how to discharge your duties legally, relative to your clients' paying sales tax.

If you are able to bill your design commissions separately, it can be very beneficial for cash flow purposes. For example, if you separate your design fees from the client's deposits and payments for goods, these two categories can be segregated into separate checking accounts. By avoiding commingling of funds, it is much easier to keep track of your finances.

If all the money is kept in one account, it becomes too easy to spend. When cash flow is tight, some designers use clients' deposits, for goods, for their own expenses. They assume they will collect other fees later and repay the money. Their concern to satisfy immediate bills overrides good judgment. They hope they will sign up other new clients soon and thus restore cash flow.

But what happens if the expected new client is a little late in arriving? What happens when the goods are ready for delivery on existing jobs, but you've spent the client's final payments and can't pay the vendor? Can you get the supplier to give you additional credit?

I knew a very talented designer who had always worked as an employee for other designers. After a long career, he obtained two very large clients and started his own business. He charged retail and kept all deposits in one account.

Although a large percentage was payable to vendors, the size of his checking account seemed enormous to him. Since he had always worked for others, he had little experience with handling money. Receiving bank statements with large balances gave him a feeling of power.

When one of his clients had a birthday, he threw a large party to celebrate. The designer felt so affluent that he gave a very extravagant present, a piece of French crystal costing $1500.

At Christmas, the designer tipped his doormen with hundred-dollar bills and bought lovely gifts for his office staff. When it came time to pay for his client's purchases, there wasn't enough money left.

The designer solved his financial problems without consciously doing anything about it. He had a nervous breakdown. His client paid double because the designer had spent the deposits on his own expenses. This is an extreme example of the price one can pay if money isn't handled carefully.

I realize that some designers work with small staffs or, perhaps, independently. In that event, it is important to engage a part-time bookkeeper, weekly or monthly. Your data must be compiled in a professional manner so your accountant can prepare a tax return properly. This may seem like a luxury, but it really is not.

If your financial data isn't properly documented, your accountant may have serious problems when tax time arrives. Try to make it easy for professionals, to enable them to use their talent and ability to give you their best.

My personal feeling is that a designer's time should be spent pursuing her creative abilities to the fullest extent possible under the circumstances. Designers should avoid becoming traumatized by financial management and cash flow problems.

You don't have to experience a financial crisis like Black Monday on Wall Street. What you must do is to implement financial management, using the concepts and techniques presented here. Make certain that some of the happiest adventures you have in life are the trips you take to the bank.

There are a number of techniques designers can use to provide financial protection. However, prior to launching into that discussion, I would like to make one special caveat that applies particularly to residential designers.

For large residential projects, and for many commerical jobs, the client usually hires a general contractor. The general contractor then hires subcontractors. On smaller residential projects, there frequently is no general contractor. The designer recommends to her clients her favorite contractors for design services (i.e., painters, mirror companies, custom cabinetry, etc.) to implement her designs.

I strongly recommend that you do not enter into any contracts on behalf of your clients for design services. If you do, your contract may be illegal. Some states require designers to have a home improvement contract license, or a license as a general contractor, to enter into contracts with other subcontractors on behalf of their clients. I would prefer to see designers avoid this issue altogether.

The further the designer distances herself from subcontractors, on a contractual level, the easier it is to avoid liability in the event the client has a problem. In a sense, this is a means of creating financial protection.

For example, if you are purchasing furniture and furnishings for a client, using your "house accounts" from showrooms, you are the direct purchaser. However, if you engage a particular mirror installer for your client, meet with the contractor at the project site. Obtain the estimate for the work, including all specifications. I would, however, strongly recommend that the estimate be prepared in your client's name, not your name. Ideally, the client should pay the contractor directly and approve the estimate in writing. I do not recommend verbal estimates or approvals, regardless of your long-standing relationships with contractors. I believe this to be one of the cheapest forms of financial protection you can use.

Your client may say, "Take care of the electrician for me. Pay him directly; I'll reimburse you. We're only installing a few lights. What's the big deal?" Tell your client that you can't do that. Have him deal contractually and financially with the electrician directly. Of course, you can inspect the electrician's work at the site, but you are not responsible for guaranteeing it. Make certain you disclaim your responsibility for any contractors in your letter of agreement. Sample language is provided in Chapter 1, "Preparing a Letter of Agreement."

There is another form of financial protection that you should use as well. Do not perform any design services if your jurisdiction would label them as "unlicensed architectural services." This description varies from one state to another. In states where designers are licensed, your limitations are clearer. In any event, find out what those limitations are before preparing design plans and supervising contractors.

Some commercial interior designers are licensed architects. Their offices prepare architectural working drawings, and these designers supervise general contractors and subcontractors. Legally, they are entitled to perform those services.

It is crucial for you to understand your legal limitations so as to be able to live within them. Check with other designers in your area to see how they cope with legal restrictions. This is a very hot issue in the interior design industry today, so it will not be difficult for you to determine how to proceed.

If your client needs services that you are not legally qualified to perform, he will have to retain those professionals who are licensed. However, that doesn't mean that you have to surrender the reins when it comes to designing. For example, many decorators know architects and general contractors whom they frequently recommend to their clients. They work together as a team. Use that philosophy for your own financial protection.

There are three other aspects of financial protection that pertain particularly to residential designers:

1. Ensuring that clients accept delivery of ordered goods
2. Avoiding the necessity to return design fees to clients
3. Preventing clients from buying behind your back

ENSURING CLIENTS ACCEPT DELIVERY OF ORDERED GOODS

A serious problem confronting many designers has been the refusal of difficult clients to accept delivery of custom-ordered goods, claiming, "It wasn't what we ordered." When clients decide what to buy, they sometimes forget their choices. Designers make recommendations based on their own taste and judgment. Some clients reluctantly agree, and then don't remember. A typical example of this involves the ordering of a wallpaper pattern. Wall coverings usually must be paid for in full prior to delivery, hence, the phrase, "collect before delivery." (CBD). Several designers have told me that their clients had forgotten their selections and refused to pay for goods ordered. Even when the designers showed their clients the approved sample on the purchase order, the clients still claimed that designer misunderstood and ordered the wrong goods. The designers, of course, had to pick up the tab.

This also happens with furniture orders. At one time, I represented a custom furniture manufacturer and saw several situations in which the designer was blamed because the client claimed the color or size of the piece was wrong. That's why custom furniture should always be specified by style, color, and size on both the order and the invoice. Trouble may result when changes are made after an order has been submitted if they aren't properly documented on the orders and invoices. When designers initiate changes, it's their responsibility to secure client approval on amended orders.

In most situations, designers bill purchases to their own accounts to obtain a professional discount. Therefore, the designer is responsible for the merchandise if the client refuses to pay for the goods. To avoid liability, I recommend the following policies.

If the designer charges his clients on a cost-plus basis, prepare separate purchase orders for each item in triplicate. Each purchase order should identify the nature and description of the goods, as well as the price and projected delivery date whenever possible. The goods should be visually identified on the purchase order as well. For example, if the order is for fabrics or wall coverings, attach a cutting to each purchase order. If furniture is being ordered, describe it with regard to size, style, color, and trim. If it is illustrated in a catalog, cut out the picture and attach it to the purchase order. Then submit these orders to your client, instructing him to sign each approved order. *Never process a purchase order or make any purchases of nonreturnable or custom-ordered goods without advance written client approval.* Keep one copy for your file, one for the client's, and one for the vendor.

If the designer charges his clients list or retail, he should prepare a purchase order for the vendor in a similar fashion. Since the client does not know the net or discounted price, a separate "Purchase Estimate" should be prepared for him. The Purchase Estimate for the client should be identical to the purchase order for the vendor, except for the price. Don't process the purchase order until you have received the client's signed Purchase Estimate with a deposit.

Difficult clients have been known to refuse to approve purchase orders or purchase estimates in writing. They prefer to make no commitment until the goods are delivered to their satisfaction. Since designers can't afford to take chances, be sure to provide the following clause in your letter of agreement:

> You will be required to provide your written approval upon acceptance of design plans and presentation, final budget, purchase orders, and all design drawings.

This is very innocuous-sounding language, and rarely will clients question it upon submission of your letter of agreement. Therefore, if a client later becomes temperamental, demanding that you "go ahead and order it," remind him of this clause and don't budge. As stressed earlier, if you change any specifications for goods that have already been ordered, always send an amended purchase order or a memo to your client for written approval.

AVOIDING THE NECESSITY TO RETURN DESIGN FEES

To protect designers financially from difficult clients, precautions can be taken in the letter of agreement if the designer has an inkling that the going may get rough once the job begins.

"Easy clients" are indeed a rare and treasured commodity. It is also beyond question that some clients are tougher and harder to handle than others. Some designers have trouble with doctors, others with attorneys, and still others with show-business people. Perhaps you don't, but most designers have their own list of troublemakers.

Difficult clients have a tendency to fire designers without warning or apparent reason. When a group of interior designers meet socially or at professional meetings, the conversation frequently drifts to anecdotes about how they were "replaced." Some designers delight in recalling stories about how they were fired by celebrities or big corporations. Their implication, of course, is that no one could ever please these clients.

Being discharged by a client is an inevitable part of working in the design business. Even the most notable designers have skeletons in their closets. However, whether you arc discharged, walk away from a job, or the project is stopped, don't be caught in the position of having to return design fees for services rendered.

There are a number of ways to avoid returning design fees. In the letter of agreement, most designers request an initial payment, submitted with the signed contract, or a retainer. Specify, for instance, that the "$2500 nonrefundable retainer shall be returned with the signed letter of agreement." Usually, there is a section of the letter of agreement that discusses payment for design fees. Once again, specify that "nonrefundable payments for design fees are requested within 10 days from billing dates." It doesn't matter how the term *nonrefundable* is incorporated into the payment section, as long as it's in there. Some designers don't like being so explicit with the use of the word *nonrefundable*. They are afraid of turning the client off with a tough contract. As an alternative, you might use the following language: "All payments made for design fees shall be considered payment for services rendered to date." I don't think this is as effective, but it does provide some protection.

The next issue is, when do your fees become "earned"? After completion? Prior to billing? When do they "vest?"

If you charge by the hour, the hourly rate should be established in your letter of agreement. Once the services have been performed, you have earned your design fee. If your client discharges you, the value of your services has been established. Keep time records so that you can provide an accounting. "Guesstimates" are not good enough and won't hold up in a courtroom or an arbitration proceeding.

Simple contemporaneous memos, made in the course of your business, are admissable. They are considered powerful evidence, documenting your time. Notes can be brief but should indicate how the time was spent; for example, "Drafting revisions: living room cabinetwork— 2.0 hrs."

If you charge for any goods at list or retail, your fee won't "vest" until the client completes the purchase and pays in full. In that sense, you act as a vendor and are held responsible as such. However, once the client accepts the goods, you have earned your built-in markup. A problem with charging list may occur after the client has accepted the goods. He may find fault and attempt to get a refund or an exchange after a month or two. If the showroom or craftsman won't accept a return or make changes, the designer has a problem. For this reason, many designers have drifted away from charging list, even though the markup is high.

If you charge on a cost-plus basis, the following language can be included in your letter of agreement: "All commissions for purchases are earned upon approval of purchase orders by the client." For example, if your client signs a purchase order for a sofa for $2500, and you are charging cost plus 30 percent, your commission has been earned once your client has approved the purchase order in writing and forwarded the deposit to the vendor. Accordingly, your commission vested once that purchase order was signed.

If you are subsequently discharged, prior to the sofa's delivery, you are still entitled to your $750 commission. You must volunteer to supervise delivery and installation, although, usually, the client won't want you involved. Nonetheless, you have specified the goods, pursuant to your client's request, prepared a purchase order with client approval, and processed the order. Even if the client changes his mind about the purchase, forfeiting his deposit, you have still earned your commission if the language specified in the preceding paragarph is incorporated into your letter of agreement.

PREVENTING CLIENTS FROM BUYING BEHIND YOUR BACK

Have you ever caught a client making his own purchases, using your design plans and specifications? Generally, when designers prepare plans, they create them with the understanding that they will act as purchasers for furniture and furnishings. After months of researching design plans, it is most disconcerting to discover that your client is trying to avoid paying your fee. Some clients are expert at manipulating their designers to work for nothing. Don't let them outwit you. The following is a typical example.

A designer prepared a floor plan for a client, including a furniture layout and fabric samples. Although the designer charged a minimal flat fee for preparing the plans, she based the bulk of her fees on cost-plus, or net plus 30 percent, for making purchases of furniture and furnishings.

Progress was slow on the shopping expeditions, but, finally, a number of choices were made. Since the designer had her own custom upholsterer, who had prototypes in muslin, all the upholstery came from one source. However, case goods—cabinets and furniture—were purchased from showrooms catering to the design trade. The client had originally intended to purchase a large dining table with eight chairs and a breakfront, or huge cabinet, and a vitrine, to store dishes and linens. However, the client never made a final selection. She had decided to postpone, she reasoned, until the living room upholstery arrived. Two months later, the client called her designer to select fabric for dining chairs that her "aunt," she claimed, had given her as a house gift.

When the designer arrived at the client's residence, she became very upset. There was a breakfront, a dining table, and chairs she had seen with her client at a design showroom. Obviously, the client had returned to the showroom with a resale number, purchasing the goods herself to avoid paying the designer a $5000 commission. She attempted to lie about major purchases so that she could use the designer for smaller purchases that would require detailed specifications and additional shopping trips.

This kind of situation happens to every designer more than once during a career. The question is, what can be done to stop it? How can you prevent a sneaky client from stealing your ideas to make her own purchases, using you to do the legwork? Try inserting the following clause in your next letter of agreement:

> It is understood and agreed that all furnishings and furniture will be purchased to implement the floor plan and other design plans submitted by my office. In that connection, I will agree to assist you in the purchase of the foregoing at my cost plus my design commissions. However, in the event that any such purchases are made or contracted for during the period of our agreement without my services or consultation, said purchases will be included in the total cost on which all commissions are assessed.

A similar clause is discussed in Chapter 1, "Preparing a Letter of Agreement." However, the loss of commissions as a result of this type of client behavior can be very severe. Accordingly, it is appropriate to broach the subject again in greater detail within this discussion of financial protection.

When I suggest this clause to designers for the first time, they invariably make two comments. The first is that the clause covers only purchases made while they are working on the project. Once the project is finished, the client can still use the designer's specifications to buy goods without paying a commission. Unfortunately, no contract, no matter how foolproof, can totally protect designers from dishonest clients. If you are working on a large project, generally, your client will want as much input and supervision as possible. She will want you to place the furniture as well as buy it. The more dependent the client is on your design judgment, the less likely it is that she'll want you to leave before completing the project.

Designers frequently ask, "Can I compel my clients to pay me commissions if they make purchases with my specifications?" The answer is, usually, no. However, placing this clause in a letter of agreement has functioned as a preventative. When prospective clients read this clause, they are put on guard immediately. They realize their designer will be watching all the purchases as they are made, which generally helps to discourage "outside purchases."

In the same vein, if your client approves your custom woodworking designs, color selections, and paint schedule but decides to use his own contractors, how do you handle the situation? Is the concept the same as making outside purchases of goods? Not exactly; it is not being done in a secretive manner. It is simply another example of how some clients try to avoid paying design commissions by hiring their own workers. In this case, designers usually supervise the client's own contractors, charging by the hour.

Financial management and financial protection for designers are important tools to protect cash flow. As your own business develops, you will discover other opportunities to maximize your profitability.

10

DESIGNERS AND INDUSTRY— EXPECTATIONS AND RAMIFICATIONS

DESIGNER LIABILITY

Designers wear many hats in the course of running their professional careers as they deal with clients, suppliers, vendors, contractors, and architects. Frequently, because of the nature of the job, a designer may play several roles with the same party, creating confusion, uncertainty, and job conflicts. Although I can't resolve all these problems, I can try to clarify certain areas to help you with your future jobs.

The factual situations in the examples presented are of no great significance. Their purpose is not to program your behavior for a similar situation, but simply to provoke thought so that you will be able to solve your own problems.

Consider this. You may approach a new project with the same design concept that you used for a previous job. However, because of the existing conditions, a totally different design may be your ultimate solution. The same flexibility is needed when dealing with people and is an important tool when playing different roles. So don't try to memorize. Simply react, and learn from your reactions.

How do designers cope with some of the problems created by industry? The following is a typical example.

A partner in a small design firm with three designers and a staff of fifteen consulted me about an existing project. He had recently been hired to renovate substantial office space and was supposed to collaborate with his client's architect. The designer was planning to specify a number of new design materials for soundproofing and insulation, as well as new office modular systems.

147

The designer was very sensitive to potential product liability. He wondered about his liability if, several years later, it was discovered that some of these materials were unsafe for the environment. Could his client hold him responsible? Could he be sued? Could his client's customers hold him responsible? How long would his liability extend into the future? The current plethora of lawsuits litigating asbestos removal triggered these insecurities. He wanted to know if there were ways to keep from being sued.

Of course, his questions were valid, but, unfortunately, I could not provide black-and-white answers to all of them. What I attempted to do was to provide him with some guidance to enable him to formulate his own approach to specifying new products created by industry.

I don't think that there are foolproof ways to keep from being sued. In the United States, we have a system of jurisprudence that virtually permits anyone to sue anyone else, for any reason whatsoever. Lawsuits in this country are a good business, and as a group, Americans are a litigious society.

Until 50 years ago, most litigation was commercial, involving such areas as breach of contract. Consumer litigation focused on personal injuries as a result of automobile negligence. Then individuals began suing doctors and lawyers. Medical and legal fees were driven up due to the cost of malpractice insurance. I have been advised that in Dade County, Florida, malpractice insurance premiums for obstetricians exceed $100,000 a year. The premiums for neurosurgeons exceed $150,000.

Many architects have been sued successfully for malpractice in connection with building defects. Some verdicts have been prohibitively high. As a result, a growing number of architects have stopped designing buildings and have become interior designers. They have changed their careers simply to avoid becoming a target for a lawsuit.

However, the reason people start lawsuits, generally, is to make money. Rarely is litigation instituted purely for the purpose of satisfying moral indignation. Furthermore, lawsuits cost a lot to start. A plaintiff must pay lawyers legal fees and court costs. Therefore, although anyone theoretically can start a lawsuit, not necessarily anyone will.

One major exception is a personal injury lawsuit for automobile negligence. Attorneys work on a contingent fee basis; they don't get paid unless and until they succeed.

Lawsuits against designers generally require the plaintiff, the complainant, to finance the legal fees. Litigation involving unsafe products usually requires the plaintiff to pay his own lawyers. That fact alone reduces the number of potential plaintiffs considerably.

Litigation over unsafe products is frequently characterized as "products liability." Originally, products liability began with lawsuits against automobile manufacturers. The courts made it possible for the consumer to sue the automobile manufacturer directly, even though he bought the car from a dealer or from an individual. Once that concept became established in the courts, products liability branched out to include manufacturers of a host of products, ranging from machines to clothing.

Therefore, as a threshold target, the manufacturer of an unsafe product, which creates a hazard, becomes toxic, or harbors a dangerous attribute, is the villian that the plaintiff will seek out. Does that mean the designer of a project is off the hook? Absolutely not. In lawsuits of this nature, rarely is there one defendant. Frequently, the plaintiff tries to sue anyone with potential liability, including the general contractor, the subcontractor, the manufacturer, the architect, the designer, and so on. This is called the "shotgun" approach.

Some jurisdictions, however, will permit a plaintiff to sue only the manufacturer for products liability. When that is the case, the clever attorneys sue all other potential plaintiffs, based on a negligence theory. It seems fairly clear that in cases of products liability, for the most part, the manufacturer, not the designer, will probably bear the burden. However, the designer should realize that there are other legal theories that can be used to be hold him liable.

The following are legal theories that plaintiffs have used to sue interior designers.

One theory is intentional tort. A designer is liable (just as any other professional would be) for fraud, misrepresentation, or misuse of funds. Thus, those designers who take kickbacks or receive secret or undisclosed commissions from their suppliers or vendors could be held liable under this theory. A second theory is breach of fiduciary duties. If a designer acts as a fiduciary for a client, that is, distributes client funds to various suppliers, such as furniture dealers and other contractors, the designer owes the client all of the customary dealings of a fiduciary, including loyalty, confidentiality, and honest dealing. A third theory is breach of contract. For instance, a designer may have breached a term of an express oral agreement with a client. If there is no express contract, a court may be willing to find an implied promise by the designer to use ordinary skill and care to protect the client's interests.

A fourth theory, probably the most common, is simple negligence. Using this theory, the plaintiff must establish the routine elements of any negligence: a duty of due care, a breach of that duty, actual cause, proximate cause, and damages. These aspects are discussed separately in the following paragraphs.

The standard of care for an interior designer is the degree of care, skill, and prudence exhibited by other designers of ordinary skill and capacity. The standard of care is higher for one who purports to be a specialist in a particular field of design. That standard is measured by the degree of care, skill, and prudence exhibited by other designers who specialize in that field.

For example, consider a state that has a title or practice act for licensing. A licensed or certified interior designer, specializing in environmental design, would be held to a higher standard of care for specifying products that are environmentally safe than an unlicensed interior decorator. This may be true even if they are both consulted for the same project to specify furniture and furnishings.

A designer is liable for negligence, but not everything that causes harm is negligence. Many states will not hold designers responsible for mere errors in judgment, so long as that judgment was well informed and reasonably made.

For example, a designer may recommend a general contractor based on the contractor's excellent reputation or on a positive personal experience. If the contractor hires poor subcontractors to work on the designer's job, the designer may not be liable for any damages.

Perhaps the designer should have verified each subcontractor, but that is not always possible. Moreover, clients sometimes ask designers to find contractors who are cheaper than those they normally use. A designer may inquire diligently, asking colleagues for other contractors who might be available. If a chosen contractor later does a poor job and the client sues for damages, the designer is not necessarily responsible.

Legally, a relevant issue is whether the designer made a diligent inquiry. Did he tell his client that his recommendation was based solely on reports from third parties, not his own personal experience? The bottom line is this: If a designer recommends any "source" to his client that later performs badly, he must be able to explain why he made the recommendation. The reasons offered must be sufficient to satisfy a standard of care that other designers would have exercised under similar circumstances.

Another important consideration is the designer's responsibility for the knowledge of design. A designer is expected to know the basic skills of interior design known by other designers of ordinary skill and diligence. Further, as a designer, you have a duty to research the basic skills that other designers know. If answers are available through basic research and you do not find them, you have breached the duty of due care. Obviously, many issues of interior design are unsettled and debatable. If you have done your research, you have fulfilled the duty of due care. This is true even if you ultimately make the wrong guess about an optimal solution for a client.

Some design problems are uniquely within the competence of a design specialist. It is a breach of duty of care for a typical designer to attempt to handle such a problem if a reasonably prudent designer would have called in a specialist. For example, suppose a brokerage firm asks a designer to create custom cabinet systems for its audiovisual needs. If the designer does not consult with an audiovisual specialist, approved by the client, and specifies cabinets and designs that are inadequate, she may be liable for any damages to redesign the system if it ultimately does not meet the client's needs.

As in any tort case, a plaintiff in a malpractice action must prove actual cause—that the injury would not have happened *but for* the designer's negligent conduct. For example, a client of an interior designer sues him for recommending unreliable contractors. The client must prove that the workmanship performed by the contractors is unacceptable. If the client has no damages, there is no case against the designer even if the contractors were known in the trade to be unreliable.

As in any ordinary negligence case, a malpractice plaintiff must prove proximate cause—that it is fair to hold the designer liable for unexpected injuries or for expected injuries that happen in unexpected ways. For example, a husband and wife hired a designer to redesign their new home. The designer neglected the job, and the house looked terrible. These problems created a psychological strain on the clients; subsequently, they both lost their jobs. A court will probably conclude that the loss of earning power by both husband and wife was not proximately caused by the designer's negligence.

A designer may be responsible for the negligence of others if, for example, they are acting as his agents or are employed by him. Thus a designer can be held liable for damages caused by a negligent design assistant, draftsman, or employee/associate when acting within the scope of his employment.

Since designer malpractice actions have increased, malpractice insurance and liability insurance have become expensive. However, many designers consider such precautions to be a necessary part of their practice.

DESIGNERS AND INDUSTRY

A designer should also be aware of how industry can place designers at risk for malpractice. Consider the following examples.

A client purchased an apartment in a newly constructed building, and his designer decided to create a very sleek environment. All the walls were covered in a silver-gray vinyl to create a background for an art collection. To produce a "minimal" effect, all the baseboards on the walls were removed. The walls were meticulously prepared for the vinyl wall covering, which had to be carefully applied to avoid imperfections.

A very expensive painting and wall covering contractor spent weeks sanding the walls so the vinyl would look as smooth as a sheet of glass. After six weeks, the walls were finished and looked like silver mirrors. The seams of the wall covering had been double-cut and were virtually undetectable.

A famous carpet showroom sold the client, through his designer, a silver-gray wool wall-to-wall carpet that had the same tonality as the wall covering. The trouble began during carpet installation.

It was very difficult for the designer or the client to gauge the progress of the installation because the numerous rolls of carpeting and padding obscured the view. The designer inspected the installation twice daily at the site and was assured by the installer that all was well. The showroom had promised the designer that it had sent its best installer. In fact, the showroom didn't have installers on staff but had subcontracted with an outside installation company.

Once the installation was nearly finished, the designer and her client could see that it was a disaster. The installer had burned a hole in one area of the carpet with his iron and had then patched it. The seaming was poor. The job also required carpeting a platform bed and a headboard. This was also poorly executed.

The worst problem, however, was the damage to the vinyl-covered walls. The installer had used a carpet stretcher, pounding it against the walls to tighten the carpet. Gouges from the stretcher appeared at the baseboard level, and because the baseboards had been removed, the marks were obvious.

The designer contacted the carpet showroom, which inspected the installation. It offered to replace the carpet at no charge to the client. However, it refused to pay for the damage to the walls. It claimed that those damages were the responsibility of the installer, the subcontractor. The showroom's attorney stated that any further claim would require resolution through litigation. This would trigger a settlement by the showroom's and installer's insurance carriers to resolve the matter.

The designer was shocked. She had been an excellent customer of the showroom for many years. She was a personal friend of the owners. Now their negligence had created damages for her client, and they had deserted her. Instead of paying for their mistakes, they had told her client to start a lawsuit.

The client hired an attorney and sued the showroom. The showroom joined the installer in the action as a third-party defendant. Then the showroom and the installer sued the designer, in the same action, for negligent supervision of the installation.

The designer was shattered when the showroom and the installer sued her. Obviously, it wasn't her fault. The other defendants were simply trying to deflect the blame from themselves.

The amount of damages sought was $60,000, which included the cost of removing and replacing the wall covering. In fact, the client had decided to live with the damaged walls, regardless of the lawsuits's outcome. He said he could not bear living through another series of installations.

The client eventually settled out of court for $23,000. Atlhough he was entitled to the entire $60,000, his lawyer enouraged him to settle. "A jury would award you $1 million if you got your arm caught in an elevator," his counsel advised, "but they might not feel too sympathetic about a bad wall covering installation. Jurors are often blue-collar workers—bus drivers and secretaries. They might not relate to expensive interior decorating problems or feel sorry for the clients."

The client also felt very bad for the interior designer. He didn't want her to have to endure a trial and exposure to liability. The showroom had abandoned the designer, claiming it was "nothing personal." Since the lawsuit was handled by its insurance company, it claimed no responsibility for having sued her for negligent supervision.

In other words, the carpet showroom refused to solve the problems it had created. It attempted to hold the designer responsible for its own damages.

As mentioned earlier, the client accepted the settlement and decided to live with the damaged walls. And then a miracle happened. When the lawsuit was over, the wall covering contractor went to the client's apartment. He planned to camouflage the damage by painting silver lacquer over the gouges. However, upon close inspection, he discovered that the gouges were merely hunks of glue that the stretcher had implanted on the walls. He removed the glue with turpentine. The walls looked perfect.

Insurance appraisers had inspected the damage during the lawsuit and had concluded that it was permanent. Obviously, they had been wrong. Ultimately, the client ended up $20,000 richer. Yet, this does not negate the fact that when the designer experienced trouble with the showroom, the showroom abandoned her, blaming her for negligent supervision.

Perhaps you may think that this was an unusual situation, that industry takes care of its designers. At least, that's what your vendors tell you. I don't believe it.

Consider another case, in which the designer also performed his duty and the vendor created problems.

A designer was retained to renovate and redesign a condominium directly overlooking Biscayne Bay in Miami. The apartment's living room had an extended terrace that had been enclosed by sliding glass doors. The glass doors, which had been tinted to protect the living room from a direct southern exposure, were made of glass panels more than 20 feet wide. The designer consulted a Miami showroom that sold only window treatments and had an excellent reputation.

The client told the owner of the showroom, as well as his designer, that he didn't like vertical or horizontal blinds. He also wanted the view to be as unobstructed as possible. The showroom owner recommended a sunscreening fabric mounted on a Roman shade. The product was manufactured specifically for use in window treatments and was made of a vinyl compound. The meshlike material, the owner advised, would screen out in excess of 70 percent of the heat and light. She felt that was sufficient, since the room was not used for sleeping, and full "blackout protection" was not required.

Ultimately, the showroom installed these shades for the living room, master bedroom, and guest rooms. The rooms all had direct bay views with a southern exposure. In addition, the guest bedroom had interlined cotton curtains, crowned with a valence. The master bedroom had silk curtains mounted on a pole with rings. The Roman shades were usually rolled down during the day, and the curtains were drawn at night.

The installations were completed, and the client paid in full. During the following summer, however, he noticed that his living room was very warm during the day, despite the air-conditioning and ceiling fans. He asked the building manager what was wrong. The manager explained that the air-conditioning system in the apartment was not engineered to cool the extra space created by the enclosed terrace. The terrace had originally been designed as an open structure but had been enclosed by a subsequent owner. It had no ductwork to release cold air. The existing cooling system wasn't powerful enough to force sufficient cold air to the terrace.

The manager advised the client to replace his central air-conditioning system with a larger one. Unfortunately, it was too late to install ductwork, since all construction had been completed. The client had his cooling system inspected by an air-conditioning maintenance service. The company advised him that the system was operating perfectly. It recommended blackout protection for the windows during the afternoons in the summer months. He was further advised that replacing the system was not necessary.

In the master bedroom, too much light escaped behind the pole suspending the silk curtains. The client was unable to sleep after 6:00 A.M., due to the amount of light that flooded into the room. After nine months, the turquoise silk fabric noticeably faded.

The client called a meeting with the designer and the owner of the window treatment showroom. They agreed on one solution. Total black-out protection was required in the master bedroom for sleeping and in the living room, during the summer months, to block out the heat. The most attractive design solution was a duette, an expensive window shade, which could be installed behind the Roman shades.

The client was relieved to find a simple solution but was appalled at the cost. If he had known his total expense from the beginning, he would have purchased lined cotton curtains for the master bedroom and installed duettes in the living room, omitting the Roman shades. He would have saved $5000.

Of course, having three different window treatments for each window was more attractive and functional. It was lovely having draping silk curtains, Roman sheer shades, and total blackout protection. However, if the client had been presented with a functional and attractive alternative, he would not have spent the money to install all of them.

He asked the designer and showroom owner, "Shouldn't you both have known how strong the sun was here? Didn't you realize that your window treatments weren't adequate?" Obviously, they both should have known. But the designer and the showroom owner had wanted to create elegant windows to frame the beautiful interior. They had fallen in love with a "look," which cost the client twice as much than if he had simply purchased blinds.

Who was responsible here? The designer, the showroom owner, or the client? The designer claimed that she was off the hook. After all, she had fulfilled her duty of care by consulting a window treatment specialist in the vicinity, who was supposed to know all about the hazards of the Florida sun.

The showroom owner disclaimed liability as well. She claimed that in all her experience, this had never happened before. She explained that she had specified the same Roman shades for other apartments with even greater exposure. However, none of them had the same amount of heat intensity that permeated these shades. She pointed out that the client was concerned about preserving the view, and that the sunscreen material was a perfect solution. She was right. It did work most of the time, but that wasn't enough.

Neither the designer nor the showroom owner even mentioned the issue of the fading silk curtains. Obviously, turquoise silk should never be used as window treatment in direct sunlight, regardless of the number of interlinings.

The designer and the showroom owner were fortunate that the client was reasonable and liked their work. He had the duettes installed and paid the full amount. The showroom gave him a discount, but the duettes were still expensive.

Obviously, the showroom was more at fault than the designer. It was the owner's business to know the effect of existing conditions on her materials. If she felt that the Roman shades weren't adequate, she should have expressed her reservations to the designer in writing. She should also have mentioned the possibility of fading materials.

The preceding cases illustrate how vendors and industry can place the designer in a compromising situation. However, the designer can do the same to industry.

A Miami designer specified pure white carpeting for her client's master bedroom and guest room wing of a massive condominium apartment on Fisher Island. The carpeting was a very expensive white wool that had been treated by the manufacturer to resist stains. It was supposed to be child-proof and cleanable.

Upon the designer's recommendation, a carpet-cleaning service was hired to clean the entire wing after six months of usage. The client told the service that it would be engaged on a regular basis. The maintenance company did an excellent, careful job cleaning the carpet, removing all the stains, However, after the job was done, the client complained, "The carpet doesn't look as white as it did when it was installed. My designer said this carpet should look as white as new for many years. Can't you do a better job?"

The owner of the maintenance company didn't know how to respond. He was afraid to tell the client the obvious truth. "White carpeting," he wanted to say, "can never look the same. It doesn't matter what your designer told you. It should be obvious that when you install white carpeting, it will never look brand new for long."

There are some truths in the design industry that are self-evident. Most clients would never believe that white carpeting would stay new looking for long. If the designer told her client that her carpet would retain its pure white color, the client believed it only because that's what she wanted.

The vendor should have merely replied, "White is white. I've cleaned it as well as possible." If the client complained to the designer, then it was up to the designer to explain the truth. The point is that any client should have known what to expect, regardless of the expertise of the designer.

A week after the carpet was cleaned, the client's cat died. The owner believed the cat had been poisoned. It had licked the carpet, the client claimed, swallowing the cleaning solvent imbedded in the fibers.

Where did this leave the maintenance company? Did it use the proper standard of care? Did it use the solvents recommended by the manufacturer for cleaning? Were the solvents nontoxic? If so, then the cat wasn't poisoned by the carpet-cleaning solution. But who is responsible to convince the client of that fact? Obviously, the maintenance company would have to prove that the cleaning process was an accepted procedure, safe and nontoxic. Since the designer recommended the company, she would have to be involved as well.

Designers sometime blame industry for problems they themselves create. Designers have learned how to pass the buck in an attempt to avoid liability. They've learned this from industry, which has passed the buck to them on numerous occasions. A perfect example is illustrated by the "aubergine incident."

A well published designer redesigned a seven-room apartment at the United Nations Plaza in Manhattan a number of years ago. The apartment, located on the 39th floor, was more than 4000 square feet. The walls of its large library had been totally lined with custom-made cabinets and moldings, hand-lacquered in aubergine, a dark eggplant color.

Approximately three months after the installation had been completed, the client's lawyer contacted the cabinetmaker, whom I represented. The attorney advised my client that the aubergine color had faded considerably and that his client was very unhappy. He wanted the cabinetmaker to pay the cost for a different lacquer finisher to repaint the cabinets.

The designer had recommended my client, the cabinetmaker, to her client. She wanted to avoid taking sides. The client's attorney then contacted me. He attempted to browbeat me into agreeing to the cabinetmaker's spending $12,000 to have the aubergine library woodwork refinished.

The cabinetmaker went to the apartment to survey the damage. In fact, there had been some fading on the woodwork, as the library faced south on the 39th floor. However, when the cabinetwork had been installed, the exposed lacquered doors and moldings had been covered in muslin to protect them from fading until the window treatments were installed.

The fabric had been removed, but the windows were still bare. All the hand-lacquered aubergine woodwork had been exposed to exceedingly harsh light for three months. Perhaps the designer and the client had removed the protective fabric to inspect the completed cabinet work. In any event, it wasn't the cabinetmaker's fault. I refused to pay the client's lawyer any money, regardless of his threats.

Ultimately, my client, the cabinetmaker, wasn't sued and never heard further. The designer apologized to the cabinetmaker profusely. In truth, the problem was the designer's fault, and she knew that she had shirked her duty.

She had obviously visited the site after the cabinets had been installed. She knew that the cabinets were exposed to the light and hadn't warned her client. The client must not have realized that his woodwork required protection with window treatments. If anyone should have known, it was the designer.

A designer's role is to inspect installations and to recommend any necessary precautions to preserve them. Obviously, the cabinetmaker hadn't removed the muslin. He wasn't responsible for damages after installation of the woodwork in first-class condition. The designer refused to accept responsibility. She avoided the conflict and allowed her client to blame the cabinetmaker.

I never learned how the problem was resolved; the cabinetmaker was never told whether or not the client refinished or replaced the cabinets. However, the designer was negligent by not warning her client to protect his cabinets from the light. It was her duty to have this knowledge as a designer and to advise her client. If she didn't know, then she should have known. Once the problem became manifested, she refused to accept responsibilty. Instead, she had allowed her own industry source to be blamed by her client.

DESIGNER RELATIONSHIPS WITH MANUFACTURERS, SHOWROOMS, AND DEALERS

When the topic of designers and industry arises, one immediately thinks of products liability and standards of care, as discussed earlier. However, there is another aspect that is also important, designer relationships with manufacturers, showrooms, and dealers.

Designers are frequently caught in territorial struggles between manufacturers, showrooms, and dealers when making purchases for their clients. A case-by-case analysis illustrates the problems that can arise.

A Miami designer had a major residential job in South Florida. She took her client shopping for furniture at various design showrooms at the Design Center of the Americas. The DCOTA is the largest design center in the Southeast; its showrooms represent numerous important manufacturers of interior design products.

One particular showroom represented many different custom furniture manufacturers. The client liked some furniture produced by one of the lines represented. However, she wasn't sure whether she should buy the designs she had selected.

Her designer knew that the manufacturer produced other designs that weren't displayed in the Miami showroom but were, however, available at the manufacturer's showroom in New York City. The designer and the client decided to go to New York to see these other designs. They also went to shop at other design sources unavailable in Miami—antique and oriental rug dealers.

While in New York, the client saw certain different samples at the manufacturer's showroom and placed an order exceeding $40,000. The showroom representative in Miami heard about the order and contacted the designer. The rep was furious. He told the designer that since she had shopped in Miami, she should have placed the order through him. Was the showroom being fair, and was this the designer's responsibility?

These are easy questions, and the answer to both is no. What makes it simple is that the designer purchased different designs in New York than the rep had offered in Miami. If the client didn't see the merchandise in Miami, how could she have bought it? The designs purchased by the client were photographed in the manufacturer's catalog available at the rep's showroom. However, the client wasn't interested in selecting from the catalog.

This is a very common situation. Major design centers often feature multiline showrooms that represent many different manufacturers. Unfortunately, not every showroom displays all the designs produced by each manufacturer being represented. Although showrooms may have catalogs or pictures, many clients resist making an expensive purchase from a catalog. They want to physically inspect a sample.

Another problem is that representatives don't always understand how to sell custom merchandise produced by their manufacturer's lines. Frequently, their sales help do not know all the options. However, when the designer consults with the manufacturer directly, she will be able to discover all its capabilities.

When designers make large purchases, they sometimes get better prices. For this reason, savvy designers prefer negotiating with the manufacturer directly to try to get a better deal.

Suppose the rep had shown the designer the same merchandise in Florida that the designer ordered at the New York manufacturer. Would the designer be responsible for creating a problem?

In my opinion, no. Territorial disputes over commissions between manufacturers and their representatives in different geographical locations are not the concern of the designer. The designer's job is to make a sale.

Many reps have territorial clauses in contracts with the manufacturers. These specify that any sales of the line made to designers in their territory are credited to them for commission purposes, regardless of where the sale is made. This is done for obvious reasons. Even if the rep doesn't make the sale, he may have interested the designer in the merchandise. Moreover, reps don't like competing with the manufacturer and other reps for clients in their territory. A clause protecting the rep from losing commissions over territorial disputes avoids that problem.

Regardless of the relationship between the manufacturer and its representatives, disputes over territorial commissions are not a concern of a designer and her client. When the Miami rep rebuked the designer for purchasing directly from the manufacturer, the designer should have dismissed him. She should have called the manufacturer's chief executive and told him to resolve the problem. If he didn't, the designer would feel reluctant to shop at the rep's showroom in the future.

Suppose the Miami designer took her client to a showroom in Chicago that represented the New York manufacturer and purchased the furniture there. Would it make a difference? Would it matter if the designer selected the furniture at the Chicago representative but purchased it from the Florida representative?

The answer to these questions is usually negative. The designer is free to make purchases for clients at any locale. There are practical reasons that this freedom must be essential. Suppose, for example, the designer had worked with the Chicago rep on other jobs and felt secure in their relationship. The designer and client should not be compelled to purchase from the Miami rep or from the New York manufacturer in that situation. After all, the designer is helping her client spend her money. Where she decides to make purchases should be her option.

As indicated earlier, financial reasons may be a consideration for a designer to bypass a rep and deal directly with the manufacturer. The Miami designer, in the example, realized that her client would place a large order if she decided to buy. Before the order was finalized, the designer asked, behind closed doors, for a lower price. The manufacturer gave the designer's client an additional 5 percent discount. Unknown to the client, the manufacturer also gave the designer an additional 5 percent commission for closing the deal.

Is such a commission legal? In this situation, it wasn't. The designer charged her client on a cost-plus basis. The client believed that the price she paid was the designer's cost. Obviously, it wasn't. The designer received an undisclosed commission, known as a kickback, which reduced her cost. Unfortunately, in the interior design business, deals of this type are made all too frequently.

I used to represent a furniture manufacturer who owned his own showroom. One of his best customers was an internationally renowned designer. One day the designer brought a client to the showroom. Several expensive selections were made rather rapidly, and the designer requested a written estimate.

On the designer's way out the door, he said something quickly to the showroom owner in French. After he left, I asked the owner what he said. The designer had remarked, "Add 10 percent onto the estimate for me."

Theoretically, if the designer and the showroom had been caught committing the fraud, they would have been subject to criminal and civil prosecution. The designer told his client that the estimate was his net cost. In fact, part of that cost was a 10 percent commission. Of course, the kickback was in addition to the commission that the designer charged his client.

If the merchandise had been sold at retail or a suggested list price, the additional 10 percent wouldn't necessarily be fraud. If a designer is the seller, not the manufacturer, he has much more flexibility in establishing a price from a legal point of view. A manufacturer can suggest a list price, but the designer is not compelled to comply with it.

Quite frankly, successful designers who place large orders often bypass reps so they can make better deals. Some of these are fair to the client, but others are not. However, the issue here is, what is legal? That really depends on the circumstances.

Suppose a Miami designer is hired by a New York-based brokerage firm to design its Miami office. The designer's fee is not an issue here, because it is charged by the hour. All purchases will be made by the brokerage firm's purchasing department through its in-house agent in New York.

The problem arises as follows. Most of the furniture will be purchased from a major national manufacturer directly through a New York dealer by the brokerage firm's New York headquarters. However, the selections will be made at the manufacturer's Miami showroom. Normally, that showroom earns a commission when selections are purchased through local dealers. Is this the designer's problem? No, it isn't, and I will explain why.

In the preceding example, I discussed the relationship between a designer and a custom manufacturer that sold directly from his own showroom and through his reps. This example involves a giant contract manufacturer. This manufacturer displays furniture in most of its own showrooms, located in major design centers in the United States. When a designer makes a selection, she usually purchases the furniture through a locally designated furniture dealer referred by the showroom.

Suppose the Miami designer makes selections for her client in the Miami showroom owned by the manufacturer. Then the showroom salesman recommends a local dealer from whom to make the purchases. Should it matter whether the designer decides to buy the merchandise through a different dealer? Absolutely not. It may be necessary, however, because of the client's needs. As stated, the Miami designer was hired to redesign a financial brokerage firm's office in Miami. The national headquarters, however, was located in New York with its own in-house purchasing agent.

The Miami designer was instructed to make all selections for the client at the Miami showroom. Then she was advised to send her specifications to her client's New York purchasing agent. He would make the purchases through a New York dealer. Will sales personnel in Miami lose commissions if orders aren't executed through a local dealer? Probably not.

The method is fair as long as the designer adheres to the following procedure. First, the designer should discuss the mechanics of purchasing with the client. He will refer her to the in-house purchasing agent in New York. Then the agent will tell her, "We will buy the furniture from a New York dealer. However, when you make selections in the Miami showroom, identify your client. Explain that purchases will not be made through a local dealer. The salesperson will understand because this happens all the time. However, he will request that his name be placed on the order to obtain credit from the manufacturer."

In this example, the designer is not attempting to extract a secret commission. She simply doesn't want to antagonize the showroom where she frequently shops. So long as she follows the correct procedures, there should be no conflicts. However, prior to the designer's discussing her New York client with the Miami showroom, the client should approve this disclosure. Obviously, the designer should be candid with the Miami showroom before she makes selections. Moreover, she must be careful to avoid violating any procedures that might make her look unprofessional.

Some large or even medium-sized interior design firms are furniture "dealers" or "stocking dealers" for specific manufacturers. Because of the volume of their orders, certain manufacturers will sell to these designers directly, bypassing showrooms. If a design firm becomes a dealer for a specific furniture manufacturer, it will pay far less for the products than if it purchases from a showroom or furniture dealer. This arrangement eliminates the middleman.

How do design firms become dealers? A typical example is a contract or commercial design firm that specifies a great deal of office furniture and business equipment from one manufacturer. Since it purchases goods on a volume basis, the manufacturer qualifies it as a dealer.

Another example is a residential design firm that specializes in designing model apartments for real estate developers. I know one particular firm that specifies the same bedroom and dining room furniture for all its apartments. Because of its volume of purchases, the manufacturer has qualified the firm as a dealer. Its discounts are double the amount it would receive for the same furniture from a design showroom.

I have known a number of designers who had small practices but developed special relationships with certain manufacturers. These designers made their purchases directly, bypassing showrooms. In such situations, the design firm acts as a retailer. It sells directly to the client, making a far greater profit than it would in buying from showrooms.

When a designer becomes a dealer, she doesn't always have the physical space to stock samples. However, in order to sell the furniture, the designer must take her client to a showroom that displays the samples. In this situation, the designer competes with the showroom but uses its facilities to make a sale.

Some showroom personnel know which designers are also dealers. In these situations, when a designer appears at a showroom with her client, she may be asked to leave. If a designer buys their other lines and is a good customer, other showrooms don't care. The designer may buy some lines directly from manufacturers, but can't be a dealer for everything.

If a designer does not tell her client that she is a dealer, a conflict of interests arises. Clients are typically unaware that their designer is a dealer, earning more commissions on some lines than others. They believe an objective selection is being offered from the entire market. In some cases, a designer frequently recommends the products she represents as a dealer. The obvious way to avoid the conflict is to show clients many different manufacturers' lines. If the client makes an informed choice, the designer has fulfilled her duty. However, all too often, it does not work that way.

Here is another example of a designer conflict with a dealer. A New York designer was renovating all the bathrooms in a Miami client's house. The client wanted all fixtures purchased to be those produced by one national manufacturer, designated for the purposes of this example as the ABC company. After meeting with the client in Miami, the designer returned to New York to prepare a presentation.

This is a very common situation in Florida. Many clients who purchase homes or apartments in that state use them as secondary residences. They frequently hire designers from their original hometowns. Likewise, some Florida designers design homes and offices for clients who reside in other locations as well.

The New York designer researched ABC products in New York prior to meeting with the client in Miami. Her local ABC dealer in Manhattan spent hours picking out fixtures and discussing availability of sizes and products for the designer's client.

When the designer met with the client in Miami, the client requested placing the orders through a Miami dealer. The designer took all the specifications researched in New York and placed the order in Florida. The New York dealer earned nothing. Was this fair to the New York dealer? Obviously not.

Yet, this wasn't the designer's fault. It makes sense to place orders with a dealer that is geographically close to the project. The client, however, wouldn't pay the designer's traveling expenses to conduct research with the Miami dealer.

Designers usually prefer to shop in their own locales before recommending purchases for out-of-town clients. But if the designer had told the New York dealer that she was shopping for a Miami client, the dealer would not have been happy. Although he wants to create goodwill with customers, he would know that he wouldn't make a sale.

Of course, ABC would have supplied the designer with brochures and catalogs in New York upon request. However, brochures do not substitute for dealing with representatives who can answer questions. Actually, since ABC earns money from any sale, regardless of the dealer, it should make life as easy as possible for the designer.

This is a typical conflict that arises when a designer purchases nationally marketed design products from various geographical areas. The designer is often stuck in the middle, between his client, manufacturers, and dealers. It should always be the responsibility of the manufacturer to resolve these conflicts, but, unfortunately, they frequently can't. They may claim to offer the designer different options, but basically, they don't work.

A real crisis may arise when a designer places an order with a showroom and the manufacturer goes bankrupt before delivery. This is not uncommon, and many designers have been faced with such a dilemma.

If a designer has sold the goods directly to his client on a list or retail basis, the designer has acted as the retailer and is personally responsible for deposits. The retailer is the guarantor.

However, if a designer has purchased the goods on a cost-plus basis from a dealer, he has acted as an agent. His liability is not automatic. If he had advised his client to purchase goods from a reputable manufacturer or dealer, he should not be held liable. Unless a designer volunteers to act as a guarantor, which is most unusual, he is not committed to guarantee each delivery.

To provide a client with a "professional discount," the designer must usually act as a purchaser. However, since he is really acting as his client's agent, he does not necessarily play a principal role in the transaction for purposes of legal liability.

In reality, many designers guarantee deposits against the occurrence of a bankruptcy to avoid a loss of their client's confidence. If the deposit is small, many designers feel it is worthwhile to refund the money. They believe it "saves face" and helps restore confidence in their ability to complete the job. If the client is valuable, it also helps to protect their client base.

If a deposit is substantial, however, the designer may be unable to refund it. Usually, in the event of a bankruptcy, a court-appointed trustee assumes control over the bankrupt party's estate. Sometimes deposits may be refunded quickly. Unfortunately, other cases can take years to resolve.

I know of several such situations, in which a designer had purchased goods through a representative's showroom. When a manufacturer filed a bankruptcy petition, the rep refunded the deposit. It wanted to avoid losing the designer's business. I am not certain that reps are automatically responsible for guaranteeing the orders; that may hinge upon the terms of the rep's contract with the designer. However, if you are going to place an order through a rep, it is wise to ask whether it will guarantee delivery of the goods.

Suppose a designer buys goods directly from a manufacturer without an intermediary and the manufacturer then files for bankruptcy. What then? The designer's liability may depend on the contract with his client. If he has specifically designated his role as an agent for purchases in the letter of agreement, I do not believe he is responsible.

However, keep the following in mind. Most professional showrooms sell only to designers. Designers purchase from them using their own accounts or "house accounts." In that sense, they act as principals. Therefore, it is the designer's letter of agreement with his client that may control his liability.

In their contracts, designers often state that they act as purchasing agents and will not act as guarantors for payment and delivery. In other words, if a vendor goes bankrupt, the designer won't be responsible. Sometimes designers won't use disclaimer language in their letters of agreements. They feel that it projects a poor image to prospective clients. I disagree. I think designers must protect themselves from forces they cannot control.

Several years ago a designer consulted me, concerned about the bankruptcy issue. The designer had selected several fabrics from a showroom and was ready to place a $15,000 order. She was concerned because the showroom was relatively new and required pro forma payment, or full payment in advance upon order.

The designer asked me about taking precautions. As an attorney, I advised her that if she was concerned about the financial solvency of her vendor, she should purchase elsewhere where she had more confidence.

Of course, there are methods available to enable a designer to secure deposits with vendors. For example, some showrooms allow attorneys to hold money in escrow accounts pending deliveries. A large deposit can also be secured with a letter of credit from a bank.

Yet, designers often feel uncomfortable making special arrangements to work with banks and lawyers. Nonetheless, if they are concerned, they should discuss the matter with their clients. If you feel reluctant to purchase from a specific source, talk to your client. If she still wants to proceed, then review your options. If you are wary about a source, don't mince words. Clients are often financially sophisticated and will appreciate your concern about protecting them.

Another dilemma presents itself when custom-ordered goods arrive with different specifications. Sometimes a manufacturer will voluntarily solve the problem as soon as possible, and the situation will be rectified. Sometimes they won't.

Serious conflicts arise when a manufacturer refuses or is unable to make the necessary modifications to comply with an order. A designer once consulted me with a seemingly superficial problem, which typifies predicaments of this nature. He had ordered an expensive dining table from a custom manufacturer. The large rectangular table had an ivory-colored acrylic lacquer finish. The top of the table was inlaid with a half-inch silver metallic band, outlining its surface around the perimeter. The bottom of each leg had an inlaid band as well.

The New York manufacturer had subcontracted the table from a French company, and the order period was three months. Upon delivery, the band was gold instead of silver.

The designer protested and would not accept delivery. The manufacturer, however, refused to return the table to be refinished with a silver inlay. In his opinion, it was not a major design defect and did not justify the expense to make the change. He apologized to the designer but refused to remedy the situation.

The designer was placed in a very difficult position. Apparently, his client's interior had a silver and white scheme. The dining room had a silver and white wall covering and silver lighting fixtures and accessories. The client was very unhappy with the table, because she felt the gold inlay was disruptive to the design.

I sympathized with the designer, advising him that his only remedy was to sue the manufacturer. Yet that wouldn't have resolved the problem either. At best, a lawsuit would have resulted in a refund, not a substitute. The client still needed to custom order another table.

The designer solved the problem by modifying the client's scheme. He kept the table, then introduced gold into the room's decor to blend with the gold inlay. He convinced his client that it was very sophisticated to combine gold and silver. Perhaps he even made her happier.

This story raises another point. When all else fails, improvise. Try to turn a negative into a positive. If a custom-ordered piece is delivered with different specifications, and there is no other practical solution, try to make it work.

The subtle difference incorporated into the design of the client's decor recalls Mies van der Rohe's famous quote, "God is in the details." Perfection in the design business, however, is a very tough challenge.

If the table had been delivered in red lacquer instead of ivory, obviously the designer wouldn't have accepted the order. There can be no justification for the delivery of custom ordered furniture in the wrong color. But what about some of the other details?

Suppose the table was delivered in the right color, but with an octagonal base instead of a round base. An incorrectly shaped base would probably provide a designer with more leverage to reject an order than a difference between gold and silver inlays.

However, from a design point of view, the difference in the finish of an inlay may be more important to a client than the shape of a base. Subtle differences may create gray areas that can be most difficult to resolve. Fabric and carpet vendors routinely label their samples with the statement, "Subject to variation." The issues are, How much variation is reasonable? and Will the showroom back up the designer if there is a problem?

An analogous case is one in which a client ordered a silver-leafed cocktail table, antiqued in gold. The table was delivered to the client, who was most unhappy. He and his designer both felt that the finish looked "much too gold."

The silver-leafed finish was specified from a floor sample in the manufacturer's showroom. The client's table was clearly more antiqued with gold than the floor sample. The manufacturer agreed to relacquer the table in silver leaf with a subtler gold antique overlay.

When the designer asked why there had been a material variation between the floor sample and the client's order, the manufacturer responded that the tables had been finished by different lacquer workshops.

Of course, the designer understood that explanation. He realized that showrooms often change suppliers and that variations do occur. However, when the table was redelivered, the client still felt that the silver-leaf finish was too heavily antiqued in gold.

This time, the designer knew that the manufacturer was right. Unfortunately, he was unable to compare the floor sample and the client's table side by side. The client had selected the finish based on seeing a large table, not a small wooden chip that could be easily transported.

The designer and his client returned to the showroom to examine the floor sample, and the designer proved that the manufacturer was correct.

The client's table looked more golden during the daylight than in the evening under artificial light. The floor sample had been displayed under artificial light and had appeared to have a less golden tonality. In fact, both finishes were identical.

Nightmares like this are typical events in a designer's workday. Fabrics and colors often look different in showrooms than on the site. Clients are often horrified when goods are delivered not looking as they had visualized. Often these differences aren't material to the design, but the designer must persuade his client to realize that fact.

Presumably, your client will trust you. If a delivered item varies from the order, you will be able to say, "Although this isn't exactly what we ordered, I think it looks fine. I wouldn't change it." If your client respects your judgment, he will listen to you.

A footnote to the story: After a year of living with the gold-antiqued, silver-leafed table, the client confessed that he liked it better with a more pronounced golden hue. Don't try to figure this out. Remember, you cannot always predict a client's behavior.

There is a famous old legal case from the 1800s in which a house had been built with square doorway arches instead of round ones as the client had requested. The client ordered the contractor to rebuild the doorways, but he refused.

Because of the construction limitations of that era, the only way to rebuild the doorways was to tear down the entire structure and start over. The judge, in a famous opinion cited in many law school texts, declared that the client was entitled to money damages only. Tearing down a structure to rebuild the shape of a doorway, he held, was not an equitable remedy.

In other words, the punishment should fit the crime. Which variations are significant enough to warrant replacement? And if replacement is not feasible, how do you convince your client to live with the result?

Designers and industry have to work together constantly to solve their problems. The relationship must be viewed as an ongoing joint venture. Only then will both prosper and continue to progress.

11

AVOIDING A LEGAL CRISIS

It often happens that a designer becomes involved in a lawsuit because of a failure in his client relationship. It may not be the designer's fault at the time, and it happens to some of the best. However, because legal action is an unfavorable outcome, an alternative is presented, with accompanying cases to illustrate.

The best way to handle a legal crisis, obviously, is to avoid one. Unfortunately, this is not always possible, and sometimes the designer must use legal means to protect himself and get paid.

Although certain client disputes cannot be settled without the involvement of a third party, many interior designers who have sued to collect fees are overwhelmed by the trauma and financial expense resulting from lawsuits. For that reason, as I have already mentioned, I always ask my clients to consider arbitration as an alternative to litigation.

Here is a good illustration of why going to court to collect unpaid fees is not always successful:

A residential designer in Los Angeles completed a $300,000 project for a client who owed him a balance of $12,000 in design fees. When the client refused to pay any of it, the designer made unsuccessful attempts to collect with letters and telephone calls and finally retained an attorney to start a lawsuit. After six weeks of the plaintiff's serving legal papers and answering pretrial motions made by the client's attorney, the case went to trial. The designer lost two days in court and ended up settling for $9000. He had to pay a legal fee ($3000) and some court costs. He ended up with about $5500, less than half of what he was owed. The designer realized that this process had been too expensive and time-consuming even though he had "won."

When this designer asked me to prepare a letter of agreement for a different client, I advised him of the existence of another vehicle, which is designed to settle differences faster than a court and, accordingly, to save on legal fees. It's called *arbitration*.

Arbitration is a legal alternative for resolving disputes without going to court. The American Arbitration Association (AAA), is a not-for-profit public service organization that provides private settlement dispute services.

Arbitration can be voluntary, and its use depends on the agreement of both parties. However, when I have represented plaintiffs in disputes and asked the opposition to submit to arbitration, generally there was resistance and I had to go to court. But if there is an arbitration clause in your contract, the matter must be settled by arbitration.

The AAA has developed a standard arbitration clause, as mentioned in Chapter 1, that can be inserted in your letter of agreement, as follows:

> Any claim or controversy arising out of or relating to this contract, or the breach thereof, shall be settled by arbitration in accordance with the Rules of the American Arbitration Association, and judgment upon the award rendered by the arbitrator(s) may be entered in any Court having jurisdiction thereof.

There is one important point to make clear. Prior to inserting this clause or any other clauses in your letter of agreement, check with your lawyer. He will undoubtedly be familiar with the AAA, which has 35 regional offices. He will tell you how or whether this clause should be modified and whether arbitration is a good method for you to use. Any further questions about arbitration can be answered by the AAA.

You are not required to retain a lawyer when you go to arbitration. If the amount in dispute is substantial, however, it's always safer to use a good attorney. Nonetheless, I have found that arbitration takes less time than most legal actions. Accordingly, legal fees for arbitration are lower than for a conventional lawsuit.

Check with the AAA about its administrative fees. The fees vary according to the amount of the claim and the claim's classification. For example, the AAA classifies some disputes as "commercial" and others as "construction."

The AAA advised me that in a recent survey it arrived at the following comparison. When filed with the AAA, an average case, from date of filing to the award date, ranged from 90 to 180 days to resolve. When litigation was instituted, a comparable case, from date of filing to a settlement or verdict, ranged from 12 to 24 months to resolve.

The AAA supplies claimants with a set of forms, and starting the procedure is generally less involved than commencing a legal action. Usually, a hearing is held before an arbitrator. This eliminates pretrial motions and pretrial depositions (hearings without a judge), which are often held prior to an ordinary trial. Moreover, many legal actions require a pretrial conference and, subsequently, a trial on a different day. In arbitration, hearings involving disputes of less than $50,000 usually require only one day.

In many instances an arbitration hearing is held before one arbitrator. This arbitrator does not have to be a judge and sometimes is not even a lawyer. Both sides are given a choice of dates for the hearing, and the AAA has always been reasonable when I have requested adjournments. On the hearing date, both parties arrive with their witnesses and documents that substantiate their claims. Your opponent may want to impose a counterclaim against you relating to the initial claim. He is entitled to do so in the original set of arbitration petitions; you are permitted to respond at the hearing.

The hearing itself is generally held on an informal basis. As it is an administrative procedure, as opposed to a legal action, the rules of evidence are generally not enforced. The party who commences the action presents his case first. All documents, statements, and witnesses are presented by him or his attorney. The arbitrator often asks questions to clarify any ambiguities. When this phase is complete, the other side presents its defense and related counterclaims with oral and written evidence.

Because of its lack of formality, this type of hearing allows participants to understand what is happening and to be more relaxed. However, sometimes this absence of formality permits a release of hostilities, and the parties start arguing. Arbitrators are not pleased with this kind of behavior, so try always to maintain control.

Most hearings in which I have participated have taken less than a day. However, if the situation is very complicated and many witnesses are needed, a hearing will continue until both parties and the arbitrator are satisfied that the case is fully heard. Both parties can produce all the documents and witnesses they feel are necessary to prove their case, within reason. As in a court of law, all testimony is made under oath.

Once the hearing is finished, the arbitrator will make his decision and grant an award promptly, if not necessarily on the same day. This award is usually final and binding. If the party who loses doesn't pay the amount of the award, it is enforceable in a court of law. Moreover, it rarely is possible to make an appeal. Once the award is made, that's it.

If you are a winner, all is well. You don't have to wait months for your money and pay more legal fees while an appeal is pending. But if you are a loser, there is generally no right to appeal in a court of law. You are compelled to comply with the terms of the award.

An arbitration clause can be a great tactical advantage to an individual interior designer or small design firm. Often, wealthy clients have a business and pay for legal help on a retainer basis. They realize that if their designer starts a lawsuit, the designer will probably lose a great deal more time, energy, and money than they will. If they have a large legal arsenal at their disposal, their attorneys might be instructed to drag out the whole affair to induce either a small settlement or the discontinuance of the action.

For example, suppose you have a claim against a client for unpaid fees and bills. Perhaps your attorney refuses to take the case on a contingency basis, that is, a fee based on a percentage of the amount collected. In this situation you may be unable to afford to pursue the matter.

However, if you have an arbitration clause in your contract, it may be a different matter. An arbitration clause decreases the risk of a protracted proceeding. Your client will be aware of this, which may, in turn affect his judgment. The presence of the clause may increase the odds of private settlement even before a proceeding is started. Without the clause, a wealthy business client may say, "Let her send me a summons and see what happens."

While all this sounds very favorable, some of my clients still don't like arbitration. They feel that a court of law is the most effective forum for their claims and that the threat of a legal action is a more menacing weapon. It's usually best to put the clause in your letters of agreement and wait until something happens. If a matter goes to arbitration, you will see firsthand all the pros and cons of arbitration. If you like the approach, continue to use the clause. If not, omit it from all future contracts.

Of course, ideally, you can always run your projects in such a professional way that neither arbitration nor lawsuits are necessary. However, as any experienced designer realizes, that is almost impossible. There are so many variables involved in a design project that it is virtually impossible to control everything, regardless of your professionalism.

In the preceding example, the designer had permitted his client to fall in arrears for bills and fees in the amount of $12,000. I'm sure the designer had a valid reason, but since he got stuck for the balance, obviously, it wasn't good enough.

Designers must always keep their billing and collections up to date. Most letters of agreement should provide that if bills are not paid within 15 days after their receipt, the designer will stop all work on the project (see Chapter 1). And most of them do just that. Of course, there are extenuating circumstances, and exceptions should sometimes be made. However, $12,000 in arrears is a serious matter, even in a project with a budget of $300,000. Monitor your contract and billing procedures to prevent this kind of legal crisis from arising.

To understand the significance of arbitration, consider the two cases that follow. In both instances, the presence of an arbitration clause would have saved the designer money and unneeded stress.

The preceding case exemplifies a common problem for designers: collecting fees due from clients upon project completion. Collecting accounts receivable is never an easy job, but in a tight economy, it has become notably worse. When interest rates start rising, corporations and individuals tend to delay creditors for as long as possible. If businesses have money available, they want to keep it to earn interest. If they aren't liquid, borrowing to amortize and refinance debt, at an exorbitant cost, is avoided.

For design projects, a portion of the design fee frequently isn't paid until project completion, for a number of reasons. Sometimes final payment is withheld as a deliberate part of the fee structure. In other words, a client may deliberately withhold part of the fee, never intending to pay the full amount.

The following is an example, given in the form of a question, of how a designer's client refused to pay both the designer and the vendor their final payments.

QUESTION: *I am an interior designer with a small business in New York City. I work alone, except for an assistant and draftsman. About a year ago I was hired by a stockbroker in New York to redesign his four-bedroom house in New Jersey.*

The cost of the project was more than $200,000. I charged on a cost-plus basis, i.e., 30 percent of all net purchases of goods and construction. I supervised all construction and saved the client the expense of a general contractor.

The client was difficult, but the project went well until the very end. There was a considerable amount of custom cabinetwork, and I hired a very expensive cabinetmaker who produces excellent quality. The cabinetmaker didn't finish on schedule and went somewhat over budget. However, I had forewarned my client that expert craftsmen were hard to find and that the plans might need some upgrading as the job progressed. The client approved each upgrade as the changes arose. In the end, the budget for the cabinetwork increased approximately 15 percent.

My client paid all his bills on time until the end. He had a final payment of $25,000 due once all cabinet installations were complete. My fee for that segment was $7500. The contractor installed all the cabinets without full payment, as my client had always paid his bills on time.

Once the work was finished, my client found everything wrong with it. For example, he claimed that the finish was in the wrong shade. Certain pieces were relacquered, in some cases, as many as four times.

The cabinets look perfect, but my client refuses to pay the cabinetmaker or my design fee. He claims that I am guilty of inadequate supervision, which delayed completion of his interior. Since he uses his home for business purposes, he contends that I am responsible for lost profits and other damages.

The cabinetmaker calls me daily, urging me to help him get paid. When I asked my client to pay the cabinetmaker, he responded, "No one is getting another cent; you've already been given more than you're entitled to." He also implied that I was taking kickbacks from the subcontractors.

I don't think he ever intended to pay his bill but is just finding excuses to avoid me. Am I liable for inadequate supervision? Is it my responsibility to obtain payment for the cabinetmaker? Should I start a lawsuit, or should the cabinetmaker? Should I wait for the client to sue me, as he has threatened?

ANSWER: The client's complaints have apparently been fabricated to avoid final payment of his bills. Based on the facts presented, I have no doubt that this designer is correct about his client's ulterior motives.

Since the designer neglected to mention arbitration, I assume that his letter of agreement did not contain an arbitration clause, as discussed earlier in this chapter. That is most unfortunate, because it would have been a perfect vehicle to resolve this designer's problems.

If an arbitration clause had been used, it would have been a mandatory substitute for going to court. It would have been useful for a small design firm such as this one, which has low operating capital. Why? Generally, far less legal work is required to resolve a dispute using arbitration, as a result of the substantial limitation on the amount of pretrial discovery. Accordingly, attorney's fees are frequently kept to a minimum.

I would have recommended taking this case to arbitration immediately. In fact, an attorney would not have been required to represent the designer. However, since the client, a stockbroker, would have retained one, I would have recommended that the designer be represented by counsel as well.

Because arbitration is not a possibility, a number of factors have to be considered prior to instituting a lawsuit. The main one is money. Litigation can be extremely costly. In addition, the client owes the cabinetmaker three times the amount he owes the designer.

One possibility is for the cabinetmaker and the designer to retain the same attorney. Counsel could represent both as coplaintiffs. If the designer and the cabinetmaker agreed to prorate legal costs on the basis of the amount of damages sought, it could result in a substantial savings on legal bills. However, there are some disadvantages. First, both parties would have to agree on the selection of an attorney. Second, there is a risk that one attorney could not pursue both claims without a conflict of interest.

As a tactical matter, it might be wise for the designer to wait until the cabinetmaker starts the lawsuit. Because of its size, he may pursue his claim soon. In fact, if the designer was the purchaser for the cabinetwork, either directly or as the client's agent, he might be sued with the client as a joint defendant. If that occurs, the designer's attorney would probably file a cross-claim against the client for the cost of the cabinetwork and his own damages.

If the cabinetmaker sued the designer for the money, the designer's attorney would sue the client, using a third-party complaint. These alternatives are presented merely to explain the format. However, my instinct is as follows: The cabinetmaker, obviously, has lost the most money. Why not wait and see what he does? If he starts a lawsuit, perhaps the designer's claims will be settled quickly. If so, the designer can avoid paying large legal bills.

There is a potential drawback to adopting a "wait and see" attitude. If the client wants to sue the designer for inadequate supervision, he may go to court in New Jersey, where his house is located. Remember, the designer is located in New York. From a practical point of view, the designer will have to find counsel in a "foreign jurisdiction" to represent him, which can be inconvenient.

Large companies are quite accustomed to defending suits in "foreign territories." In my experience, however, small business people feel more comfortable dealing with litigation in their own jurisdiction. If that's how the designer feels, he might be better off to proceed alone, or to team up with the cabinetmaker.

However, if there had been an arbitration clause in the designer's letter of agreement, naming his own jurisdiction—New York City—as the locale for engaging the American Arbitration Association, the issue of foreign jurisdictions would not arise. This point underscores the usefulness of this clause.

Based on the facts, it doesn't appear that this client has any realistic chance to avoid liability for payment. An expert can be hired to document that the work was well executed. There is always the possibility, of course, that the designer and the cabinetmaker might reduce their claims for a quicker out-of-court settlement once a lawsuit begins.

Aside from these issues, another important question is, how could the designer have prevented the client from holding out on him financially until all the work had been completed?

It is very common practice in the interior design field to permit a client to withhold a percentage of the design fee until job completion. Ten percent is frequently used. Some designers believe that if a client is allowed to withhold something, he will feel more secure about the designer following through on the job.

I don't disagree with this philosophy if the client is known to be financially reliable. On commercial jobs, for example, large companies with good credit ratings usually pay their bills. Residential clients may be a different story. In this case, the client is withholding the fee simply to be vindictive. Accordingly, be very careful before providing a client with this option.

Allowing an "absentee client" to withhold part of the fee sometimes makes sense. One of my designer clients was approached to create a million-dollar residential interior for an oil-rich South American. Because of the size of the fee, the designer agreed to have 10 percent of his fee withheld until the job was completed. Ultimately, he was fully paid. These facts may be unusual, but the rationale is obvious. The scope of the job and size of the fee made the risk justifiable. Generally, however, before permitting it, think twice.

Suppose a client asks you to allow her to withhold 10 percent of your fee until project completion. What would you tell her if you want to refuse? I would use the following explanation as an answer.

A major part of the interior design process, that is, design planning, is frequently completed before construction begins. However, if a designer charges on a cost-plus basis, he usually doesn't get paid until purchases of goods and construction commence. This doesn't happen generally until midway into the project. Consequently, designers have to depend on their retainers to sustain them during the interim. Few such amounts are adequate. Therefore, withholding payment until project completion can cause the designer to sustain an undue financial hardship.

There is another "catch" to fee withholding: When is a job completed? In theory, a job is completed once all installations have been finished. Minor odds and ends don't count. But clients don't always think that way. Many designers have experienced having the last 10 percent withheld because of complaints about petty details or incidentals. In this example, all work had been finished. The client's reasons for withholding payment were totally unjustified.

One way to prevent clients from withholding payment is to watch vendors carefully. In this example, the cabinetmaker shouldn't have finished the installation without more payment. In that case, the designer would have also been paid a larger portion of his fee when billing for the cabinets.

Most furniture showrooms won't deliver anything until full payment has been received. Some will take orders only pro forma, that is, with full payment in advance. Others require a substantial deposit (e.g., one half) upon order, with the balance due prior to delivery. It is important to adopt this line of thinking. When I tell this to some designers, they react negatively.

It is easier for furniture showrooms to operate this way, they claim, because selling goods, rather than services, is a much more impersonal process. Showrooms adopt policies and enforce them without flexibility. Designers, on the other hand, have a more personal relationship with their clients. It's not as easy for them to "deal tough."

I agree with that philosophy. However, I don't think that it should make a difference in regard to bill-collection policies. Designers must make their method of operation clear from the beginning. It shouldn't interfere with client relationships unless the client wants to use it as a weapon.

The client, in this example, must have signaled the designer and cabinetmaker during the project that he would be a problem. Instead of becoming more cautious, they tried hard to satisfy him by finishing quickly. In this case, accommodation bred disaster.

I can't prescribe a formula guaranteeing that you will always receive your final payments. Occasionally, even the sharpest designers lose money at the end of a project. However, when entering into a letter of agreement, be wary of this potential problem.

Take precautions in preparing your contract. Think about using an arbitration clause. Watch billings and collections carefully during the project. Prior to making installations, be certain that payments are up to date. In other words, watch for all these cues. You'll know before the job ends whether you can trust your client. Prior to taking any risks, decide whether they are justified. Naturally, it's essential to satisfy clients. Personal referrals are the most important source of new business. But it's also important to be a smart business person and to collect final payments.

In the preceding two cases, I discussed how arbitration can be used as a speedier economical vehicle to help designers collect unpaid fees. In that sense, arbitration, as opposed to litigation, is useful as an "offensive technique." It is a mechanism that a designer can activate to achieve a result. Arbitration can also be very useful as a "defensive technique." It can protect a designer who is attacked by a client.

A specific instance in which a designer may experience difficulty is when she decides to terminate a client relationship prior to project completion. Arbitration may be a useful defensive technique under these circumstances to protect her and to save money. Following the presentation of an example, an analysis is given to explain the usefulness of arbitration in that event.

However, as an introduction, a few dynamics of the designer-client relationship are reviewed here. Most of the advice I provide to designers relates to how to strengthen relationships. To maintain a successful business and keep it growing, a designer must complete her jobs, right down to the last detail. She should keep her clients happy. As you well know, this isn't always easy.

Once a designer is hired, the job should begin on a positive note. A client does not usually sign a letter of agreement, paying a fee, unless he feels that he's in capable hands. Generally, a conflict doesn't arise until design plans are in full swing and serious decisions and financial commitments must be made. At that stage, a client may become reticent about spending his money and attempt to postpone progress by refusing to make choices or changing plans.

When this behavior is manifested, the designer must recognize its cause and "hang in there." She should hold her client's hand, making necessary changes. Hopefully, the client will become more relaxed about continuing the project and will take the necessary steps to proceed.

Occasionally, a client may limit his commitment to a project simply because he's not convinced that his designer knows what she's doing. In fact, the client may have the money to create a complete interior, but feels insecure about design plans. Frequently these doubts are erased once construction starts, furniture is delivered, or installations are completed. As his anxieties become minimized, he'll take a deep breath and decide to go "all the way."

It is my experience that once a designer is able to surpass these early hurdles, she will capture her client's confidence. Other rough spots that crop up later, such as construction problems and late deliveries, can somehow be resolved. However, the ability of a designer to produce plans and drawings that please a client is often the true test of her professionalism.

Sometimes, unfortunately, even the most professional designer cannot handle a client, as the following example illustrates.

QUESTION: *I am a free-lance contract designer with 15 years experience. For the first time in my career, I have met my match. I entered into an agreement to design a showroom, approximately 10,000 square feet, with a clothing manufacturer approximately three months ago. My clients are two partners, successful businessmen in their fifties, who have never worked with a professional designer before. Financially, I am being paid a flat fee of $20,000 for preparing all construction drawings plus 20 percent for all purchases of goods and construction, on a cost-plus basis. I was paid a $10,000 retainer upon signing the letter of agreement.*

After my completing an entire set of drawings, based on hours of consultations, my clients refused to approve them. I made endless changes, which they still didn't like.

I decided to try another tactic to move the project along. I put aside the drawings and attempted to interest my clients in furniture and fabrics. For example, I showed them more than 75 different upholstery fabrics, in colors they requested. They couldn't agree on any of those either.

Although I like my clients, I don't think that this project will ever get finished. I have used up the retainer, calculating my hours, and even if I quit now, I won't be money ahead. How do I withdraw from this contract? What are my legal responsibilities?

ANSWER: Walking out on this client could expose the designer to two types of damages. First, she is liable for the $10,000 retainer. The fact that her clients "used up the retainer" is not the issue. She signed a contract, agreeing to produce satisfactory plans for a flat fee. If she breaches it, she is liable for a full refund.

Second, if she refuses to continue with the project, the clients may contend that she wasted three months. They could sue her for consequential damages, that is, three months' rent for loss of use of their space and other damages.

I don't think these clients would succeed in that type of action. However, I do believe they would recoup most of the designer's retainer. Of course, both parties would have legal fees to pay, which makes a lawsuit a losing proposition.

When a designer parts company from a client prior to completing a project, she forfeits a number of things. She loses a measure of self-respect. Even if the client created the problems, the loss of a client is still, to some extent, a personal failure. An experienced designer should be able to determine whether a client will be a potential problem. A professional usually knows when to avoid involvement in a relationship. If a designer-client relationship fails, the designer loses her design fee. Moreover, she loses a subject for photographing, useful for publication and her portfolio. Finally, she loses a personal referral, a lifeline for staying in business.

The best way to end this relationship is for the designer to try to negotiate her way out of it peacefully. She should schedule a routine design meeting without arousing any suspicion about her intentions. Both clients should be requested to attend.

I feel that it is important to handle this situation face to face. Writing a letter or discussing it on the phone may be less painful but will probably be far less effective. The designer should tell her clients, frankly, how she feels about the project. The clients shouldn't be blamed, but the designer should not accept responsibility. She should state that she can't finish the project. She should also state that her clients would be better suited working with another designer.

She should stress that she has used her best efforts to provide every viable design alternative, but that none have been acceptable. If the clients protest, the designer should take that opportunity to resign. Then the meeting should be ended quickly. The designer should avoid saying anything further and wait a few days for her clients' reply.

Probably, one of two things will happen. First, the partners may review the situation and realize that they have been unreasonable. People generally don't like to admit when they're wrong. However, if the clients trust their designer's ability, they won't want her to quit. If possible, the designer should give her clients another chance. If she can survive this impasse, her worst troubles may be over. Certainly, these clients will never be easy, but perhaps she'll be able to finish the project and get paid.

Second, if the clients agree to the designer's resignation, in all likelihood they'll ask for the retainer to be returned. Of course, the designer will refuse. The clients will reason as follows: She had a contract to design their showroom; she breached it by resigning. Since she did not produce satisfactory plans, they are entitled to a full refund.

I have been involved in a number of situations in which designers have wanted to quit and have requested my intervention. This was my advice: If a client is paying by the hour, or on any time basis, termination isn't difficult. Simply request payment for services rendered to date. In this situation, if the clients had already accepted the drawings, the designer would have been in a stronger position.

However, since the designer was paid a flat fee and her plans weren't accepted, she is in a more difficult position. The smart thing to do, of course, is to stay with the job until the drawings are accepted. If this is not possible, the designer should try to negotiate a release with her clients for $5000.

If the clients will not negotiate, the designer could simply keep the money and wait. If the designer had an arbitration clause in her contract, her position would be a lot stronger. As stated earlier, arbitration is cheaper and less time-consuming than litigation. However, if there is no arbitration clause, a lawsuit may be started, which can be expensive. The clients can use a threat of litigation to force the designer to return the whole retainer.

Many designers complain that their projects never seem to end. Even after all construction and installations are completed, certain clients may continue to harass their designers on any pretense. Ignoring these clients is the only alternative. It is a necessity and is not the same as walking out on a client in the planning or construction phases.

Before discharging a client, consider the following: Have you earned your design retainer, or are you prepared to offer a refund? Have you charged by the hour or must your plans be approved for you to earn your fee? Are you in danger of being sued for breach of contract? Is there an arbitration clause in your letter of agreement? Have you been reasonable in making every effort to accommodate your client? In any case, before making a decision, proceed with caution.

In the preceding three case studies, I have discussed the benefits of using arbitration as a means of settling client disputes. There is, however, yet another method of solving disputes—mediation. Both parties select a third person to listen to their conflict, who makes a recommendation. There are professional mediators who charge a fee for their services. Under certain circumstances, the American Arbitration Association will agree to perform mediation.

Mediation is even less formal than arbitration. However, there is one major difference: an award is nonbinding. In other words, the decision of the mediator is not enforceable in a court of law.

I don't like mediation, generally. On a conceptual level, I think it is a good idea, and sometimes it works. The problem is that since the mediator's decision isn't binding, I find that it works against the designer. In my experience, many of the lawsuits that are instituted against designers are as much a vendetta as an effort to recoup fees. Clients tend to blame their designers for every aspect of a project that goes awry, regardless of whether it is the designer's fault. Unfortunately, the mediations involving designers that I have experienced were not brought in good faith by the clients. Clients sometimes use mediation to intimidate their designers and to stall payment.

If a client submits to arbitration, as stated before, both parties must accept the award, legally. Being knowledgeable of that fact, some clients refuse to allow a designer to insert an arbitration clause in the letter of agreement. If a client refuses to allow you to use an arbitration clause, be wary.

Yet, sometimes clients aren't troublemakers, even though they won't allow arbitration. I have a design client who designed a house for an entertainment executive. He refused to allow an arbitration clause in his letter of agreement. The designer was concerned, but signed the contract anyway. The job ultimately was completed with no problems. It turned out that the executive had been involved in an arbitration proceeding in his business, in which the decision had been unfavorable to him.

The point is, if a client will not allow you to use an arbitration clause, find out the reason before you permit its omission.

There are several points to remember. First, if there is no arbitration clause in your letter of agreement, your client doesn't have to submit to arbitration and probably won't. Most clients who sue their designers want to inflict pain, emotionally and financially. Going to court runs up expensive legal bills resulting from pretrial motions and discovery, which are eliminated by arbitration. Furthermore, an arbitration award cannot be appealed, whereas a court decision can.

Second, you still should hire a lawyer for arbitration, which does cost money. Arbitration fees are graduated, depending on the amount of relief requested by the claimant and the amount of the counterclaim requested by the respondent. Although it is not compulsory to retain legal counsel, chances are your client will, and you are advised to do so as well.

Third, if you are sued by a third party, even though the cause of action may relate to a client's project for which there is an arbitration clause in your agreement, you cannot compel the use of arbitration. For example, if a client and a contractor become embroiled in litigation over a breach of contract for construction, you may be sued as a codefendant by the contractor. In this case, you cannot compel the use of arbitration. If the contractor, however, has an arbitration clause in his contract with your client, then the case will be settled by arbitration.

Fourth, arbitration does not guarantee a better result for the designer. It all depends on the facts of the case and how sympathetic the selected arbitrator may be to your cause of action. For example, if the arbitrator has had a poor personal experience with a designer, I find that works to the designer's disadvantage in an arbitration proceeding. However, it's very hard to know the situation in advance. You can't predict who the arbitrator will be.

What I like best about the arbitration clause is the psychological effect it seems to have on some clients. So often, designers tell me that when they discuss the clause with a potential client, a common reaction is, "Well, I guess that means there won't be any lawsuits." Isn't that what you want?

Of the numerous other ways to avoid litigation, preventative measures are always the best and, generally, the cheapest. As the following example illustrates, it is important to be sure that the right party is signing the agreement.

QUESTION: *I am a designer in Denver. Recently, a commercial client returned my letter of agreement bearing the signature of a "ranking" employee of his business. Although I was quite concerned about alienating the client, I returned the agreement to the company's owner. I requested his signature since our arrangement was initially made on a personal basis. The client returned the agreement to me with his own signature; however, he added a note stating that his employee had the authority to bind his company and that I was being overcautious. Was I?*

ANSWER: The designer's decision to obtain the signature of the owner of the company was correct. Although such action may not have been absolutely necessary from a legal standpoint, his logic and instincts were practical and sensible.

When you enter into a relationship with a new client, problems may arise that will be difficult to resolve. Accordingly, it is better to eliminate this particular potential problem now with a letter or telephone call. Unless a client is trying to avoid responsibility, he cannot reasonably object to signing himself. Therefore, if a client still refuses to sign the contract after a detailed explanation, you should probably forego the entire project.

Legally, however, the signature of a "ranking employee" may be adequate to bind a client. It depends on the position of the employee in the client's company and the organization of the business itself.

When dealing with a partnership, you are wise to obtain the signatures of all the general partners. In many states, if the partnership defaults, the general partners will be personally responsible for compliance with the terms of the agreement.

A corporation's liability is generally limited to the assets of the company itself. Therefore, when doing business with a corporation, bind the corporate entity unless you can get a personal guarantee from officers or shareholders.

Personal guarantees are not usually provided for designer contracts unless the company is new or its financial situation is unknown. Moreover, a request of this nature often hinges on the balance of power in an existing designer-client relationship. If, for example, the designer is well known and the client is a small company, the request for a personal guarantee might be delivered as a polite ultimatum. On the other hand, if the designer needs the business and the corporate client appears solid, the request should be made carefully.

Corporate officers are usually empowered to execute agreements that bind their company. Ranking employees in large corporations are sometimes authorized to enter into agreements as well. For example, the officer of a major corporation would not necessarily sign a designer contract to renovate three floors of office space. The authority would probably be delegated to a lesser executive, such as a vice president. On the other hand, if you are designing the same space for a small, recently organized corporation, perhaps you should accept only the president's signature.

If a contract is executed by a ranking employee who is not authorized to sign agreements, all is not necessarily lost. For example, suppose an unauthorized company employee signs a designer contract. However, later the treasurer signs a retainer check as initial payment for a design fee, and the vice president approves the design plans and purchase orders. These actions will "ratify" the initial agreement, subsequently binding the corporation to its entire terms.

Furthermore, if an employee is not designated to bind her employer, a delegation of this authority may be validated by a company officer. For example, a corporate president may advise the designer in a letter that the ranking employee has the authority to sign contracts. His delegation of responsibility grants the employee sufficient authority to bind the corporation. However, this fact should be established in writing. Oral assurances by company executives or other personnel may give the employee "apparent authority." But this may be very difficult to prove in the absence of written documentation.

As a practical matter, however, it is best to rely on legal means to enforce an agreement in a court or arbitration hearing. These proceedings can be expensive, time-consuming, and energy draining. The purpose of this chapter, in fact, is to point out how to avoid litigation. It is always smart to quietly investigate the solvency of small corporate clients in particular and to be conservative if the question of authority arises.

There is one circumstance relating to the issue of signing contracts in which I would not accept a delegation of authority. In any designer contract with a married couple, regardless of whether it's a commercial or residential project, always try to get the signatures of both husband and wife. The following example illustrates the importance of this precept.

QUESTION: *I am a residential designer in the Houston area. A married couple retained me six months ago to design and complete all installations for their large, expensive suburban home. The budget, without my fee, is in excess of $200,000. Recently, when the project was about halfway finished, the couple had an argument and the husband moved out. Now the wife says she hasn't enough money to pay my commissions or the balance of the deposits for the furniture on order. I know the husband has plenty of money. What do I do next?*

ANSWER: Dealing with an estranged couple requires finesse, perseverance, and determination. In this situation, it doesn't sound as though the designer can expect to complete the job. He has to extricate himself as quickly as possible. Obviously, he needs to collect his fees and secure payment for vendors and contractors.

The exact steps that you must take under similar circumstances will depend on your letter of agreement. But the husband and wife must sign the contract to ensure joint responsibility.

Some designers operate on a "direct payment" method. Their clients pay vendors and contractors directly, and the designers supply supervision and purchase orders. Consequently, the designer is literally liability-free, except for the collection of his own fee. However, if the designer has purchased goods and services for the clients in his own name, a variety of alternatives should be considered.

First, the designer should immediately contact the husband and wife to request a comprehensive accounting. In this case, the husband was affluent and realized that he was responsible for payment. If spouses are not irrational, a solution can usually be found.

The designer should be candid, telling the couple that he will not continue with the project. Even if a couple reconciles and decides to complete a job, it is probably unwise for a designer to resume. Once a designer is warned about trouble, it is best to end the relationship. If the couple refuses to cooperate, all claims should be documented and sent via certified mail to both husband and wife.

As previously indicated, all vendors and contractors should be notified by telephone, and the notice followed up with a letter.

If the designer's letter of agreement is properly structured, problems should be minimized. For example, full payment and design commissions should be requested on order for wallpaper, fabrics, lighting fixtures, accessories, plants, and retail items (i.e., flatware, china, crystal, linen, and other household items). Although the designer may not actually pay all these vendors in full before delivery, the client's money should be on deposit.

For other furnishings and fixtures, 50 percent of wholesale cost and design fees should be deposited with the designer on order. Cancellation fees rarely run this high, so this deposit will protect the designer. Certain vendors will cancel orders on stock items for a minimal charge.

As noted earlier, custom ordered merchandise may present different problems, and manufacturers have varying policies. If an order is not yet in progress, cancellation should be simple. If the items are ready for shipment, a manufacturer may cancel the order when the deposit is forfeited. If the manufacturer insists on full payment, there is a problem. In rare situations the designer may be forced to accept the merchandise and seek legal recourse from his client.

Antiques, usually, do not present much of a problem. If the designer has a good working relationship with reputable dealers, they will often accept the merchandise and give a full refund.

For labor and construction, a 50 percent deposit on wholesale cost and design fees should be paid to the designer upon purchase order approval by the client. In this connection, many contractors refuse to proceed with custom installations unless they are paid at each stage of their work. Therefore, if the clients refuse to continue payment, monies for most of the work performed to date should have been held on deposit.

Consider now the grimmest of all possibilities. If payments have been stopped, after the designer has ordered a lot of merchandise on his own account, he may require legal help. If you are ever in this situation, don't wait. Institution of proceedings may frighten the parties into immediate restitution. Advise all unpaid vendors about the situation, and they may join you in the action. If an arbitration clause was included in the agreement, relief may be speedy and inexpensive. Just remember that if payment is due, a designer should not stall vendors and destroy his own credit rating. Make the vendors aware of the situation. Take immediate corrective measures.

When billing on a cost-plus basis, I always stipulate that payment for design fee commissions is due on all goods and services that are ordered. Therefore, even if the client cancels the order, the fee is still payable to the designer. If the client denies liability for these commissions, the designer may use legal means to collect his fee.

Generally, when a designer is faced with this situation, his initial reaction is one of shock and bewilderment. However, quite frequently, resolution of the financial difficulties is quick if the designer takes immediate action.

When the designer insisted on full payment from the Houston husband mentioned in the example, he paid immediately. Under similar circumstances, you might not be that lucky, so remember *all* of the strategies described here.

In summary, preventive measures should be taken to avoid a legal crisis whenever possible. These include the following:

1. Provide an arbitration clause in the letter of agreement.
2. Keep client billings and collections up to date.
3. Be sure the right party executes the letter of agreement.
4. Make sure both husband and wife sign the letter of agreement for their personal, joint projects.

12

PURCHASES AND DELIVERIES

The subject of purchases has been discussed throughout this book from different vantage points. In many jobs, purchasing is a central function of the interior designer. In others, designers prepare design plans only and have their clients purchase goods and design services. This second arrangement is much more common in commercial jobs than in residential projects.

This chapter discusses how purchases are influenced by the timing of a project and deliveries. Case studies present various problems that arise in the purchasing process as well as illustrations of how to deal with them.

The discussion begins with a review of how designers specify purchases through the use of a purchase order.

PREPARATION AND ISSUANCE OF PURCHASE ORDERS ON ALL GOODS AND DESIGN SERVICES

It is essential to incorporate, systematically, everything contained in the budget on purchase orders. Be careful not to leave anything out. Usually, the most complex purchase orders are those for design services and construction. For residential projects, some designers use their floor plans and prepare the orders on a room-by-room basis.

If you intend to act as the client's agent for payment, you will usually prepare an estimate for her and she will forward you a deposit as required. Then you will prepare a purchase order to be sent directly to the vendor.

If the client is going to make her own purchases and payments, you will prepare the purchase orders for her use in triplicate. One copy is retained for your files. Another is forwarded to the vendor by the client. The third is retained by the client for her own files. Have the client initial your copy indicating her approval. This is extremely important, so as to protect yourself if unauthorized changes are made without your approval.

When forwarding purchase orders to the client, many designers wisely include a cover letter, as the following example illustrates:

Date

Dear (Name of Client)

Atteached please find enclosed purchase order #_____, dated: January 15, _____. Please send one copy with your check directly to the vendor and fill in the following information for our records:

Amount of Check:

Name of Vendor:

Name of Bank and Check Number:

Please process this letter as soon as possible and return a copy to our office to enable us to check on your order.

Very truly yours,

Name of PRINCIPAL of Design Firm

Once the cover letter has been returned to you, you will know that the order has been processed and will be able to check up on it if necessary.

Before preparing any orders, ask your client what name should be listed as the purchaser. For example, some residential clients may instruct you to list their business as the purchaser for tax reasons. Some commercial clients own several corporations and may prefer one of their corporations to be the purchaser, rather than their main organization. Therefore, don't prepare the orders before checking with the client, so as to avoid the possibility of having to redo them because the incorrect name was used.

After each purchase order is processed, the matter is out of your hands. Or is it? Unfortunately, as most experienced designers can testify, trouble may be in the offing.

THE SIDE EFFECTS OF LATE DELIVERIES

Late deliveries create serious problems for interior designers. Not only can project completion be delayed, but frequently clients withhold payment of design fees until all installations are finished. When clients become anxious about late deliveries, they sometimes take out their frustration on the designer. Although the designer isn't responsible, he is the easiest target.

Delivery problems must be expected in any business in which numerous purchases and installations are commonplace for a single project. In fact, many designers have their own techniques to prevent problems. For example, some won't order imported furniture unless it's in stock. Others avoid specifying custom-dyed fabrics or carpeting or imported stone, such as Italian marble, unless the client specifically makes the request. Many designers focus only on perfecting their design with merchandise in stock. They believe it is much easier to complete projects with available goods rather than to specify unusual materials that may create problems and liability.

In recent years, designers have advised me repeatedly that some clients have held them financially responsible for the effects of late deliveries. The following question gives an example of a contract designer who was a casualty of a late delivery. She lost her client and design fees and sustained money damages as a result of an unpredictably late delivery.

QUESTION: *I was retained by a clothing manufacturer on Seventh Avenue in New York City to design a new showroom. I had ordered 20 chairs from an expensive contract furniture manufacturer whose reputation has been foremost in the field for more than 30 years. A 12-week delivery was scheduled but never met.*

My client moved into his new space without the chairs. After 12 weeks, I asked the manufacturer to lend chairs temporarily until the order was delivered. He refused. After 21 weeks, my client, without consulting me, purchased different chairs directly from another manufacturer. He insisted that I return his deposit, and, since I wanted to finish the job, I paid him with my own funds.

After 25 weeks, the chairs arrived. I requested that my own deposit be returned by the manufacturer, but he refused. Rather than forfeit the deposit, I took delivery of the chairs, paid the balance in full, and warehoused them. My hope is to sell them to a future client at a discount.

When I told a few other designers this story, they related similar experiences with other major manufacturers of domestic goods. Apparently, some are independent, refusing to be responsible for compliance with their own specified dates. Can something be done to prevent this?

ANSWER: A preliminary comment: When the manufacturer refused to provide substitute chairs, the designer might have rented some for her client. Designers often find substitutes for a temporary crisis such as this one. Even if the client hadn't reimbursed the designer for the rental, she would have had a better financial result.

I suspect the designer never foresaw her client's impulsive purchase. This is an example of why a designer must be responsive to her client's needs. She had to create an operable showroom by a certain date if at all possible. Certainly her client complained, but she didn't find the right solution. When designers are clever enough to overcome obstacles, they receive repeat business and recommendations.

Regarding a designer's personal liability for late deliveries, the following clause should always be stipulated in the letter of agreement:

> Our role is to expedite and double-check your purchases and to follow up in case of loss or damage. Please bear in mind that we do everything possible to keep furniture deliveries on schedule, but we cannot guarantee specific dates. Just before move-in, we compose a punch list of outstanding items and concentrate on expediting the delivery and installation of the same.

I don't believe that designers are liable for damages as a result of late deliveries. However, the purpose of this language is to ensure that you won't be held responsible. A similar clause appears in Chapter 1, but it is repeated here to emphasize its significance.

If your client is acting as his own purchaser, either directly or through a purchasing agent, obviously you are out of the line of fire. If a designer doesn't make purchases, he avoids a lot of headaches.

However, many designers do act as purchasers. They deal with the vendors directly and act as the client's agent for payment. They obtain a professional discount, charging the client cost-plus or retail. In these situations, they must cope with delivery problems. When net prices are disclosed to a client, the designer frequently asks the client to intervene in the event of a delivery problem. Since there is no secrecy about prices, there is no reason for the client not to complain directly.

If the client in this example had submitted the purchase order and a check to the vendor, the designer would not have been forced to return the deposit. Her only financial role would have been to prepare the order, offering the client her professional discount.

Many designers never allow their clients to intervene with vendors, insisting that it is unprofessional. However, after experiencing a financial loss, some change their minds. Many designers have dealt with too many clients who refuse to pay balances on ordered goods and with contractors who don't complete jobs after payment. Now they insist that clients act as direct purchasers and sign all purchase orders and contracts directly.

Sometimes "holding a client's hand" when a delivery is late may soothe him until the merchandise arrives. Most designers, however, are extremely busy and find it difficult to attend to each detail. Nonetheless, clients usually relax when designers show concern. It is helpful to prove that you are doing everything to expedite delivery. For example, some designers calendar all major deliveries. If any are late, they follow up with telephone calls and "Speed Memos," sending copies to the client. Once this practice becomes automatic, it's a strong argument for your own credibility as a professional.

For those designers who do make purchases, there is a technique that may be useful to pressure vendors when deliveries are late. When you prepare, for example, "Purchase Order #100," include a delivery date for the goods ordered. When attaching your check, write in one corner, "As Terms of Purchase Order #100." This makes the time of delivery a material term of the contract.

If there is no delivery by that date, the vendor is liable for breach of contract. However, vendors sometimes provide their own purchase orders or confirmations that release them from liability for late deliveries. Read the fine print on any document you sign that is supplied by the vendor. However, I am amazed by the number of vendor order forms and confirmations that don't even mention delivery.

If you use the technique described here, the vendor doesn't have to acknowledge your order to be responsible for its terms. Acceptance of the check is sufficient, because it "incorporates by reference" the terms of the purchase order. Each case is different, of course, and laws vary from state to state. However, if you are concerned about deliveries, you have nothing to lose. Try it.

Whether it is fair to hold vendors liable for late deliveries is a policy question, and the answer varies according to the facts. As mentioned earlier, if the product is imported or handcrafted, the vendor's hands may be tied. He may be unable to control production or delivery if he acts only as a middleman. For example, if your client wants furniture lacquered in France or handprinted fabrics from Italy, the delay may not be the showroom's fault. Designer showrooms can't control every situation. Make sure your client understands that when you place orders.

The example in the question, however, reflects a different situation. The designer showroom was owned by the manufacturer, which produces its own products. It was responsible for providing the chairs and should have done something to accommodate the designer's client during the delay.

Sometimes manufacturers deliberately delay completing orders, taking advantage of the designer. For example, in some cases, manufacturers delay production while waiting for a minimum number of orders. That allows them to increase their profits on a per-order basis. However, designers are rarely told the truth about a delay. They're always given an excuse that makes it appear unavoidable.

However, designers have begun to compare experiences and voice their disapproval. At meetings of designer organizations, such as the

American Society of Interior Designers (ASID) and the International Interior Design Association (IIDA), they are comparing notes to see whether some manufacturers are routine offenders. I have heard designers make announcements at national design conferences about which vendors to avoid. This costs manufacturers countless profits, as a result of poor public relations.

Late deliveries can no longer be ignored. Unfortunately, they can also be commonplace with a number of large domestic furniture manufacturers. Some of these manufacturers are considered to be important sources by designers and architects because of their contemporary designs and quality workmanship. For that reason, they have gotten away with late deliveries. The following question provides an example of a designer who, with the assistance of his client's attorney, survived a traumatic experience with a major manufacturer.

QUESTION: *I am an interior designer in New York City. Recently, a major furniture manufacturer created a very serious problem for one of my clients because of a late delivery. Although the furniture finally arrived, it was almost six months late. During the order period, the manufacturer's employees knowingly made false statements, which jeopardized my own credibility with my client.*

I had ordered a sofa for my client one year ago, at a total cost of $9000. The manufacturing price of the sofa was $6000. The price of the fabric, the customer's own material (COM) purchased from a different company, was $3000. One half of the price was required on order, i.e., $3000, the balance being due immediately prior to delivery.

The fabric required 10 weeks for delivery and was also ordered a year ago. Full payment was made on order, pro forma, and it was delivered to the furniture manufacturer two months after the order. The furniture manufacturer sent me an acknowledgement for the receipt of the material. After the fabric was received, the sofa was promised within 10 weeks to three months.

In fact, the sofa never arrived until a month ago, being six months late. Prior to that time, the manufacturer kept promising "immediate delivery," but then delayed, using endless excuses. My relationship with my client became tense and difficult.

Once the sofa was several weeks late, it became clear that there were problems. The client called me for weekly status reports. I kept calling the manufacturer for an explanation. I was told several different stories. The first was that the sofa's frame, imported from Italy, had arrived late. The second was that there had been a major theft of materials by certain employees within the company, delaying all deliveries. My client listened with disbelief.

Three months ago, the manufacturer advised that the sofa was, at last, available for delivery. The final payment, $3000, was required in advance. My client made the payment, disbursing a total of $9000.

The day before the delivery, the manufacturer cancelled it. The representative claimed that the fabric, accepted about seven months earlier, had been received partially damaged in certain areas, and several extra yards were needed. I told him that his request was an impossible one. The imported fabric wasn't available in stock and took two months to deliver. Further, any additional yardage would come from a different dye lot and would not match the original fabric.

After I informed my client, he called his lawyer at once. The lawyer demanded an immediate delivery or a full refund from the manufacturer. My client was overwrought. Almost a year had elapsed and, even with a refund, he still had no sofa.

The manufacturer then called a weaver who repaired the fabric. I warned them not to ship the sofa if it appeared damaged.

Finally, delivery was made. The rewoven areas were inconspicuous and eventually disappeared with wear. There was some minor shipping damage, but my client refused to have any further contact with the manufacturer to correct it.

My design fee for all this work was $2700, i.e., 30 percent of the net cost of the sofa, including the fabric. Financially, because of the extra time I spent, I sustained a substantial loss. My client endured extreme emotional turmoil, and while the sofa did look beautiful, it was not in perfect condition.

Although the crisis is over, the underlying problem still exists. My confidence in this manufacturer has dwindled. What else should I have done for my client? How can I function as a design professional if merchandise doesn't arrive on time?

ANSWER: The designer in this situation handled everything correctly. Nonetheless, I have presented this case as a basis for a meaningful analysis. One point illustrated by the facts is that a late delivery can cause other complications that can create irreparable harm. It's not simply a question of a deadline being delayed.

First, note that the designer purchased a European fabric from a different showroom prior to its submission to the furniture manufacturer. Coincidentally, the furniture company sells its own line of fabrics. The designer, however, picked a different line. Unfortunately, when more than one source for a custom item is specified, the risk of mistakes increases. If the fabric had been supplied by the furniture company, it would have been completely responsible.

Legally, in my opinion, the furniture company was responsible, nonetheless, for the damaged fabric. If the reweaving had not been satisfactory, the company should have been responsible for the replacement cost. In fact, the fabric had been delivered to the company nearly 10 months earlier. Proof of delivery had been acknowledged in writing. If the fabric had been timely inspected, upon delivery or within a reasonable time, it should be have been returned immediately if it was damaged. The company cannot disclaim responsibility now after taking possession of the fabric without a complaint 10 months earlier. It failed to fulfill a duty to inspect.

This case raises a corollary issue. The manufacturer acknowledged its receipt of the fabric by forwarding the designer a confirmation. However, if the designer hadn't received the acknowledgement, legal responsibility may have been unclear. Therefore, this emphasizes an important point. If a designer specifies upholstery, curtains, or any furnishings for which the fabric is the customer's own material (COM), a written acknowledgement should always be obtained from the final manufacturer, whether it is a large company or a local upholsterer.

Second, note that the manufacturer made false representations to the designer. It collected the balance of the price of the sofa, $3000, after promising immediate delivery. Then it cancelled the delivery shortly afterward, disclosing the fabric damage. In my opinion, this conduct was fraudulent. The manufacturer surmised that the customer wouldn't pay the balance if it revealed the fabric damage. Furthermore, inasmuch as the fabric hadn't been rewoven at that time, the furniture was not ready for delivery.

The client obviously realized that there was fraud involved and contacted his attorney. Outside help was necessary to resolve the situation. It is uncommon for a reputable company to act fraudulently. However, if it happens, a client should be notified immediately in order to take the necessary steps.

Third, this designer asked what she could have done to help expedite the matter. I recommend the following course of action: Once a manufacturer indicates that a delivery will be substantially overdue, the designer should request that a company officer send a letter to the client directly. This will put the client directly in touch with the problem, mitigating the designer's intermediary role.

The designer also raised another important issue. When manufacturers create delivery problems, it reflects on the designer's credibility. For protection, designers must keep paperwork in first-rate order. Designers should also communicate with one another, using their professional networks, to command the service and respect to which they are entitled.

THE SIDE EFFECTS OF EARLY DELIVERIES

Regardless of how quickly designers are able to work, many clients still complain that their jobs aren't completed soon enough. Frequently, this is due to the waiting period when ordering furniture and furnishings. Since installations are carefully scheduled, one late delivery of an important item can delay job completion until the goods finally arrive.

Psychologically, however, the real problem is the client's perception of the design process. Once merchandise is ordered, even though a client is told that delivery will take four months, he still may think that it will arrive sooner. Many designers believe that if clients really understood how long it takes to complete a project, they would start their jobs earlier.

Designers, of course, always treasure the rare client with foresight. This client retains a designer far enough in advance to accommodate her needs. This allots sufficient time to create design plans and order merchandise. After plans have been completed, furniture and furnishings are warehoused prior to installation dates. Designers tend to feel more in control. It's a comfort to know that the headaches accompanying late deliveries will be avoided. Paradoxically, the luxury of adequate time, an invaluable aid, can cause other problems, as the following case illustrates.

QUESTION: *I am a residential designer in Chicago with a staff of three and require a minimum budget of $50,000 for any new client. About seven months ago, I signed a contract with a client who has purchased a new two-bedroom condominium in a building under construction. Installations cannot begin for another three months.*

My office completed design plans and ordered all merchandise within two months after I was hired. One order was for curtain fabric for the whole apartment—one hundred yards of an expensive sheer material. The fabric was shipped to my curtain maker to store until the construction was finished. The fabric arrived several weeks ago and has some flaws in the selvage, i.e., at the bottom.

My curtain maker said that since the damaged area is at the edge of the material, it won't show on the curtain panels. Unfortunately, the curtain maker doesn't own a rolling machine and won't examine all the material until the curtains are made. Since that will take a while, I don't know whether or not to keep the material. The fabric was paid for pro forma *, i.e., in advance upon order. If I hold onto the fabric without inspecting it for two months, I'm afraid the manufacturer won't let me return it if serious damage is found later.*

Is there any way that I can keep the fabric for two months without risking my office's liability for the cost if it's badly damaged?

ANSWER: Most clients anxiously await the delivery of ordered merchandise. Usually, when fabrics are received, either for upholstery or curtains, the material is inspected and utilized at once. This case is unusual because the designer was hired far in advance. All major purchases were completed before some were needed. In a sense, the time lag has now become a potential liability instead of an asset. However, although this situation isn't common, issues relating to timing are important.

Although this delivery occurred while the condo was under construction, the case would be the same if the apartment were an older unit undergoing architectural renovation. When designers are able to plan, they frequently order goods that are stored and utilized later. Therefore, designers have to be watchful when projects are "under construction" and goods ordered in advance arrive prematurely.

Issues relating to designer liability may arise if goods are faulty or nonconforming to specifications once installed. Cases may vary from commercial projects for which open office planning systems are ordered, to residential jobs for which curtain fabric arrives early. It's important to spot a potential problem and deal with it immediately, as the designer in this case has done. The logic is usually the same, but the plan of action for a solution varies, depending on the goods involved.

This case is relatively simple. The designer should contact the fabric manufacturer, advising of her inability to make a complete inspection. Then she should volunteer to keep the fabric for two months, until the curtains are made. The designer should reserve the right to exchange the goods or obtain a refund if the fabric is found to be damaged. If the fabric showroom objects to the waiting period, the designer should discuss the situation with her client. The client can decide whether to keep the fabric, taking his chances, or to return it immediately. Either way, the designer should ask the showroom to send her a letter so she has written proof of where she stands.

The designer's letter to the showroom reserving her right to return the fabric should be sent by certified mail, return receipt requested. A copy should be sent to her client. If there is no reply after two weeks, the letter should be proof of adequate notice. This is particularly important if the vendor isn't represented in a local showroom or if the designer has no previous history with the vendor. Providing notice prevents the vendor from claiming later that it had no knowledge about the situation.

It's unlikely that any problems will occur, but why take the risk? It's also important to follow up the correspondence with a phone call. If the vendor agrees to allow the designer to hold the fabric until she's ready, she should ask for permission in writing, explaining that the client is insecure and would like written confirmation as reassurance.

These negotiations are often handled with sales representatives, who can be helpful while making a sale but may be slow to make adjustments later. A frequent response is, "That's not my department. You'll have to contact 'customer service' for help." Does this sound familiar? Your answer can be, "You're my sales representative. If you can take my order, why can't you help me with a problem? Why don't you call customer service and give me an answer?"

If you aren't being helped immediately, don't waste time being shuffled from one company employee to another. Each one may make a separate judgment, which is of no use to you. If your questions aren't answered quickly, send a certified letter to the company's president. If the company is responsive to its customers, either you'll receive a direct reply or a specific company employee will be assigned to solve your problem.

When I have discussed these issues with designers, they frequently reply, "The vendors I deal with simply wouldn't do that. They wouldn't refuse to take back damaged fabric merely because I hadn't inspected it for two months." Perhaps some wouldn't. However, think about what some vendors do when their deliveries are late. Usually, they apologize and make excuses. That doesn't help if your client is waiting for delivery.

Logically, therefore, don't trust these vendors to help you out with other problems either. Your own liability is at stake. Take written precautions, as I've suggested, to circumvent potential problems about notice.

What may change your approach is your client's reaction. Discuss your situation with the client before contacting the vendor. A client may tell his designer, "If you tell the vendor that you want to reserve the right to return the fabric for two months without inspection, he may refuse. If so, I'll have to return it now to get a refund. I don't want to lose the fabric. I need it for the curtains. Let's wait and see what happens. Don't rock the boat. If the fabric turns out to be damaged later, we'll deal with it then. In the meantime, don't return it simply on the possibility that it's not usable."

Of course, you should follow your client's instructions, but make sure to send him a letter confirming his request. Moreover, if you charged the fabric to your open account with the vendor, make sure your client pays you for it immediately. If a problem develops later, you've done your job and can prove it. You will still be caught in the middle between client and vendor; however, it will be clear that you have no liability for the damage.

Each design project creates a separate set of relationships, many of which become interwoven. Because of the large number of components, even for the simplest jobs, the number of things that may go wrong is endless. No designer can possibly be astute enough to foresee all potential problems before a project starts. That would be an impossible task. It would also take such a negative frame of mind that it would probably hurt more than it would help.

However, what's useful to remember are the categories of problems that may arise. Learn the general approaches needed to deal with them. Most designers acknowledge late deliveries as a major issue to be carefully watched. Obviously, early deliveries can also be a problem when goods must be stored for a long period. If any risks have to be taken, let the vendor assume them.

CONTRACTS WITH SHOWROOMS

Purchasing custom-ordered goods for clients is an important component of an interior designer's job, for both residential and contract projects. When dealing with showrooms and furniture dealers, designers need an encyclopedic amount of knowledge, which, I find, is acquired by practical experience.

A note of caution must be heeded in regard to placing large orders pro forma. Some manufacturers require full payment in advance prior to processing orders for goods, such as fabrics, that are not in stock. For example, suppose a designer is ordering fabric in a custom color for restaurant chairs. When the designer places the order, the showroom requires full payment to process the order. Should the designer instruct the client to submit the full amount?

Most designers have open accounts with showrooms where they conduct business. However, don't charge a client's purchase to your own account until the client sends you the money. If the client decides to cancel an order, you'll find that most showrooms will permit cancellations with a restocking charge that varies, generally, between 5 percent and 25 percent. If the goods are custom ordered, the client may have to forfeit his deposit.

It is sometimes hard to convince clients that they must pay in full for their purchases, in advance. Designers have to explain the "pro forma concept." If you transact business at reputable showrooms on repeated occasions, there is very little exposure to risk. However, if you are not familiar with a particular showroom, you must advise your client of that fact. It is then up to her to make the decision.

Several years ago, a designer consulted me about a problem. He had designed a suite of offices, for which he had ordered expensive furniture. One grouping, for a large reception area, was a series of custom leather sofas purchased from a showroom that represented a prestigious Italian line. When the sofas were delivered, the color of the leather, a shade of taupe, was distinctly different from the sample. The board chairman's wife complained about this small detail; otherwise, the sofas were in perfect condition.

However, the designer had other problems on the job—with various orders and with the general contractor. He tried hard to resolve them, as an intermediary, but the wife refused to relent about the sofas. On this project, it was the "straw that broke the camel's back."

The designer consulted the showroom manager about the conflict. He compared the leather sample, used for the order, with the sofas that were delivered. The manager tried stalling. He took a month to check with the national sales manager, located in California. Then he tried checking directly with the manufacturer in Italy. Ultimately, the manager told him that company refused to make any changes because the variation was "not significant."

The designer was shocked. He had always wanted to purchase these sofas for a client. He had been thrilled when he finally got the opportunity. Unfortunately, when he found a customer, he had trouble with the order.

Ultimately, there was no happy ending. The designer was sued for the cost of the sofas and damages relating to other orders. Since the designer had sold the sofas on a retail basis, he was the vendor responsible for their quality. After a year, an out-of-court settlement was reached. The designer had to pay damages plus his legal fees.

There is a very important lesson to be learned from this case. When considering placing a large custom order, investigate the reputation of the vendor first. In this case, the showroom refused to cooperate with the designer. It wouldn't reupholster the sofas or reduce the price. Full payment had been made prior to delivery. The showroom refused to refund the money.

Prior to paying pro forma, ask yourself these questions: Have you done business with the showroom before? For how long? Are you acquainted with the manager? Have you ever had any problems with orders before? If so, how were they resolved? If the showroom is new, should you place the deposit in an attorney's escrow account? If you have any reservations, have you explained them to your client? If you have, then it's up to the client to decide.

In this case, the designer should have told the client the following, before placing the order: "This is an established showroom that sells 'high-end' imported goods. I haven't ordered from it previously. Also, any problems with custom imports are usually harder to correct than with domestic goods." These warnings should have been made to the client in a letter. Obviously, you can't do that with every order, but this was a special situation.

Realistically, what would have been the best remedy in this case? Since the showroom made no effort to bend, it made the designer look unprofessional. If the designer had had a previous relationship with the showroom, perhaps a compromise could have been reached. For example, the showroom might have offered a discount to calm the client. It's amazing how 10 percent off a price can placate irate customers.

If the leather had been damaged, or even a different color, then the designer should have sued the showroom. In that case, the showroom may have reupholstered the sofa without charge. However, in this situation, the showroom had a point. While technically the client was correct, she was being unreasonable to demand the cost of purchasing new leather and redoing the sofas. The variation in the shade of the leather from the sample was minor.

If the showroom had made any effort to accommodate the designer, a satisfactory financial arrangement may have been found. Then the designer wouldn't have lost his client or been sued.

In summary, before placing any large custom orders for clients, scrutinize the showroom carefully. If you have any reservations, discuss them with your client. Let it be the client's option whether or not to proceed. If your client approves, send her a memo carefully listing any potential problems. If anything goes wrong later, you will have strategic protection.

REACTING WHEN A CLIENT CHANGES HIS MIND

Unfortunately for designers, clients often change their minds about purchases that have been ordered. Changes can be handled more easily if the order isn't for a custom item, if the change is made prior to shipment, or if the order is not yet in production. Very often, however, clients request changes after their orders have gone past the point of no return. Designers and vendors are then in an uncomfortable, if not costly, position.

Here is a typical example of a last-minute change whereby a vendor, who tried to cooperate, was wedged between a designer and his client. The dilemma is related from the vendor's point of view to show how a supplier thinks when a client tries to victimize both vendor and designer.

QUESTION: *I am the owner of a small furniture company that produces all merchandise on a custom basis as ordered through designers. Two months ago, a designer ordered a $3500 cocktail table for his client. He had specified a 36-inch round table lacquered in Chinese red with an octagonal brushed-brass base. A 50 percent deposit accompanied the order, which was standard procedure with my firm. About two weeks later, before work began, the designer called and said the client wanted to change the color to beige, the shape of the base to round, and the base's finish to stainless steel. I made the changes on the original purchase order and called my craftsmen.*

When the table arrived seven weeks later, the designer and client came to inspect it. The client was horrified. She told us that she wanted the table as originally ordered. When we reminded her about the changes, she said that she never made any. The designer protested and insisted that she had to pay for the order.

The client refused to accept delivery until the table conformed to the original specifications. She blamed the designer for the error. The designer is an old and trusted customer. I want to know the fairest way to proceed, as well as my own legal responsibilities.

ANSWER: I advised the owner that, of course, he is probably not legally liable. His merchandise is sold only through designers, so he is responsible to the designer, not the client. This is usually the case unless a purchase order specifically indicates that an owner may deal directly with a client.

The rationale for this relationship is simple. The owner's merchandise is sold to a professional market. His customers (designers) make profits on the resale of the merchandise by obtaining the consumers (clients) and specifying the goods to be produced. Designers have to keep their clients under control and ensure that there are no errors in processing orders.

In this example, the owner had handled the order in the proper manner. The purchase order prescribed definite requirements with a full description of the merchandise to be produced. Before work started, the owner's customer, the designer, issued changes, and written notes were made to confirm them.

Ideally, the owner should have issued a new purchase order to the designer, having him initial his approval. Alternatively, it would have been smart to confirm the telephone conversation about the changes with a letter. However, as matters stood, the owner was still in a fairly secure position.

The designer could have claimed that the changes were never confirmed. He could have insisted that changes were merely mentioned and that the owner was responsible for the terms of the initial purchase order. The designer, however, was honest. He admitted, in front of the owner's employees, that he had specifically requested the changes.

If the designer hadn't been honest, it would have been the owner's word against the designer's in a legal proceeding.

How could the owner have substantiated his own position? In most states, "books and records kept in the ordinary course of business" are accepted as credible evidence. The burden of proof is then shifted to the designer, who must prove these records are false or incorrect. He could, of course, prepare his own correspondence or alter records indicating the confirmation of the initial order. Of course, any court or jury would seriously question the veracity of this documentation.

In its final determination, the court, after proof is submitted by both parties, decides what makes sense. It certainly seems unlikely that the owner would have made such drastic changes unless they had been requested. Furthermore, the changes were routinely recorded on the owner's records.

The owner in the case did not go to court. The designer was a good customer, so the owner wanted to keep his goodwill.

It is not uncommon for clients to change their minds yet again when faced with reality, as in this case. Consequently, the owner tried to resolve the situation peacefully. First, he offered to deliver the controversial table to the client's residence. Improbable as it seems, this tactic is often successful. When an item is seen in place in a room, the client often begins to like it and wants to keep it.

Then the owner gave the designer a different alternative. He offered to relacquer the table and change the base below cost if the designer would absorb the change. This was still expensive, so he offered to sell the table to the designer for his production cost. He suggested placing the table on his showroom floor for resale with a special reduced price.

The designer agreed to this strategy, and the table was sold to another designer within a month. The designer recouped his money for the table and had another one made for his client. This time the client initialed the purchase order and accepted the table with the new specifications.

By providing these options, the owner felt that he had done his part. In any custom business, incidents of this nature invariably occur. Loss of profits in such cases must be accepted as part of the cost of doing business. This designer was fortunate to end the episode so cheaply. Naturally, he continued doing business with the owner. The designer learned the hard way how he could be victimized by a client.

The "change of mind" in the preceding example is typical of many cases. Clients are frequently overwhelmed by anxiety after a purchase is made, even with their designer's assistance, and they feel that they must make some change.

Until now, this chapter has dealt solely with the purchases of goods. In the following case, however, the client changed his mind about the whole project after all the plans had been approved.

QUESTION: *I am a New York designer specializing in the architectural renovation of residential interiors. A year ago, a client retained me to totally redesign his townhouse. He paid me a $5000 flat fee plus a 30 percent commission on all purchases of goods and design services. I prepared a materials presentation, which he approved.*

All design plans were prepared. About a week before they went out for bid, the client put the house on the market, selling it two months later. Shortly afterward, he bought a large apartment in a high-rise building overlooking the city. Then he called me to design his new apartment.

I offered my client the same terms as in our original agreement—a $5000 design fee plus 30 percent commission on all purchases of goods and design services. Then the client asked me to waive the $5000 flat fee. He said he had already paid it once and didn't want to pay it again.

I refused, because this is a different project and all the other plans had no value. Was I correct?

ANSWER: I advised the designer that he was not required to design his client's new apartment for free. He was not obligated to give any credit for the new plans from the design of the townhouse.

Fortunately, the terms of the designer's original contract for the town-house were very specific. The importance of precision in your letter of agreement cannot be overemphasized. As indicated in Chapter 1, the first paragraph of the agreement should always contain a clause listing all the design areas.

In this case, the designer had agreed to design the whole townhouse for $5000. However, if he had intended to design only part of the house for this fee, then the letter should have been precise on this point. For instance, suppose the $5000 fee had covered only the designer's cost for five of the rooms. In the absence of specific details, at some later date the client could have requested additional plans and insisted on their preparation at no additional charge. The client could also have conceivably changed his mind about *which* rooms he wanted designed. The designer would have been forced to comply with the client's request if his agreement didn't spell out the extent of his obligations.

Generally, a designer spends a great amount of time on initial consultations and design plans. Design fees, whether they are flat amounts or retainers to be applied against commissions, only partially cover the cost of initial efforts. The real profits come later when purchases are made and the commissions are collected. In this example, the $5000 design fee did not compensate the designer for all his plans.

Many design contracts provide that as soon as a purchase order is completed, with the client's written approval, the commission is due. That applies even if a client changes her mind and never makes the purchase. Of course, this is a tough clause to enforce. If a client changes her mind about making a purchase, she won't want to pay her designer a commission even if she did approve a purchase order.

If the client in this example refused to pay a second $5000 design fee, for design of his new apartment, the relationship with the designer would have ended. If the client threatened to sue the designer to obtain a refund for the first design fee—$5000 for the townhouse—the client would have lost the case.

Ultimately, the client finally relented and agreed to pay a new design fee of $5000. However, I told the designer to consider carefully whether to handle the new project. First, he had lost money on the first project, the townhouse. Moreover, he had had difficulty with his client over the fee. Second, if the client changed his mind once, he certainly could do so again.

To completely design a project that is never executed is a very frustrating experience for a designer. You lose not only financially, but emotionally. You also lose a project for photographing, useful for your portfolio and publication. This may not be a significant loss for a large firm with a substantial number of jobs in progress. However, a small, growing practice needs continuous new projects to show prospective clients.

The designer agreed to design his client's apartment. He weighed all the pluses and minuses and decided to go ahead. He and his client had gradually developed an extended personal relationship. The client's taste, needs, and budget were explored, and solutions were found. Obviously the client had enough respect for his designer's ability to pursue him relentlessly.

When the designer decided to risk the second project, I told him to be particularly careful with the budget. Many designers don't prepare a budget with the initial presentation. If a client doesn't like the designer's selection of goods, it has to be redone. However, if a client isn't overconcerned about the budget, it can be postponed until final selections are made.

The designer proceeded with caution in this situation. He prepared a detailed budget with his visual presentation. The client initialed all the selections he approved. The designer left very little room for error before preparing any design plans. The client approved the drawings in writing before the designer started implementation. The job was completed quickly, and the designer was fully paid.

In summary, purchasing is an essential component of a designer's business. There are many nuances to the process that a designer must learn through practical experience. Even the most seasoned professionals run into occasional difficulty. However, if you manage your business properly, you will avoid being stuck with losses. You must take responsibility to avoid misplaced liabilities created by the whims or mistakes of clients and vendors. You will then make more money.

13

WORKING WITH ARCHITECTS

Designers are often confronted with the challenge of working with architects on commercial and residential projects. When a client decides to build or renovate any structure, he must often consult with an architect before planning any construction. Building permits must be obtained and licensed contractors will be hired, requiring an architect's services.

Some designers are licensed architects or work in firms in which architects are on staff. Others have working relationships with architects whom they consult as necessary. However, a client may have her own preference. She may choose her architect independently, advising her interior designer that he must collaborate.

It is very important for the designer and architect to establish a relationship that is beneficial to the project. Innumerable conflicts can develop, resulting from different tastes, varying design preferences, and personality clashes. Designers frequently don't like to surrender their territory to architects, and vice versa.

MAXIMIZING YOUR DESIGN FEE

When collaborating with architects, designers should never overlook the money issue. Many designers charge on a cost-plus basis, that is, charging a percentage of the cost of goods and design services that are specified. So do many architects. Problems arise on occasion as to *who* specified *what*.

For example, assume that an architect is designing a four-bedroom house with three baths. The client would like a custom-designed master bath with certain features, including special plumbing and cabinetry. The architect prepares an architectural drawing and shows it to the client. The client reviews it with the designer, who advises the following: The basic layout is fine, but detailed cabinet drawings are needed and specialty plumbing fixtures and lighting should be purchased. The client subsequently decides that she likes the designer's ideas. She tells the architect that he will be receiving the designer's specifications.

The designer then prepares a new set of cabinet drawings. He revises them three times with the architect and the general contractor until they are satisfactory. He shops with his client to select plumbing fixtures, hardware, and lighting. He meets with the electrician to supervise the lighting plan and is present at the installation. He shops with the client for materials, including marble and granite, and hires a special mirror installer.

All the goods are ordered through the general contractor, and the installations are completed. The architect submits his bill. He includes all the goods and services specified by the designer, as a basis of the budget for billing his commission. When the designer hears this, his reaction is, "How am I going to get paid?" The architect and client respond that he is paid on the budget for the furniture and furnishings. The designer may lose out financially because he didn't plan ahead for dealing with construction.

At first, this situation sounds ridiculous. However, it happens all the time. The architect's fee is frequently geared to the budget provided by the general contractor; this is typically part of his standard contract. As far as many clients are concerned, the designer is paid enough for his services through design of the interior furnishings, so he should really throw in other services for no extra charge. Frequently, interior designers lament, "I spent so much time redesigning a kitchen (or bathroom or powder room) and never got paid for it."

So what is the best way to ensure payment? The easiest alternative is to charge by the hour for any consultation services where your client requests your supervision. Designers typically charge an hourly rate between $75 and $300, depending on the strength of their practice, the size of the job, and their reputation.

Charging for consultations can help a lot. If you decide to do so, keep good time records. It is amazing how much time is spent on design meetings with architects, general contractors, and subcontractors. If you're not getting paid cost-plus for construction, why should you design and supervise installations for nothing?

Another method is to charge cost-plus on all materials that you specify for the project. This has to be made clear from the inception of the job and included in your letter of agreement. The following clause, discussed in greater detail in Chapter 1, should be included in your letter.

> With respect to your budget, it is agreed and understood that all items for the interior that are specified by our office are included in the budget for commission purposes. This includes, but is not limited to the following:

1. Custom plumbing and hardware fixtures
2. Lighting and switching
3. Wall covering and interior paint schedule
4. Window treatments
5. Flooring and floor coverings
6. All cabinetwork, including kitchen cabinets, custom vanities, buffets, bookshelves, banquettes, and interior doors

Obviously, this applies only to goods that *you* specify. If, for example, you specify three lighting fixtures, the cost of those fixtures will be included in your budget only for commission purposes. However, if you do not provide a list in your letter of agreement, be prepared to lose out on your fees to the architect. Instead, fight to get paid for the work you perform.

The following is an example of how to maximize design fees when collaborating with an architect on a corporate project:

An architect is engaged to renovate 8000 square feet of a client's corporate offices. The client also retains an interior designer to customize the interior for the president's executive office (including a suite with a master bath) and the corporate boardroom.

The architect's plans contain the basic architectural layouts. All other design decisions for the president's executive office and boardroom remain the responsibility of the interior designer. Although the designer plans to purchase all the furniture and furnishings for these areas, all construction, including material finishes and built-ins, is to be implemented by the general contractor.

If the architect bills on a cost-plus basis for the general contractor's budget, this may create a problem for the designer. If the interior designer charges cost-plus too, the designer must specify all custom materials and specialty construction in order to be paid for his services.

There should be no conflict between the architect and the designer on the furniture and furnishings budget. The designer will select all the furniture, furnishings and equipment, known as the FF&E, for the corporate boardroom and the president's office. These will include the desk, chairs, occasional furniture, the boardroom table and chairs, and all fabrics, window treatments, and accessories.

Construction, however, may be a different matter. Suppose the designer and his client select custom architectural paneling, manufactured and to be installed by a special woodworking company. Normally, all construction is handled by the general contractor and is supervised by the architect. However, since the designer specified the paneling, it should be included in his budget, not the architect's. The designer will have to coordinate the installation through the general contractor and, possibly, the architect. However, the commission belongs to the designer.

Suppose the president wants a customized master bath for his executive suite. The architect has prepared a general construction layout, but the designer must create an elegant, personalized bathroom. The designer shops for various types of marble. He selects all the specialty bathroom hardware, including the lighting fixtures. Finally, he prepares all the cabinet drawings for the vanity and recessed cabinets.

If the designer is allowed to process all these purchases through his office, it is easier to retain these items in his budget for billing purposes. However, if he must prepare these specifications to be purchased by the general contractor, the architect may bill for the commissions.

How should the designer handle this situation financially? If a designer bills for his services on a straight hourly basis, this is never a problem. However, many designers believe that it is more profitable to bill on a cost-plus basis for custom jobs utilizing expensive materials. Therefore, when a designer prepares a letter of agreement for his client, he should state that he will charge, for example, 30 percent on all furniture, furnishings, and customized installations that he selects. In this case, such charges include the cost of any materials, cost of construction, and installation costs for the president's office, executive bathroom, and the boardroom.

In addition, the designer should charge by the hour for meeting with the architect and general contractor. This should be made clear by adding the following to the letter of agreement:

> If it is necessary, upon the client's request, to prepare any interior cabinet drawings or to confer with the architect, general contractor, or other personnel for implementation of design plans, there will be an hourly charge of $.

Using this method, the designer will be paid a commission on everything he specifies. If he supervises the installations with the general contractor and the architect, he will be paid for his time. On your next contract job, keep this approach in mind to maximize *your* profits, rather than the architect's.

The following question offers another example of a potential conflict between a designer and an architect in regard to fees. This case is cited because it introduces a subtle strategy that can be used in handling a client, following the principles outlined earlier in this chapter.

QUESTION: *I am a residential designer in the San Francisco area. A former client consulted me recently. He plans to build a huge, expensive house. An architect has already been hired. He is interviewing general contractors and consulting engineers.*

I plan to charge cost plus 30 percent for my design work. The client told me that the architect is charging cost plus 15 percent. I'm concerned about being taken advantage of, since I don't want to design all the interior architectural work without being paid. How should I handle my client?

ANSWER: The designer's concern is justified. Negotiations with his client and the architect should be handled very delicately until the letter of agreement is signed.

This situation has become very typical. Until the 1960s, an interior designer was rarely asked to help plan the space for a new commercial or residential structure. Architects generally preempted that role. They designed the space from the outside in. When they finished, the designer was hired. Generally, there wasn't much left to "design." Construction was finished, and, basically, the designer's job was to decorate the space with furniture, accessories, floor and wall coverings, and so forth.

Things have changed a lot since then. Some of the spaces created by great architects are uncomfortable, lack warmth, and are uninviting. Sophisticated clients begin consulting an interior designer before approving their architect's plans. Spaces are now designed from the inside out.

Architects, in many cases, have preferred to isolate themselves from interior designers. Some want designers excluded from initial planning stages. In every respect, interior designers must use affirmative measures to defend their vantage points. When design fees are involved, one must begin in the letter of agreement, which is initiated of course, during the project planning phase.

This designer should begin consulting with her client without preparing any sketches or drawings. Simultaneously, she should negotiate her letter of agreement. She should attend joint meetings with the client and the architect, never mentioning fees at first. The client, it is hoped, will become impressed with the way she integrates herself into the project. Then the designer and the client should meet privately to discuss the letter of agreement.

If the designer decides to charge a flat fee, hourly fee, or any type of time-based fee, obviously there is no problem. Compensation is totally independent of any third-party relationships, (i.e., with architects, contractors, or engineers). However, if the designer wants to charge cost-plus, she must explain to the client what belongs in his budget.

In an analogous situation, you might have to do the same. The client must be advised orally, as well in the letter of agreement, as to what belongs in the budget. Refer to the clause, provided earlier in this chapter, that lists includable items. This should be done as early in the project as possible.

Explain that all items you select are included in your budget for commission purposes. This rule of thumb is the easiest way to define your territory. All selections should be documented by a purchase order and signed by the client. Specifically list items, such as custom plumbing and hardware fixtures, lighting and switching, wall coverings and interior painting schedule, window treatments, flooring and floor coverings, and cabinetwork.

It's obvious how this approach might operate for your benefit. Recall the example of the master bathroom discussed earlier. You might be called upon to create a special bath with custom fixtures. If you provide the drawings and specifications, the selection of materials and fixtures should be incorporated into your budget for commission purposes. This is a typical example and a fairly easy situation to handle. A more difficult one might relate to flooring and floor coverings. Suppose, for example, that the architect specifies hardwood floors for the entire residence and the client approves. Obviously, the cost of installing those floors will not be in your budget.

However, a "one-floor treatment" is rarely the pattern for an expensive residence. Marble or slate could be used in the foyer or dining room; carpeting might go in the bedroom. These choices are generally made by the client and the interior designer. The cost of any custom choices should be included in your budget.

The same logic applies to wall coverings and interior painting. The interior designer selects custom wall coverings and makes selections for custom colors. The costs of material and labor necessary to implement these design decisions may also belong in the designer's budget.

However, if the designer is simply picking a paint color, the painting cost probably won't be included in her budget. If she retains her own painter to provide a special finish, then she can bill for a commission. If the designer purchases wall coverings, she can bill a commission based on the cost of the goods. However, if the general contractor has the wall covering installed, the installation cost probably won't be included in the designer's budget.

One other item to be considered is cabinetwork. If the architect supplies the drawings for the kitchen cabinets, those will be included in his budget. However, the client may want the designer to design the kitchen. The designer may prepare her own drawings for custom work or purchase cabinets from a specialty manufacturer. If so, this cost should be incorporated in the designer's budget.

Generally, all custom bathroom vanities, dining room cabinetry, bookshelves, and banquette seating are custom cabinet items created by the interior designer, not the architect. Make sure they are listed in your agreement under "cabinetwork."

All these items are fairly expensive. If you can persuade your client to pay your commission on items in these categories, you will have a large budget. You will earn a substantial fee on an expensive, custom-built residence. One way to encourage a client is to offer certain services at no charge. State any such gratuities in your letter of agreement immediately after you have outlined your budget.

For example, you might act as a consultant for exterior architectural materials. Because the exterior must complement the interior, it's only logical to extend yourself in this area. You could also offer your services for landscaping and the pool area. If the architect keeps you out of that decision-making process, at least you have made the offer. Your goodwill looks sincere.

Don't feel compelled, however, to donate any of your services at no charge. Some designers feel that there is no reason to perform any services for nothing. Any free advice, of course, is optional. The project may be so difficult that you will only consult with the architect and general contractor for an additional hourly charge. If that's the case, tell your client and so indicate in your letter of agreement. If you don't do this, your client will probably expect you to provide this consultation without charge anyway.

If you do consult at no charge on pool areas, terraces, and gardens, you should still charge for any furniture or furnishings for these areas. Accordingly, when you list the areas included in your budget, add "outdoor furniture."

Items generally excluded from the interior designer's budget are stereo equipment, burglar alarms, fire detectors, and intercoms. However, if you design cabinets to house this equipment, the cabinetwork itself should be included.

In the last case cited, the architect's cost-plus commission is 15 percent, whereas the interior designer's is 30 percent. This disparity is frequently the case. The architect's budget, often the same as the general contractor's, is frequently two or three times larger than the interior designer's. Many clients, of course, prefer to put as many items in the architect's budget as possible in order to pay a lower percentage in fees. They want the designer to include her consultations for nothing. Be prepared for this attitude.

Sometimes the client will have a closed-door discussion about your fee with the architect to find out the "usual practice." If the architect or contractor wants to discuss your budget with you, simply refuse. Your relationship with your client is confidential. You don't have to justify your fees to anyone other than your client. If the client advises you that he has "surveyed the situation and finds your fees overreaching," merely respond that this is your method of charging. If he wants to compare pricing, he should check with other designers.

Of course, you can always compromise if you're getting close to signing your contract. For example, you could offer to waive your commission on a dining room chandelier, a coffee table, or some other token luxury item. That is simply good business sense if the fee warrants it.

Yet it doesn't pay to give in too much. Advise your clients that although you will be flexible, you will not consult in major areas of decision making without being paid.

MINIMIZING YOUR LIABILITY

A conflict over design responsibility often arises in the construction phase of a project, as illustrated by the following example:

QUESTION: *I am an interior designer in New York City. I was hired to design a renovation for a Manhattan townhouse and have been working with an architect, consulting engineer, and general contractor. The architect and general contractor have tried to minimize my design input as much as possible, but my client has insisted that they utilize my schematics and cabinet drawings*

Once construction started, I visited the site frequently to inspect the progress with the subcontractors. The first serious problems arose with the kitchen and master bathroom.

A number of my specifications were changed without my being consulted. The fixtures were rearranged, and many of the cabinet details were eliminated. I told my client about the unauthorized changes, and he called the contractor and the architect. They said they had to make changes because my drawings were wrong. Neither one of them had ever mentioned this to me. How do I handle the situation?

ANSWER: There is no single solution to this predictable sort of problem. The situation reflects a very poor working relationship between an architect, a contractor, and an interior designer. The architect and contractor openly resisted working with the interior designer. They changed his drawings without his approval, and when construction errors were made, they attempted to shift the responsibility and blame to him.

There is one easy and effective way to prevent this problem from arising. A number of my clients, established designers with excellent reputations, refuse to work on a project unless the client will select a contractor from their list. This is a very restrictive condition to impose. Clients usually reserve the option to select their own contractors when plans are sent out for competitive bids.

I was once instructed by a designer to specify the name of a particular contractor in a letter of agreement for a prospective client. I suggested leaving the decision up to the new client.

"Absolutely not!" the designer protested emphatically. "My cabinetwork has very special detail. One contractor understands my work and gets it finished at budget and on schedule. If I can't work with him, I'll let the client go. It's not worth it. I'm not going to try to educate a new contractor about the way I design, particularly with an architect looking over his shoulder."

Although the ability to control the selection of a contractor or subcontractor is ideal, it is hardly realistic to expect. Many designers would lose prospective clients if they insisted on making their own choices. The interior designer must generally adapt to the contractor, not vice versa.

Fortunately, the circumstances in the example are unusual. The responsibilities of the architect, general contractor, and interior designer, in supervising subcontractors on the site of a project, frequently overlap. Among professionals, the precise delineation of duties may not be terribly important so long as there are no personality conflicts or costly construction mistakes. In this example, both adverse elements are present.

If it becomes clear, during the construction phase, that the architect or contractor will be hostile, stay very close to your client. Once your design drawings are complete, deliver a copy of the plans to the architect. Indicate in a cover letter that you are willing to make any necessary changes. Send a copy of the letter to your client. If the architect finds fault with your drawings at some later time (as in the example), it will be easy to prove that you provided sufficient notice to make any changes. You will have put him on his guard. Chances are that the architect will recognize this and, it is hoped, will be cautious about making modifications without consulting you first.

Once your plans have been submitted and all changes have been finalized, make sure your client signs the drawings. Then submit them to the contractor(s) with the architect's plans for competitive bidding. Because drawings must be precise, indicate on each one, "Spot-check field dimensions." Once the contractor has been selected, send him a letter requesting comments if he wants any changes. Send a copy of this correspondence to your client as well.

When construction starts on the interior, visit the site as frequently as possible. Make sure the contractor is following your drawings. The quality and supervision of the work are his responsibility. If there is anything wrong, make notes and report to your client immediately.

If the designer in the example had followed all these precautions, he could not have been held responsible for sanctioning unauthorized changes. They would have been the fault of the architect or the contractor. If the client blamed the designer, he could have replied, "These mistakes aren't my fault. I prepared the original plans. First, they were submitted to the architect. He approved them. Then you signed them. Finally, the drawings were sent to the contractor. You have a copy of my correspondence. He had every opportunity to make changes, but didn't. I watched construction carefully. As soon as I saw the changes, I notified you at once."

With that type of procedure, you can avoid being held responsible for the mistakes or interference of others. Your professional responsibility will be discharged at every juncture.

This strategy is basically defensive. A better way to handle the situation is to plan an offensive strategy with the architect and the contractor. Once your initial plans and material selections have been completed, call a meeting of the architect, contractor, and client at your office. It is wise to meet with them on your own territory.

Review the plans carefully. Make sure your client pays attention, participates, and expresses his approval to the others. In effect, you must state to the architect and contractor, "Here are my plans. This is what the client wants. He has approved my ideas in the presence of us all. If you can't use them or want to make important changes, you had better say so now."

Of course, this doesn't mean that the architect and contractor must make all revisions at that moment. But if they don't object to your design plans within a reasonable time, it will be much harder for them to make major changes later.

Overall, it is the responsibility of the interior designer to take a careful approach to ensure the proper implementation of his own design plans. He must effectively delegate some of this responsibility to the architect and the general contractor. It takes teamwork to bring a project to life.

There is yet another area in which the interior designer must maintain control: the taste level of the completed project. Generally, any client who hires an interior designer to help create architectural plans is fairly sophisticated. He probably wants the architect to be given direction so the interior will reflect his taste. Architects often overlook or neglect this aspect.

The interior designer must become involved in the selection of materials in as many areas as possible. For example, he should act as a consultant for exterior architectural materials, which should complement the color schemes for the interior. General landscaping, pools, terraces, and gardens are other areas in which the designer should provide guidance.

If an architect objects to your "interference," merely explain that the project must be designed from all vantage points. For example, the designer typically selects all outdoor furniture for all outdoor living areas. It certainly follows that he should be consulted for architectural materials as well.

Watch your client's reactions while you are expressing your opinions during this process. He'll appreciate your efforts on his behalf.

All too often the architect and contractor lose sight of what the client wants during a design project. They like to complete the project according to their own specifications. The interior designer must ensure that the results will suit the client's needs. The designer's success, in most cases, hinges upon his diplomacy with other professionals. Sometimes, as in the example, the architect and the contractor may be impossible to handle, joining forces against the designer. Usually, the situation isn't so dire. How well the designer is received depends largely on his client's support and his own tact.

Such expertise on the designer's part requires many hours of consultation. It is much more challenging to design a space prior to construction than to decorate it after it's finished. As discussed earlier, you must structure your letter of agreement so that you are properly compensated for these extra efforts. If your requests are reasonable and your client really wants your input, he'll agree to pay you what you deserve.

In the preceding example, the client hired his own architect and the designer had to cope with defending his territory. The parameters of his client relationship were defined by the outcome of a power struggle.

Sometimes, however, the interior designer hires an architect himself. When a designer is retained by a client to design a project, the client may rely on his judgment completely. The designer, in that case, hires all outside consultants. Suppose a consultant makes a mistake and the designer doesn't catch it until it's too late. Who picks up the tab?

Consider what happened to this interior designer. She was retained by a small advertising agency to design an office in a loft space which was presented without interior walls. The agency hired the designer based on her portfolio and personal recommendations. The job required an architect to create a suite within 3000 square feet by preparing interior architectural drawings. The designer told the client that an architect would be necessary, and that she knew one who was excellent at planning lofts.

The client agreed, and the designer hired the architect. She gave him all the data, describing how she wanted the space to look and function.

Once the plans had been completed, the designer showed them to her client. The agency approved them and paid the architect directly. All structural renovations were created pursuant to architectural working drawings stamped by this registered architect, who was a member of the American Institute of Architects.

The interior designer's favorite general contractor came in at a reasonable bid and was hired by the client. Although the client signed a separate general contractor's agreement, the designer was paid on a cost-plus basis of 20 percent for the entire budget. The budget for the project was $150,000, so the designer stood to make a $30,000 fee.

Construction began, and things progressed well. Halfway into construction, the designer found several architectural details out of scale. Fortunately, she had been closely inspecting the construction, and she met with the contractor immediately. The contractor told her that he was simply following the drawings and proved that his work conformed exactly. After reviewing the situation with her two associates, the designer was forced to admit that the contractor was correct. The architect had apparently made some incorrect measurements, and neither the designer nor her associates had caught the mistakes.

The general contractor told her that it would cost about $3500 to make the changes. The designer was in shock and didn't know what to do. She came to me for advice, and we reached the following conclusions.

The fault, obviously, was with the architect. He was guilty of malpractice. The damages sustained from his errors amounted to several thousand dollars. However, the designer didn't feel secure about telling her client and blaming the architect. His fee had been only $2500. He worked free-lance and wouldn't have been expected to pay for the damages. The designer would have to sue him, cost more in legal fees than the claim was worth. Furthermore, any lawsuit involving the client could have cost the designer her job.

The expense to correct the errors was approximately 10 percent of the designer's fee. Viewed in that light, it didn't seem as catastrophic, so the designer decided to assume financial responsibility. In fact, she was partly to blame. She had inspected the drawings with her associate's approval and told her client they were excellent. How could she afford to disclaim responsibility now?

We were able to reduce her liability in an unexpected way. The designer had recommended the general contractor for a number of other jobs on prior occasions. He needed work and liked the designer. When the designer explained the situation, he agreed to absorb nearly half the loss. It was ironic that the contractor partly paid for the architect's mistake, because he was the least responsible of all the parties.

There are several lessons to be learned from this case. *If a designer hires an outside consultant, the designer shares more responsibility than if the client selects the consultant independently.* I don't think that is true from a strictly legal point of view. So long as the designer uses careful scrutiny when retaining an architect, or any other outside consultant, the designer should not share any liability. However, from a practical standpoint, as this case points out, it's not always easy for a designer to disclaim responsibility for the negligence of a hand-picked consultant.

If the client had hired the architect directly, it would have been easier to force the architect to assume responsibility for his mistakes. Of course, the other complication was that the designer had approved the architect's drawings. A designer, however, does not act as a guarantor for an architect's plans.

Here, the designer fared better solving the problem alone. *Sometimes it makes sense to absorb certain losses to avoid losing an entire job.* Once the designer settled with the contractor, it cost her only about $2000, or 7 percent of her fee.

Finally, it is important for designers, when they need help, to use economic leverage with contractors or vendors who owe them favors. Designers keep their sources in business by making recommendations. If they are responsible for profitable referrals, they should ask for outside help when necessary.

However, a caveat when using outside consultants: Check and double-check their drawings and specifications to protect your own credibility with clients.

DESIGNER'S PERFORMANCE OF ARCHITECTURAL SERVICES

Designers must be careful not to perform any services as an unlicensed architect or home improvement contractor. This is a prohibition consistently ignored by many interior designers. They're not clear as to what "architectural" means, and they have provided such services frequently without any consequences.

On large commercial projects, this is rarely a problem. A major architectural firm usually assumes all responsibility for any architectural work. It is on smaller projects that designers are likely to exceed the scope of their legal authority. Quite frequently, such projects are residential, but not always.

To those designers who have been involved in a lawsuit or arbitration proceeding, it is no secret that many judges take a dim view of interior designers. For a multitude of reasons, the designer is often viewed by the court, at best, as an unlicensed professional who is frequently incompetent and sometimes dishonest.

I appeared as an expert witness in a lawsuit in federal court, in which the defendant, a designer, was being sued by an angry client. All the complaints in the lawsuit related to mistakes made by the general contractor and subcontractors. The designer was being sued for two reasons: project delay, and inadequate supervision. In fact, the client had interfered with the designer's supervision, which helped cause the delay.

Many things had gone wrong on the project, but most of the problems weren't the designer's fault. They were things that happen in renovating, restoring, and redecorating an old building. When numerous craftsmen interact with contractors and a crazy client, sparks fly. Ironically, the project was finished, turned out beautifully and was published in several magazines. However, the client tried to blame the designer for all his troubles, and, despite my testimony to the contrary, the court believed him.

Unfortunately, this is not an isolated instance. Several years ago, a designer lost a similar case in New York. The designer was attempting to recover the balance due on a contract for services rendered in the design of a condominium apartment that involved combining two units.

The court denied recovery. It stressed that the designer had operated as an unlicensed architect and had billed the client for an architect's services. In fact, the designer had hired a licensed architect to file the renovation plans, but not until most of the alterations had been completed. The court concluded that since the designer had acted illegally, his contract was void. Therefore, the designer was prohibited from recovering any of his fees.

As a practical matter, I was shocked by the decision. For many years I have advised interior designers never to use the word *architect* or *architectural* in their letters of agreement to describe their services. However, it still surprised me that a client could evade paying his client for that reason.

Furthermore, I have always advised interior designers to avoid providing architectural services. If a project requires architectural work, the client should deal directly with a licensed architect, who should then prepare the necessary plans. In the case cited, that is what happened. However, the plans weren't filed until the renovations were under way, and the designer billed directly for the architect's services.

Large interior design firms frequently have registered architects on staff. These firms are quite familiar with the laws of the states in which they practice and are usually careful about the necessary procedures in supplying architectural plans.

Smaller design firms are not always as cautious. If you are not aware of the regulations in your state, find out about them. It is common practice for designers who are providing interior architectural plans to do so through a licensed architect. Some designers, though, never bother to engage an architect. Their jobs are completed by general contractors, who have their own architects stamp the plans and, when necessary, obtain building permits. In some cases, when plans border between structural and nonstructural, permits are not obtained and the services of an architect are not used.

Although many designers are capable of preparing architectural working drawings, many refuse to do so. They prepare design plans, with schematic drawings. Then they confer with an architect, approved by the client, to prepare the necessary architectural documents. Therefore, if a designer taking this proper approach decides to have walls removed or to relocate plumbing pipes or fixtures, she can't be accused of providing unlicensed architectural services. If these changes are documented by a registered architect prior to construction, a client cannot avoid payment of fees, claiming that the designer acted illegally.

Does this mean that a designer should bill clients through an architect for any borderline architectural service? Check carefully with knowledgeable designers in your own state.

As stated earlier, if a designer hires contractors directly for her client, she may require a home improvement contractor's license or a general contractor's license, depending on state laws. To play it safe, have the client hire the contractor directly.

Providing a service that a court deems "architectural" can be illegal. Keep in mind that a court will not enforce a contract it deems to be illegal. Find out where you stand in your own state—knowledge is power.

The interior designer is one of the newest professionals in the design field. When a designer collaborates with an architect, she must define her role, determining her fees and areas of authority and responsibility. Many of these are gray areas for the designer. The burden rests on this generation of designers to clarify, define, and illuminate.

14

DEALING
WITH RESPONSIBILITY

The implementation and execution of design plans by the interior designer places him in the center of a huge web of responsibilities. If the designer doesn't know how to handle his obligations he can become hopelessly entangled.

REACTING WHEN A CLIENT CHANGES PLANS

Unfortunately for designers and vendors, clients often change plans about completed design plans or merchandise on order. Frequently, it is their personal circumstances that cause clients to have a change of heart. Regardless of the reason, however, the designer is frequently stuck in an untenable position.

I always advise designers to be extremely scrupulous about their responsibilities to their clients; unfortunately, the reverse is not always true. Sometimes clients act irresponsibly, placing their designers in a very difficult situation, financially, as the following example illustrates.

QUESTION: *I am an interior designer in Los Angeles and have been in business for more than 15 years. I am known in the trade as a "society decorator." My clientele is small, but select, and uses me on a repeat basis.*

I have a problem with a client, a married couple, and my upholsterer. Apparently, the wife went way over budget on her choices without her husband's agreement. I had no idea the budget would be a problem. I had worked with her before when she had been married to someone else, and money had never been an issue.

In any event, the wife approved all my upholstery designs. They cost about $15,000, retail. I told the upholsterer to start work. Then I ordered the fabric from a showroom, about $8000, retail, and charged it to my open account. My client told me she was in a hurry, so I rushed the order.

Then I sent the wife a request for a 50 percent deposit. I usually charge retail, asking for half on order, with the balance due before delivery. Normally, I receive the deposit in advance, before ordering anything. In this case I made an exception, which was a big mistake.

The wife returned my estimate. She said she couldn't afford the order and had never approved it. She asked me to design something different that would cost six or seven thousand dollars less. I told her that she had approved my designs and the fabrics. It was too late to cancel the order. She told me that she was very sorry, but there had been a misunderstanding. Then she said something that sounded "legal." She told me that if she had approved the order, why didn't I have a written confirmation?

I had hoped that she would convince her husband to honor her commitment, because the work was in progress. Now the upholsterer is ready for delivery, but I've been stalling. He's beginning to get very upset. I have to placate him since he's my most important source. I use him for all my jobs. What do I do next?

ANSWER: I advised the designer that several courses of action were available, but first he had to consider his responsibilities and priorities with all parties involved. Obviously, he couldn't satisfy everyone. Someone had to take a loss, and he had to decide who it would be before taking any action.

This particular upholsterer's quality and service had been crucial in establishing the designer's reputation. It is well known that fine craftsmen in the trade are not easy to find. Consequently, when a successful working relationship is established, it should be treated with great care and respect.

The designer also had to consider his own reputation. He had been in business for a number of years and was very well known in the design community. A designer's stock-in-trade includes his credit rating and reputation for integrity. Although many vendors refuse to accept orders from designers without a deposit of 50 percent or more, reputation still counts for public relations purposes and should be saved at any cost. Clients will hear it through the grapevine if a designer doesn't pay his bills. Publications often overlook a designer with a bad reputation.

Certainly, it's important to please clients, even those who don't always behave well. In this case, the designer had to be practical. The client was a repeat customer from a select social circle who would probably use him again or recommend him to prosperous friends.

The designer was left with the following alternatives. The fabric showroom had to be paid or the designer's credit would be ruined. The upholsterer had to be paid or the designer would lose a key workman. And, finally, the client had to be satisfied so the designer could finish the job and obtain referrals. Resolution of all these elements required the designer to swallow his pride and open his wallet.

If you find yourself in an analogous situation, contemplate using this strategy. Begin sending checks for small amounts to vendors (e.g., the fabric showroom and the upholsterer) to demonstrate your good faith. When issuing payment, call the vendors and explain the situation. Try to stall for time. The designer in this example owed a fabric showroom $4000 (i.e., $8000 at retail). He sent 10 percent immediately, before delinquent bills began arriving.

The designer owed his upholsterer about $7500 (i.e., $15,000 at retail.). He sent $1000 with a bottle of champagne and asked him to hold the merchandise for 30 days. If you can stall for time, you may be able to straighten things out with your client. Since the orders were on a retail basis, the designer was the seller. He was legally responsible for final payment in any event.

Now comes the hardest part. Contact your client at once. Review the situation and apologize for the misunderstanding even though you were not at fault. In the spirit of compromise, waive part of your commission or design fee on one particular item (in the example, it was the upholstery). If that doesn't work, find out what your client would be willing to spend. If the client offers 70 percent or more of your net cost, settle on that amount if possible.

The situation will then be resolved. You'll have saved face with your client and protected your reputation. Of course, you'll have to weigh the cost involved and arrive at your own conclusion. If you retain an attorney and end up in litigation, you can spend an equal amount or even more on fees, and you will lose a client.

The designer in this case sold his client the furniture for $17,000 at retail, instead of the estimate's price of $23,000. In fact, he reduced the price by $6000. His cost was $12,500 so he still made a profit of $4500. However, he earned a total design fee on the job of nearly $20,000 and received two referrals from the client over the following year. The client was thrilled because she received exactly the furniture she had ordered for $6000 less.

If your client refuses to accept merchandise on generous terms, you may have to resort to legal means. An arbitration clause in your letter of agreement makes it possible to resolve the matter in one series of hearings without an appeal. As discussed earlier, this will reduce time, effort, and legal bills. Assure your vendors that they will be paid for the cost of the goods. If you are legally responsible for payment and will ultimately require their cooperation, this only makes sense. Finally, one additional cost must be absorbed that cannot be measured financially—the aggravation cost.

Once you extricate yourself from a predicament of this nature, the following axioms should be branded into your memory forever. When charging retail for custom orders, always have your clients sign detailed estimates prepared by your firm before you place the orders with vendors. Obtain a deposit of at least 50 percent, based on the retail price.

All orders should thoroughly describe the goods, and, if possible, include a sketch with dimensions, a picture, or a sample (fabrics). If a husband and wife are involved, try to get them both to sign all orders. Operating any other way is not only unprofessional but an invitation to disaster.

Under certain circumstances, you may be duped by a client, and, consequently, may not want to maintain any further relationship with him. Still, your responsibilities to certain vendors may make it necessary to settle for less than you're owed. The following example illustrates a typical situation in which compromise is necessary:

QUESTION: *I am a young interior designer in metropolitan Chicago and was hired last year by a wealthy builder to design a model apartment for a 30-story luxury building. I charged my client cost plus 30 percent for all the furniture and custom construction. The builder paid all his bills as the job progressed. The budget was approximately $100,000, and I had collected approximately $28,000 in fees and commissions at the time the trouble developed.*

When I sent my client a final bill of $2700 for design commissions and $9000 for custom-ordered accessories, he refused to pay but gave no explanation. When I called him, he told me that he had paid enough for the job.

I continued to bill my client, but he ignored me. He also refused to return the accessories. A month later, I was sued by the showroom that sold them to me. My lawyer brought the builder into the lawsuit. Now, the builder has offered to pay $9000 for the merchandise but refuses to pay my commission. I have already paid my lawyer $1200. He advises me to accept the settlement. It seems unfair. Should I accept?

ANSWER: I told the designer that his attorney's advice was correct. Further, I advised him to settle the claim immediately. I told him that he should consider himself fortunate for concluding a potentially hazardous episode so economically.

I never discovered why this designer's client wouldn't pay him. However, the designer had been careless in his business practices. Specialty accessories generally require either a 50 percent deposit upon order, with the balance due before delivery, or pro forma payment (100 percent) due on order. Obviously, the designer delivered the merchandise without receiving any payment from his client.

In this case, the client paid his bills until the job was nearly completed. I know several designers who believe, "They always try to cheat you at the end of the job." Of course, that's not true, but it certainly applied in this situation.

Clients, unlike leopards, often change their spots for no apparent reason when it comes to paying bills. Do not be lulled into a sense of security by a client's record for dependable payment. Simply remind your clients: "Deposits must be made upon order. It's nothing personal, and no negative inferences are intended. It is simply a question of uniform business practice for all of my clientele."

The wealthy builder in the example would have understood that language very well. We must assume that he simply chose not to pay his bills. If you find yourself locked into such an impossible situation, settle it quickly. A client may be dissatisfied with a designer's work or feel that he has been overcharged. His motivation is not the crucial factor. You must minimize your losses as much as you can.

Designers have neither the time, energy, nor money to waste in litigation. If you do sue a client for unpaid fees, he has the right to make a counterclaim against you for the same amount of damages or even more. True, the counterclaim may be groundless and without merit. Nonetheless, protracted litigation can result in soaring legal bills. Wealthy clients have formidable weapons that they often use without hesitation, or even good reason.

Most designers cannot afford to absorb too many financial losses. Accordingly, as explained earlier, I strongly recommend using an arbitration clause in the letter of agreement. Of course, an arbitration clause won't prevent *third parties* from suing a designer for unpaid bills, as shown in this example. However, it does help to resolve disputes between a designer and his client more cheaply and quickly.

The designer's indignation at having to absorb the loss of his commission was certainly understandable. The job had been completed, and his compensation was arbitrarily denied. Unfortunately, his credit with a showroom was also destroyed.

If the designer had contacted me before the showroom sued him, I would have given him the following advice: *Pay the showroom.* The designer should have paid the showroom regardless of the outcome of his lawsuit. In fact, he should never have charged the merchandise to his open account or released it to his client prior to full payment. However, once he delivered the merchandise, he was responsible for payment.

Unfortunately, a few clients will always try to squeeze a designer at the end of a project. Guard yourself against this eventuality by insisting upon signed purchase orders, deposits, and arbitration clauses. However, if you fail to take these precautions and suffer the consequences, don't compound your error. Retrench, consolidate, and learn from your mistakes.

Sometimes, unfortunately, a designer may find herself entangled in the personal affairs of his client in such a way to cause the worst kind of trouble. In the following example, again, the client had a change of heart, this time because of a change in matrimonial status. If a designer has not managed her financial affairs with a certain degree of precision, she may find herself in the most adverse circumstances, as the following question illustrates.

QUESTION: *I am a successful Miami designer. I've always operated on an informal basis with my wealthy and prominent clientele. However, I've unexpectedly run into some real trouble and don't know how to handle it.*

Old clients of mine, a married couple, recently engaged my services. The husband is a real estate executive from a wealthy family. More than a year ago, the couple bought a mansion in Coral Gables and called me to redo it. I hired an architect and completely redesigned the house. The budget was about $1,000,000. The clients approved my design and told me to proceed with all the orders.

Construction was finished about six months ago. All the furniture, fabrics, and accessories were ordered. The couple never signed anything but supplied me with all the deposits, which were at least 50 percent in most cases. I have charged some things to my open accounts at a few showrooms, but nothing extreme.

About a month ago the wife called me. She told me that she was getting a divorce and leaving Florida. Her lawyer had worked out a settlement for her share of the house. She told me to be prepared to deal with her husband.

Soon after, the husband called me and asked me to meet him at the house for a conference. When I arrived, he introduced me to a young woman, his fiancée. He was very cordial. The woman was pleasant but made it clear that she didn't like the way I had decorated the house. I don't know whether it's personal or whether she wants everything different from the wife's choices. I have the feeling that she doesn't want me to finish the job.

Until now I have handled all the bookkeeping and payment, without any problem, with the husband's office administrative assistant. He still owes about $300,000 on custom merchandise that has yet to be delivered.

What do I do now? I'm afraid I won't be paid for some of the furniture because the fiancée doesn't like it.

ANSWER: This predicament was one of the worst in which I had ever known a residential designer to become entrapped. In a simple divorce situation, a designer can usually extricate herself without too much trouble. Here, however, the designer had unwittingly became involved in a situation that placed her in great financial jeopardy.

The designer had insisted on deposits for most of the goods. However, she had charged $12,000 to her own accounts. Moreover, if her client had forfeited the deposits, refusing to accept the orders, the designer would have lost nearly $75,000 in commissions.

Unfortunately, the husband and wife had never signed purchase orders. The husband's office staff had simply forwarded the deposits, and the designer had not pressed the issue.

A designer's informal style of conducting business can prove to be a very expensive mistake. Too often a designer is awed by her clientele, and if the relationship also develops into a social one, she loses perspective on *the* most important fact: She is running a business.

This situation is a typical illustration of how, even under the most favorable conditions, an unexpected event can cause insurmountable problems. Nothing should have gone wrong. First, the designer had been in business for a considerable length of time. She was experienced and had rich clients. Second, she had worked well with these clients before. Unlucky? Definitely. But sooner or later, such complications will crop up. If you haven't organized a tight and sound operation, you will wind up losing money.

I agreed with the designer about her future with the client. She had to be prepared to leave the job. Unless she had a chance to establish a relationship with the fiancée, she would probably hire someone else.

The designer's purchase orders were meticulous. Since they weren't approved in writing by the couple who ordered the goods, naturally, the designer had every reason to be uneasy. Fortunately, however, the deposits submitted by the husband's office confirmed the orders.

For your own jobs, take the following advice. Have all purchase orders or estimates approved by both husband and wife in writing. If a client provides written acknowledgement of an order, it substantially removes financial liability from the designer. Following an improper ordering procedure was the designer's first mistake.

Her second mistake lay in charging any purchases for the client to her own accounts before being paid. In the scheme of things, it hadn't seemed too important to the designer at the time. After all, the job was a big one and the client had paid all other deposits as requested. However, once a crisis arose and the designer saw that her job was in jeopardy, she was very sorry that she had placed herself at risk.

Never assume financial responsibility for your clients, or for any third parties. Use your credit line or open accounts to make purchases only after you have received payment from your client. In this situation, instead of obtaining *all* deposits from the client upon placing orders, the designer collected only *some* of them. She planned to bill her client upon delivery. When the designer consulted me, payment had not yet been refused. However, since she knew trouble was on the horizon, she was very apprehensive.

The designer ultimately found the perfect, easy way out. She prepared purchase orders for all goods on order that had been charged to her own accounts. She itemized all deposits and requested immediate payment. As she had dealt with the client's office administrative assistant, she continued to submit all the documents to him. She inserted a note with the purchase orders, requesting the client's signature. When the office administrator questioned her, she advised that she was now processing orders this way. She didn't appear anxious, and the orders were finally signed.

Fortunately, all this paperwork was completed at the client's office, away from the scrutiny of his fiancée. Once the papers were signed, they confirmed the orders by "relating back." Legally, the client "ratified" all previous orders that the designer had placed orally.

The designer was extremely fortunate that the husband decided to finish the project. For example, when faced with the purchase orders, the client might have stopped the project, making no further payments. Of course, the husband would have forfeited his deposits. However, sometimes people act irrationally under trying personal circumstances.

If payment had been refused, the designer would have been forced to go to court. I generally advise every other avenue of recourse before advocating legal action. Yet if payment had not been forthcoming quickly, drastic steps would have been necessary.

When he wants to discard his designer, a client often resists dealing with her on any level. In situations of this nature, a lawsuit forces settlement, because the designer is already a very painful burden for the client. A legal action may conclude dealings quickly and favorably.

HANDLING TROUBLE ON THE JOB

Supervision, one of the designer's hardest jobs, is discussed in several other chapters. This role of the designer is a central theme of this book because it is so important to a designer's practice.

One of the easiest ways to avoid problems is by learning from the mistakes of others. That is why there are so many case studies in this book. It's one thing to discuss why using certain procedures is a good idea. It's quite another to show what happens when designers don't use them and things go wrong.

The five cases that follow involve designer responsibility for defective goods and faulty installations. They are organized according to product to help you remember them. I hope that you will identify with the examples and that you avoid similar problems.

Fabrics and Upholstery

QUESTION: *I am an interior designer in Minneapolis and have a small but very busy office. I have a partner and two junior designers as assistants. My partner and I divide our clients, enabling us to work separately. Now I am in a difficult situation and don't know what to do. I have a residential client who owns a 10-room house. The job had been going well. All the plans are finished, and many deliveries have been made.*

The problem involves the den. An expensive hand-printed fabric was purchased from a quality fabric showroom in Minneapolis to be used for upholstery, curtains, and some of the walls. Before placing the order, the showroom mentioned that the fabric might vary from the sample, due to the hand-printing process. I told my client not to be concerned, as I had used the identical fabric for a different job with no difficulty.

The showroom called to advise when the fabric had arrived in their local warehouse. Ordinarily, I would have inspected it, but I was on my way to Canada for a three-week business trip. To keep the job going, I called my upholsterer. I told him to pick up the fabric and start work on the curtains, upholstery, and walls. The client's house was empty, as he lives in Europe a great deal of the time. I wanted all installations completed before his return.

When I returned from my trip, I went over to inspect the work. It was a disaster, and I was horrified. Something must have gone wrong with the printing, and the fabric is a mess. It is totally irregular and doesn't conform to the sample. The colors are off and vary from one "repeat" to the next. The designs barely resemble each other and look like several small rolls were combined.

I called my upholsterer and asked him why he used the fabric at all. He told me that he was just following my instructions because I was out of town. I called the fabric showroom. When the owner came to look at the den, he went into shock. My client will be back in a week. What should I do?

ANSWER: I told the designer to call his upholsterer immediately. He removed the furniture, curtains, and the fabric that had been upholstered on the walls. When the client returned, the designer told him that the fabric had been delivered but looked different from the sample. He explained that although that rarely occurred, he wouldn't reorder the fabric. Then he went shopping with his client and found something "in stock" so that work could start immediately.

The designer was able to conceal any evidence that work had been done with the original fabric. Although he had been a victim of circumstance and, to some degree, bad luck, the primary responsibility was the designer's. He had to take immediate measures to avoid losing credibility with his client. If he had done his job properly, he would have avoided sustaining any damages.

Ordering hand-printed fabrics can be risky. The odds are always higher that the order won't conform to the sample than when using conventionally screen-printed fabric. However, if you're dealing with a reliable vendor and all the potential hazards are explained to the client, fine. Take the chance.

When the fabric was delivered, it was the designer's obligation to have it inspected. Never accept a delivery on a custom item prior to inspection. The designer should have had his partner inspect it. Even though they didn't share clients, partners do come to each other's aid. Of course, it would have been inconvenient to have the showroom put it on a rolling machine to examine it, but it would have been well worth the time.

When designers have small offices and are overworked, one of their most important jobs is to delegate authority appropriately. This designer had accepted responsibility for approving a major order. Through his inadvertence, he compounded the risk by authorizing expensive "finishing" work as well. Any damages sustained were his immediate responsibility.

That didn't necessarily mean that the designer had to bear the ultimate cost. Even though the fabric was "accepted," it had been manufactured into other products, making it impossible to return. However, the showroom gave the designer full credit toward another fabric in stock.

Suppose the showroom hadn't been so cooperative. Then, the designer would have had to start a lawsuit. It would have probably resulted in, at least, a partial settlement. The probability of success in this type of case varies, depending on the jurisdiction. Consulting an attorney would be necessary to gauge one's chances of success more precisely. Unfortunately, it costs money to hire lawyers. This is not the type of negligence case that many attorneys would take on a contingency, that is, with the fee being a percentage of the recovery.

At first the upholsterer insisted on being paid for his work in full. He had been paid only a deposit. He claimed that he had followed the designer's instructions and was entitled to be compensated for his work. The designer then insisted on having a meeting with his attorney and the upholsterer with his own lawyer. The upholsterer agreed.

The designer made the following clear. Hand-printed fabrics must be accepted, even if there are slight irregularities, especially when language to that effect is printed on the showroom's purchase order. However, in this case, there were "gross imperfections." The product was totally unacceptable according to the standards of the trade. The fact that the fabric showroom provided a full credit was evidence of that.

The designer's attorney elaborated on the upholsterer's responsibilities. A custom upholsterer, he explained, is charged with the duty of having a certain amount of knowledge. He is responsible for knowing whether a fabric is defective. He should not have worked with obviously damaged goods unless the designer had physically approved them. This was not a case in which the fabric was "marginal" in quality. A serious error in judgment had been made, the attorney argued, and the upholsterer should at least absorb the cost of his own services.

Ultimately, that was the result. The upholsterer did not charge for all his initial work; however, the designer gave him the opportunity to redo the job with the new fabric. The upholsterer was very stubborn, but even his own attorney convinced him that he had been wrong.

Suppose the upholsterer hadn't cooperated and the designer refused to pay him? He may then have sued the designer and his client as joint defendants. The designer would have had to indemnify his client for any recovery, but even so, the entire fiasco would have been revealed. The designer would have appeared unprofessional. However, this designer was willing to take that chance. He refused to pay the upholsterer "hush money" simply to keep the matter quiet.

The upholsterer ultimately made the wisest decision, economically. It would have cost him considerable legal fees to sue the designer, and, ultimately, his lawyer advised, he had a good chance of losing the case. Although the curtains and the wall coverings were worthless, the sofas had already been built and needed only to be recovered. Financially, he still made a profit on the job .

Obviously, designers make mistakes. The interior design business is too detail oriented to maintain a near perfect record of decision making. However, keep one thought in mind. When taking shortcuts, deliberate for a moment about the financial consequences. If this designer had explored the potential repercussions of his snap decision, he wouldn't, for one second, have sacrificed time for money.

Wall Coverings

QUESTION: *I am a residential designer in Atlanta and have recently had a great deal of trouble with a wallpaper installation. My client lives in an old house. When I called the wall paper hanger, he said the walls needed special preparation because of the layers of paint that had accumulated over the years.*

The installer said that the solution was to apply two coats of a special primer. After the primer was applied, he started hanging the paper. While I was out of my office, he called my assistant. He told him the old paint was coming through the primer and the paper was peeling off the walls.

My assistant volunteered to supply a special adhesive glue. The adhesive ruined the paper entirely, and nine rolls needed to be replaced. I immediately hired another wallpaper installer, replaced the paper, and completed the installation. The original wallpaper hanger has kept the deposit for his services and refuses to pay for the paper, which he claims was ruined because of my assistant.

Am I responsible for replacing the paper and refunding the deposit to my client?

ANSWER: The designer would be liable for damages if he was negligent. Before the designer's behavior can be deemed negligent, it must be established that he had a *duty* to the wallpaper hanger, and that he breached that duty.

Did a duty exist? I don't think so. The designer specified the wallpaper. He delivered it to the installer. It was the installer's duty to state: "I can't hang it because of the condition of the walls," or "I can try, but I don't guarantee any results." But that's not what happened.

The wallpaper hanger assumed the responsibility of installing the paper. He advised the designer that certain preliminary steps were necessary and then started work. Unfortunately, he didn't select the proper method of application.

However, assume for the sake of argument that the designer did have a duty to the wallpaper hanger. Did he *breach* that duty? The duty would have been breached if the designer failed to act with the standard of care required. The standard of care is ascertained by predicting the actions of a "reasonable man." In other words, how would any reasonable designer have acted under the circumstances?

The answer is, the same way. Most designers hire reputable wallpaper installers. Once craftsmen are hired, designers generally follow their advice since their judgment is trusted. Assuming the first wallpaper installer was a reasonable choice, the designer complied with the "reasonable man" standard by following his instructions.

Was the interior designer the *cause* of the damage? It is true that it was the designer's idea to hang the wallpaper. He also hired that particular installer. Without those two events, the damage never would have occurred. However, were these decisions the "proximate cause" of the damage? No. While they were connected in the chain of events, it was the installer's application that caused the damage.

Was the damage *foreseeable*? Absolutely. However, the wallpaper installer assumed the risk. He identified the potential problem and recommended a special application. However, during the process, the wallpaper hanger took the advice of the designer's assistant. That was not foreseeable by the designer. Once the wallpaper hanger applied the primer and started the installation, it was *his* standard of care that came under scrutiny, not the designer's.

It appears, therefore, that the designer complied with the standard of care. But what about his assistant? Although the designer is responsible for the acts of his employees, that applies only if those actions were pursuant to the designer's authority. Certainly, a designer would never authorize his assistant to give a professional technical advice about a specific application. That information is not within the scope of his expertise. Therefore, the wallpaper hanger should have known better than to use the assistant's adhesive.

Obviously, the designer was not responsible for the damage. The liability rests with the wallpaper hanger. He should refund the deposit and pay for the damaged wallpaper. Since the answer is obvious, isn't this a tortured method of reaching a simple conclusion? However, some jobs require 15 installers to work on the same area. When something goes wrong, a methodology is necessary, sometimes, to place liability correctly.

How can you figure out when a designer is liable for negligence? Try asking these questions once again: Does the designer have a duty to act? Was the duty breached? Did the designer act using the "reasonable man" standard as a guide? Did the designer cause the damage? Was the damage foreseeable? Was the damage closely connected to the designer's actions so as to impute liability?

It is sometimes very difficult to determine a designer's liability. The task can be compared to searching for a design solution for a given space. There are many alternatives, of course, but which is the right one?

Mirror Work and Cabinetry

In this category, two cases are discussed. Since glass is a fragile medium, it is of the utmost importance that experts perform any installation. The two casualties described here may remind you always to use extreme caution.

QUESTION: *I am an interior designer in Seattle and am known for contemporary interiors with custom installations. I designed a mirrored sliding door for a client, who was thrilled with the concept. I had the door built by an excellent carpenter. It was hung on a track that was bolted into the ceiling. After construction* *was completed, the mirror work was applied at considerable expense by one of the finest mirror vendors in the state.*

I didn't design a lower track, and the carpenter and mirror man didn't think one was necessary. Apparently, it was. One panel shattered, possibly because the door swung too freely. At that point, a lower track was installed. I called the carpenter and mirror man to help determine the reason for the broken panel. Neither of them knew, but both were quick to avoid any blame.

I think my client, or one of his guests, simply knocked into the panel, but I can't prove it. My client claims the damage occurred because there was no lower track. Now he insists that I have the door repaired for no charge.

I don't feel responsible, although I haven't told my client yet. My client hired me because of my unique design ability. All other aspects of the job are innovative and perfect. As far as I'm concerned, this is just a "design casualty" for which there is no explanation. However, I am concerned that I will have to pay for this. Aren't my carpenter and mirror man partly responsible?

ANSWER: This was a typical situation that required analysis of responsibilites before coming to a conclusion. Unfortunately, some of the most innovative and creative designers don't use common sense when resolving troubles on the job.

This designer emphasized that he had earned his reputation with custom designs that required special installations. Any design must be fit for the purpose for which it is intended.

The designer's attitude disturbed me for two reasons. First, he had defended himself by saying that all other aspects of the job had been completed with no problem. Why shouldn't they have been? That logic can't be used as an excuse to justify a design error.

Second, the designer also mentioned that he had been hired because of his unique design ability. He believed that a client should be willing to endure a design casualty when taking innovative risks. I think that is an unprofessional attitude. A designer shouldn't produce anything for a client that doesn't work. If a designer thinks that there could be a risk, then his client should agree in advance.

In this situation, the designer conceived the design and convinced his client to create it. He had been careful to select fine craftsmen. However, it was his first experience in designing a hanging mirrored door, which was fragile and expensive. A designer with a different outlook may have taken the same risk. However, he could have minimized his own liability by using the procedures described in the following paragraphs.

If you are ever in a similar situation, consult with your craftsmen before you build an untried design. If they have reservations, note them and proceed with caution. Then talk to your client. Tell him the truth: The design is untested. It should work, but the material is fragile.

Don't guarantee success. Indicate that repair costs might be necessary in creating a prototype. Then leave the decision up to your client. It is simply amazing, despite all these warnings, that some clients will proceed nonetheless. In any event, the designer can protect himself even if the outcome isn't ideal.

If no damage results, the designer is a hero. If problems do arise, at least the client has been forewarned. Before building a prototype, warn the client about any risks in a letter. Then, if a problem arises later, the client can't conveniently "forget" that he was warned.

Obviously, it was too late for the designer in this example to use these strategies. He had to repair the damage immediately to rectify his relationship with his client. As the client hadn't been warned about a potential design problem, he had naturally expected his designer to assume full responsibility.

As far as litigation was concerned, I told the designer to ask himself several questions before suing his suppliers: Are their services unique? Do you want to use them again? Were you warned about potential damage before building the installation? Did they perform the work according to your instructions? (Was the track hung securely? Was the mirror work finished properly?) If a designer's instructions are followed and he does not object after work has been performed, it is unlikely that he has any recourse against his craftsmen.

The fact that a subsequent installation of a lower track corrected the problem was proof of the faulty design. The designer found the solution, but too late. Obviously, the door swung too freely and needed to be stabilized. The design required modification. Furthermore, the client believed that design error was the reason for the broken panel.

Ultimately, the designer ended up paying for repairs—a very costly outcome. Always remember one crucial point before embarking on this kind of venture. An innovative designer, who wants his client to take risks to satisfy mutual creative endeavors, must develop great skill and style in client relations. Otherwise, he should specify only safe design solutions that will meet his client's needs.

QUESTION: *I am an interior designer in Scottsdale, Arizona, and have been working with an older couple on their condominium for almost a year. They have prolonged the job with their obsession for the wrong details and have insisted on using their own carpenter. While his work is adequate, I do not consider it to be fine cabinetwork.*

The wife had several storage cabinets, including dressers, custom-built for her walk-in closet. She wants them all mirrored, including the doors. The carpenter has finished the cabinets and says that they are ready to be mirrored. Based on the construction, I don't know how good they will look if they're mir-

rored. Also, since glass is fragile, I'm concerned about damage once the work is completed.

The mirror company says that the cabinet imperfections won't show when the mirror work is finished. However, it won't assume any liability for damage. When I explained all this to my client, she told me in an exasperated voice, "I'm leaving all this in your hands." I don't want to assume responsibility. What can I do to protect myself?

ANSWER: I told this designer that she was being very conscientious about providing adequate supervision. However, since her client insisted on using her own carpenter, it was not the designer's responsibility to guarantee the result.

After hiring her own contractor, the client had no right to place the responsibility for the mirrored furniture on the designer's shoulders. Before the mirror work was undertaken, the designer had to disclaim all liability. Therefore, the designer's next step was to send her client a letter.

The letter contained the following information: The designer recommended using a skilled cabinetmaker to build the furniture and doors; however, the client hired a different carpenter against her advice. Although the designer would continue to supervise, at the client's insistence, she did not feel that the finished product would meet a minimum standard. Although the mirror company is an excellent choice, it will not be responsible for subsequent damage due to faulty construction of the cabinets or doors. Before proceeding further, the designer would recommend hiring another cabinetmaker to attempt to make necessary corrections prior to the mirror installation.

After receiving the letter, the client called her designer and told her that she was satisfied with the cabinetwork. She also told her to proceed with the mirror work. Then, the designer asked me what her liability was at that point.

I told the designer that since the client chose to ignore her warnings, she was covered regardless of the outcome. If the job turned out well, fine. However, if the work didn't look good or the doors subsequently cracked, the designer was in the clear. Of course, that didn't mean that she would be exonerated in her client's eyes. In fact, the client might become angrier because she had no one to blame but herself.

This case brings another factor into the discussion of designer liability. If the furniture were lacquered or covered in fabric, for example, the designer wouldn't have been saddled with this problem. Of course, the finished product may not have looked as good as the designer had hoped. However, that's not the designer's fault. Since the client had selected her own cabinetmaker, it wasn't the designer's responsibility if the workmanship was inferior. The added risk lay in dealing with a fragile material, such as glass, that could ruin the entire installation if it wasn't handled properly.

There are different procedures that can help circumvent a situation like this one. The easiest is to insist on a client's hiring the contractors of the designer's choice. Some clients will agree. Others, however, want to send plans out for bid to compare prices. If a designer insists on using specific contractors, clients sometimes assume that he is obtaining kickbacks, or illegal commissions.

A less stringent but still effective approach is to encourage a client to select her own general contractor but to use the designer's "specialty" subcontractors for areas requiring particular expertise. For instance: A well-known New York painting contractor usually charges at least one third more than "quality painters." However, a number of prominent designers hire the company specifically for specialty treatments, such as glazing or lacquering walls. A New York manufacturer of custom furniture is an acknowledged expert in producing goatskin-covered furniture of flawless quality. Since goatskin can discolor, peel, or deteriorate if it isn't applied properly, many designers refuse to specify furniture in this finish unless it's purchased from that company.

The time to insist is the moment the design issue arises on the project. So, for example, when the client told the designer that she wanted mirrored doors and furniture, the designer should have said, "I'll be glad to design them, but not if your carpenter is going to build them. I'll supervise his work in all other areas. But when it comes to mirrored furniture, that's another matter. Unless you hire my cabinetmaker, I don't want any involvement with that part of the project. Mirrored furniture and moveable doors are too risky to attempt unless experts are used. My cabinetmaker is the only one I trust."

Many younger designers are sometimes reluctant to use this approach. They feel it makes them appear too overbearing, tending to "turn the client off." However, the crux of the matter is that they're too insecure about themselves, financially or professionally, to insist on using reliable contractors who will spare them from undue problems. Frequently, once designers mature, they refuse to design and execute special details unless the client employs their craftsmen.

General Construction and Carpentry

QUESTION: *I am an interior designer in Indianapolis. I finished designing a suite of commercial offices, approximately 5000 square feet, about six months ago. My client called me last week and sounded very angry.*

Some of the installations are falling apart, and he acted as if it is my fault. I went over to inspect the site and was very disappointed with the condition of the office. The wall paneling is buckling in several major areas. Many of the carpentry details look shoddy, including custom cabinetwork that has begun to delaminate. Even the paint job has started peeling in some areas.

The client had insisted on hiring a contractor who had done a lot of work in his office building. I know he used him because he thought he got a special deal. I had recommended my own contractor, who does excellent work but was much more expensive. When I told my client that he would be better off using my contractor, he claimed he couldn't afford him.

I suggested consulting with my contractor to provide an estimate to make all the necessary repairs. My client claimed that I was partly responsible for the damage because I allowed his contractor to use second-rate materials and didn't properly supervise.

That is not true. Once construction started, I had very little to say about the implementation of my drawings. My client and the contractor made most of the decisions. Every time I made a suggestion, I was basically ignored. Do I have any responsibility?

ANSWER: I advised the designer not to panic. As he insisted that he had performed his services diligently, I didn't think that he had any liability for his client's damages.

The client had selected the building contractor and had dealt with him directly. Therefore, the designer had no responsibility for the defective workmanship. He hadn't been an important part of their working relationship, but, on the contrary, had recommended a different contractor.

Under similar circumstances, when supervising construction for a client, your obligations are (1) to provide a workable design plan, (2) to specify appropriate materials, and (3) to inspect construction to make sure the work conforms to the plans.

The defects in this case had no relationship to the design plans, schedules, sketches, or floor plans. For instance, there was no improper partitioning of an area as could have resulted from errors on a partition drawing or plan. Further, the designer had prepared purchase orders for all goods and design services, a standard procedure. These purchase orders served as a record of the designer's competence in terms of material authorization. They had been approved by the client prior to submission to the vendors and contractor.

A specific problem was the buckling of the wood paneling on the walls. Obviously, that damage can stem from a number of different sources unrelated to the designer's work. Improper installation or leaks in the walls of the structure itself can cause buckling. As far as the designer was concerned, he recommended appropriate wall paneling for the job. It was the contractor's job to install it properly. Of course, the designer had the duty to inspect the installation. In this case, however, the contractor basically ignored him. Since he wasn't recommended by the designer, the designer had very little leverage to enforce his suggestions.

If you are supervising design applications and become aware that the contractor is ignoring the manufacturer's specifcations and your advice, tell your client immediately. Send him a written memorandum to protect yourself from any subsequent reprisals. Some designers refuse to undertake projects unless they think that the contractor has the technical competence to implement their plans. Most designers, unfortunately, don't have that luxury, as the example illustrates. Accordingly, if a contractor refuses to acknowledge your supervision, you can only document every error during the course of the job, making certain that your client receives a written memorandum to that effect.

You are not ultimately responsible for the supervision of workmanship. Even if you make an error or omission, the contractor shares the responsibility. He must perform the work according to minimum standards of craftsmanship. For this reason, it is most advantageous to the client if the designer and contractor have worked together before.

The designer in the example advised his client that the material specification was appropriate and that he had adequately supervised installations. He also mentioned that the damage was the result of the contractor's poor workmanship and reminded the client that he had recommended another contractor.

The client, unfortunately, wasn't pacified with this explanation. He replied that, surely, the designer must have noticed the poor quality of workmanship during construction. The designer then produced copies of three letters that he had sent his client during construction. Each letter was a criticism of the work by the general contractor. The client said that he had never received the letters.

Ultimately, the case went to court. The designer was sued as a codefendant with the contractor. The designer presented his own evidence on "summary judgment" and was dismissed as a codefendant before the case ever went to trial.

In any event, if you ever become involved in a similar situation, respond to your client at once. Indicate that you are willing to help supervise the repairs but also advise that you have satisfied your obligations. Feel free to charge for your additional services if your client wants your assistance. Don't be placed in a defensive position when you are not responsible for any damages.

WHEN IT'S WISE NOT TO SUPERVISE CONTRACTORS

Do you have clients who hire their own contractors, using your plans and specifications, in an attempt to pay a cheaper price and avoid paying design fees? Do these clients ask you to supervise these installations without any payment? The following illustrates a typical situation:

QUESTION: *I am a residential designer in Aspen, Colorado. I prepared a complete set of design plans for a client's house, including a furniture layout, cabinet designs, painting and wall covering schedule, and specifications for all flooring and floor coverings.*

I charged a small flat design fee for preparing these plans because I also charge cost plus 30 percent for all purchases and contracting. This includes supervising the installations. My client approved the design plans.

I sent the plans for cabinetry and flooring to excellent contractors with whom I've worked before. I also contacted two painting contractors who do quality work.

The project was a complete renovation of a four-bedroom house. It took several weeks to prepare the plans and schedules, meet with the contractors, and obtain the bids. Once I had all the estimates, I met with my clients, a husband and wife, for review. They approved the purchase orders for the furniture and furnishings but told me to wait on the contracting.

Ten days later, the husband called me. He said that the estimates for the contracting were outrageous and that he was going to hire his own contractors. Then he told me that he wasn't going to pay me a percentage on the contracting, because he was using his own sources. He still wants me to supervise the contractors but wants to pay an hourly rate.

I feel that I have been manipulated but am not sure of what to do. What is your recommendation?

ANSWER: When the designer consulted me, I asked her whether she had any inkling of this problem during initial client interviews or during the design planning phase. On the contrary, she said the clients had wanted to use her sources.

Of course, I told her that the decision was hers, but by charging by the hour for supervision, she would have to sacrifice income. From a financial point of view, she would earn about half as much on an hourly basis as on cost plus 30 percent, the fee the clients agreed to in the contract. It seemed also that the husband was breaching the contract and renegotiating on his terms without the designer's consent.

When the designer showed me her estimates, they appeared within reason, indicating two other factors: Her clients may never have intended to pay a commission on the contracting, merely using the letter of agreement as bait to obtain design plans for a low fee. Even more provoking, to obtain appreciably lower estimates, they may have hired inferior contractors.

There is nothing worse for a designer than being involved in a botched job. If contractors provide poor installations, they can invariably drive clients, as well as the designer, to the breaking point.

If these clients had wanted to substitute only one contractor, that would have been understandable. However, a complete substitution told a different story. It is much more difficult for a designer to work with contractors who are an "unknown commodity" than to work with sources with whom she has an existing relationship and prior history. Since the designer didn't know the clients' contractors, she felt she had no authority to supervise. She had also been compromised financially.

The designer advised her clients that she would supervise the delivery of the furniture and furnishings but refused to supervise the contracting. The husband became extremely nervous when the designer refused to bend. Ultimately, he agreed to use her sources and pay her on a cost-plus basis, the terms of the original contract.

I know several very successful designers who handle this problem in a different way. The have a clause in their letter of agreement to this effect:

> In the event you do not use any of the contractors or sources or workmen recommended by our office, there will be an additional 10 percent design fee on the cost of these sources that you obtain on your own behalf.

Obviously, this statement shows a very independent attitude, waving a red flag early in the relationship. It really forbids clients to hire any sources of their own. However, some designers have had such bad experiences with clients' contractors that they don't care how this pronouncement is received.

Supervising contractors on a residential job is quite different from working with a general contractor for the renovation of an office building. A residential job is a painstaking process, requiring a great deal of attention. If a designer can't work with reliable sources, make a reasonable fee, and control the job, it's not worth the effort. The need to face financial compromises and uncertainty as to supervision are issues confronting designers repeatedly. They must be dealt with carefully.

CONCLUSION

The designer should not bear the responsibility for the quality of the work on a job. If a general contractor is retained, he is liable. If there is no general contractor, the designer must make certain that the contractors are legally responsible to the client.

Of course, the designer must make periodic visits to the site to be certain that the contracting work conforms to the design plans. If "simple decorating" is involved and there is no general contractor, the designer must supervise closely but is not responsible for faulty workmanship. As heavily emphasized in this book, using quality craftsmen makes life easier.

The same logic applies to goods that are ordered by the designer. The designer should not be personally liable for any defects. However, designers often lament, "I know I'm not responsible, but my clients always point the finger at me. I am always placed on the defensive, as if everything is always my fault." That's because designers are the most visible and available targets. The key is to specify and supervise carefully, using caution as a precise weapon.

When faced with a predicament in which a designer might be liable for damages, I initially consider the presumption in regard to our system of criminal justice: "A person is presumed innocent until proven guilty."

15

CONSULTING WITH CLIENTS

This book discusses how to run an interior design business mainly from the legal and financial points of view. Also important to any designer is how to consult with clients and acquire new business. The following discussion is not intended to be a comprehensive treatment of the subject, but presents techniques that may be helpful to designers in consulting with clients.

PREPARING A PORTFOLIO

It is extremely important to own a portfolio that will help you get clients. You must learn what to put in and leave out, what the total effect should be, and how to present yourself as successful and professional. You can study how the experts make their own dramatic statements. Experience will teach you what you have to do to capture the client's attention, gain his confidence, and convince him that you are the best possible choice.

Although your portfolio evolves continuously, when finished, its style, look, and flexibility should make a statement that will help to close deals successfully.

It isn't a very difficult task for a seasoned interior designer with a number of finished projects to assemble a portfolio. All completed work *must be well photographed*. If the material has been published in shelter magazines, all the better. The real problem arises when a designer is beginning his career and desperately needs a portfolio to attract new clients, as the following question illustrates:

QUESTION: *I am a young interior designer and have just started my own business with another young designer. After graduating from design school, we worked for different firms—one a large contract firm, and the other a small residential one. A number of clients have been referred to us. Unfortunately, we don't have a big portfolio to show prospective clients. We need new jobs, not only* *for fees, but also to build up our portfolio. What do we use now to show new clients?*

ANSWER: Since the designers had worked for firms where their work had been published, their first step was to assemble tearsheets from the magazines of the published articles. In some cases, the designers had been given written credit for their participation. They used these articles in their portfolio, explaining to clients their participation in each project.

Both designers had saved the projects they had completed in design school, and several of the floor plans looked very professional. The designers had them photographed, reduced in size to fit their portfolio.

After their existing materials were assembled, they reviewed a list of techniques that many designers use in assembling their first portfolios.

Some designers have their own residence and office photographed for their portfolios. These may often be used as backdrops for a color story. Many designers borrow furniture, accessories, and antiques from friends or on "memo," or consignment, from vendors. They hire a photographer and photograph the rooms from different angles, styling them in various ways using indoor plants and flowers. The same location can be made to look like two or three different interiors by a clever designer.

A word of caution: Express your own design philosophy but don't make it too extreme. If you have a limited number of photographs, choose designs that are distinctive, tasteful, and saleable. When meeting with prospective clients, display an environment to which they can relate. You want them to visualize how your ideas can be used for their own project.

Photographs of table settings can also be useful additions to a portfolio. They demonstrate the taste and ability of a designer in selecting and assembling accessories. Borrow dining rooms of friends or persuade vendors to let you photograph their furniture on showroom floors. Table settings are relatively simple to assemble and can be completed in a short time. You can photograph two or three compositions within a matter of weeks.

"Before and after" stories fill out a portfolio. A typical favorite is a temporary vacation residence such as a summer beach house. In a rental or newly purchased home, for example, the "before" photograph may show a nondescript interior. When the space has been redesigned with furniture, accessories, and plants, the "after" photograph will demonstrate your ability. Moreover, because budgets are generally limited for this type of project, you might say to your client, for example, "I redesigned this rental beach house for $20,000." Resourcefulness on a low budget always creates a positive impression.

Some designers begin with a typical design layout for one specific space. Then they create several alternative designs for the same space, using black-and-white or full-color renderings. For a project like this, hire a professional if you don't draw well. It will be expensive but worth the cost if the product looks professional.

Many portfolios contain the designer's resume, a summary of his education and work history. It is also wise to include a business card, which should have a professional logo using a creative graphic approach. Resume and card are particularly important if it is necessary to send the portfolio to a prospective client in a different geographic area.

Once a portfolio becomes substantial, it can be divided into separate volumes—one for residential work and the other for corporate or commercial work. If time allows, show all prospective clients both portfolios. A residential client might like an approach used in a commercial project, and vice versa. In any event, separate portfolios illustrate that you have two different areas of expertise.

It is sometimes smart to edit a portfolio prior to presentation to a particular client. For example, if you will be meeting with a client who likes traditional design, omit some of your contemporary work. Add photographs of traditional projects that might not otherwise be displayed in your portfolio.

Knowing how to assemble a portfolio is an important skill to master. Presenting it properly to potential clients may be of equal importance. A designer should use his portfolio to show his versatility in meeting his clients' needs. For example, when showing some of the photographs, point out why certain design decisions were made.

Contemporary spaces, for instance, are often designed specifically to accommodate a client's art collection. Interiors with minimal furniture and neutral backgrounds are often designed for single clients who want environments as maintenance-free as possible. Ceramic tiled floors are favorites with home owners who have pets and children. The rationale should be explained when displaying a photograph of an interior designed for a specific purpose. Most clients have particular reasons for choosing specific design solutions. Emphasize these reasons when explaining "background" design.

Preparing a portfolio is, to some degree, an acquired skill. But even at the beginning, the more work a designer puts into its development, the better the result will be and the more clients it will attract.

Other chapters of this book have provided instruction on preparing financial proposals for commercial and residential projects. When successful designers prepare a proposal for a potential client, or even a brief letter responding to an inquiry, they frequently enclose a color brochure showing photographs of a project. Ideally, the brochure is a reprint from a prestigous magazine. Some designers use special binders containing several reprints with a list of completed projects, both commercial and residential. Others list names of prestigious clients, with their addresses, to be used as references.

A handout portfolio, containing reprints and recommendations, is an invaluable tool for a designer. If you haven't had your favorite projects photographed by a magazine, consider photographing a project and having brochures printed. Clients often interview a number of designers before making a decision. They may become confused or forget the interiors they liked after viewing the portfolios. Reprints leave a lasting impression. A wife can use one to remind a husband about which designer she wants to hire. An officer of a corporation can use one at a meeting of a board of directors to show why he wants to retain a specific firm. This is a very important marketing tool and is well worth the investment.

CONSULTING WITH THE CLIENT AND GETTING THE JOB

The skill with which you conduct your early client consultations can determine whether you get the job. After a certain amount of practice, you will eventually learn how to develop a relationship in the early phases.

Generally, your contact with a new client begins with a telephone call. Always ask how you were recommended—through a personal or professional contact, a publication, or another source. Encourage the client to describe the project. Let him do most of the talking. Chances are, he will anyway. Be an attentive listener and show enthusiasm. Assuming that the phone interview is successful, the next step is a face-to-face meeting.

The first meeting often sets the stage for the entire relationship. The client will size you up. Many designers are uncertain as to how to present themselves at a first meeting, as the following example illustrates.

QUESTION: *My partner and I have recently started a business after working for small but well-established design firms for several years. Our former employers were widely published and had impressive offices and large portfolios.*

Our old bosses generally had one or two brief meetings with prospective clients and always acted very low-key. We think we need to be more assertive, since we are totally unknown. How do we maintain our professional image while assertively marketing our company?

ANSWER: Less experienced designers may have to use different approaches than their more experienced competition. For example, some designers travel to the project site before their clients meet them at their offices for the initial interview. That way, they can speak knowledgeably with the client about his project at the first meeting. These designers also avoid talking about fees and budgets until they have personally met with the client, visited the project, and decided how to charge.

One way to "sell" to a client is to outline, with a fair amount of precision, how you will handle the project. Many designers develop a step-by-step working procedure that tells a client what he will get for his money. A proper presentation of this procedure can serve two purposes. First, it will educate the client about the way a design project operates (many have no idea, having had no prior experience). Second, it will emphasize that a massive amount of work needs to be done and will clarify the designer's roles and responsibilities.

If you use a project assistant, he should be present at all initial meetings as well. Although most designers have their own specific methods of handling a project, the following paragraphs outline a typical working procedure that you can adapt as you wish when being interviewed by a prospective client.

Step-by-Step Working Procedure

1. **Space Evaluation.** Many clients consult designers before buying or leasing residential and commercial space. At that time, the designer is often encouraged to give her opinion about various issues, such as "usability of space," aesthetic appeal, and the functional aspects of design. Most designers feel much freer to be totally frank about the space *before* the client has taken it. Don't talk a client out of the space if he really wants it. He'll just end up hiring another designer. In commercial situations, designers often advise their clients about the conditions relevant to signing a lease—painting, construction, partitioning, flooring, and so on.

2. **Interview on Space Requirements and Personal Preferences.** Clients, particularly in residential cases, react to the personal. They love to talk about what they like. They want to be convinced not only of the designer's professionalism, but also her responsiveness to what they want. There are a number of ways to do this. Many designers ask their clients' "likes," "dislikes," "must haves," and "don't wants." When you request the preparation of these lists, ask the following questions:

a. *Colors.* Does the client like pastels or primary hues, bright colors or muted, subdued tones with accents? Does he prefer light living rooms? Dark bedrooms? In commercial situations, should colors from a company's stationery or packaging be incorporated?

b. *Style of design.* Does the client favor contemporary, traditional, neoclassical, or minimal design? Some clients have strong preferences; others don't know what they like. Your portfolio should be broad enough that the client will feel that you can give him what he wants. If it's not, consider showing slides or assemble a portfolio with several different styles of interiors.

c. *Materials.* What kinds of basic materials does the client like? Does he like marble, wood, or ceramic? Does he prefer a traditional approach of taffeta or velvet or the informality of leather and canvas? Some designers elicit these preferences by showing sample boards from previous jobs exhibiting different materials.

d. *Lifestyle.* Is the client single, married, or divorced? Does she have children? Does she entertain, enjoy cooking, listening to music? What are her hobbies? How does she spend her leisure time? Does she like antiques or collect art? Does she need space for a piano or other large musical instrument? Does she own a pet—perhaps a large dog that destroys furniture? Does she have any health problems—allergies or a heightened sensitivity to noise or light? Does she need special accommodations for guests? Does the client insist on a dining table that seats 12, which will be used only at Thanksgiving? Clients should be thoroughly questioned to determine whether their "musts" are really as important as they may initially believe them to be. Would an expandable dining table be more appropriate than a large, permanent dining space that would be used infrequently?

   An extremely important issue for many clients is the amount of storage space. Clients are often obsessed with storage, particularly those who are collectors or compulsive shoppers and savers. You should find out whether the space requested is for primary or secondary use. It is always important to know how long your client has lived in the space and what he likes or dislikes about it.

e. *Existing furniture or antiques.* What does your client own now that he wants to put in the newly designed space? Ask for a complete inventory. It is important to know what furniture he has before discussing materials or preparing a visual presentation.

Some clients are better than others about expressing their preferences and making these lists. Some cannot easily visualize. A designer once told me that a client of hers said, in an exasperated tone, "I can't make these lists. I don't know what I like or what I don't like." Ask these particular clients (although you should suggest this to all clients) to submit pictures from books or magazines of interiors that they like. Let them also submit pictures of furniture, window treatments, rugs, fabrics, and so forth.

One very important caution: Find out which client is going to be making the design decisions. With married couples, you can usually tell immediately. Single people often have someone in the background whose opinion is solicited before a decision is made. Find out who it is and meet with him from the very first interview. For example, a designer complained that one client made final decisions on Fridays but always changed his mind completely by the following Tuesdays. Finally the client revealed that before signing any purchase orders, he always checked with his business partner to see what he liked.

In dealing with corporate clients, you need to know who has the final design approval and who issues purchase orders. Request that only one person be designated so that you don't have to answer to several individuals separately.

Most of the preceding considerations pertain to both residential and commerical clients. Life-style preferences tend to be less exacting for commercial projects, however, because the client is generally more pragmatic. The space must function well and be aesthetically pleasing, but the client doesn't live there. Of course, at times, especially in part- nerships, none of the partners or their wives can agree on what is best for the firm. For this reason, apartment buildings and hotel lobbies are notoriously difficult to design.

3. *Survey of Existing Architectural Conditions.* Surveying and measur- ing the space are, of course, prerequisites of any serious design plans. Never rely on building floor plans or existing blueprints. Generally, there is no way to vouch for their accuracy, and if there are errors, you will be held responsible. Tell your client, during your early inter- views, that you will undertake a survey of existing conditions. How- ever, make sure your letter of agreement is signed and that you have received a retainer check before you spend any time or money. Even before entering your client's premises, obtain written permission to present to the building manager and the superintendent. Keep a copy for your own files. These letters are legal safeguards. Naturally, you'll also need a set of keys.

4. *Feasibility (Space) Study.* As I have emphasized, you have to con- vince a prospective client that your design ability will satisfy his

needs. Your residential client's needs should be researched in the first or second interview, as indicated earlier.

However, in commercial situations, feasibility studies are sometimes quite involved and often don't commence until your client has signed the contract. In the early interviews, however, you can explain the purpose of a feasibility space study and indicate that it takes the following aspects into consideration:

Type of business
Number of principals involved
Number of employees
Number of private offices and departments
Number of clerical and secretarial spaces
Space requirements for office machinery, computers, telephones, faxes, etc.
Traffic flow pattern

Depending on the type of commercial client, the list can be endless and will vary markedly from business to business. For example, one of my clients, a commercial designer, has frequently been retained by brokerage firms to design specialty desk and telephone systems for traders. This requirement necessitates an intensive study to analyze the client's precise needs. During the initial interviews, define the scope of the feasibility study and its purpose.

5. *Visual Presentation.* During your first meeting, explain to your client how the visual presentation operates. For example, designers generally present a floor plan, furniture layout, some schematic drawings, and even full-color renderings. Material samples and pictures of furnishings may be attached to display boards that mark and describe each area and room. You may display samples of flooring; mirror, wall, and window treatments; fabrics, pictures of furniture, and lighting, and so forth. The designer should allow sufficient time at the meeting for a complete presentation and should insist that his client earmark the same period of time on his own agenda. All work presented should be thoroughly researched, and the designer should be prepared to answer any questions.

Some designers stage the visual presentation at the design site to enable their clients to visualize easily how the space will look. Most designers, however, want to conduct the presentation at their own offices. Generally, clients change at least 20 percent of the proposal, and if the designer can show alternatives from examples and catalogs on hand in his office sample room, final decisions can be facilitated. It also helps to have a member of the design firm's staff available to take notes of client objections and to document the approved changes.

Before the presentation, double-check to make sure that all proposed selections are still available. A designer once designed a living room and a library, with all selections approved by his client. Then he discovered, to his dismay, that most of the selections had been discontinued six months previously.

Some designers provide their clients with a preliminary budget at this stage. If you do, make sure that all prices are current. (The psychology of presenting and discussing budgets is thoroughly covered in Chapters 2 and 4).

After all substitutions have been resolved, be sure your client indicates his final approval by initialing all sample boards and other presentation memoranda.

6. *Preparation of Schematic Drawings and Design Plans.* Most prospective clients are unfamiliar with the amount of work that goes into a full set of design plans. Accordingly, many designers show them a sample set from another project so they can understand what is entailed.

For commercial projects, designers who are licensed architects may prepare a full set of architectural working drawings. As discussed in Chapter 13, "Working With Architects," designers who aren't licensed architects must not prepare any documents that are legally required to be prepared by an architect. However, designers often collaborate in a joint venture with architects to prepare a set of drawings for a project. The following is a typical list of drawings:

Existing conditions
Demolition
Construction
Reflected ceilings
Electrical and telephone
Finish schedules (paint and wall coverings)
Cabinetwork
Hardware

Advise your clients that preparing the drawings is probably the costliest and most difficult phase of the project, as drafting is expensive and time-consuming.

Don't prepare extensive, detailed cabinet drawings for residential projects unless you are fairly certain that the client wants to finance the construction to implement the plans. In their enthusiasm about a total design concept, some designers prepare all the drawings without first obtaining preliminary estimates. When the contractors bid on the job and the client balks at the cost, much work has been wasted.

If clients are shown sample sets of drawings during initial consultations, they often complain that they cannot interpret them. Explain that you will take them to the project and measure out furniture and cabinetwork with tape or chalk so they can visualize your designs. Remind them, also, that you will supply a rendering and sketches at the visual presentation (if that's part of your program).

Once the drawings have been reviewed and approved by the client, send them out to the contractors for written bids. A dated cover letter should accompany them and include any last-minute changes not incorporated, perhaps, in the drawings. Before sending the drawings, notify the selected contractors in advance, so that they will be aware that your drawings are being submitted for bid. Specify a deadline date. Tell your client that you can't proceed on the project until all bids are received, so that he won't make any needless revisions or additions until the budget figures have been analyzed.

The next three steps—7 through 9—do not usually have to be explained in great detail in the initial client consultations. Brief summaries for each step are provided here for purposes of continuity and information if, in fact, a prospective client does question you about them.

7. *Review and Evaluation of Construction and Cabinet Bids.* Once all bids have been received from contractors and subcontractors, most changes and eliminations will usually be made for budget reasons. Clients often eliminate some of their earlier "needs and requirements" once they see hard budget figures. Bids are analyzed, changes are finalized, and contractors and subcontractors are consulted again to determine the revised budget.

8. *Submission of Final Budget.* After the final budgets for construction, cabinetwork, and furnishings have been revised, they should be carefully organized and presented to the client at a final meeting. Don't forget to include sales tax and delivery charges. Some designers add an additional 10 percent contingency in the event of price increases or substitutions.

9. *Preparation and Issuance of Purchase Orders on All Goods and Construction.* Information on preparation of purchase orders is presented in Chapter 12. However, for purposes of continuity, it is repeated here.

Systematically incorporate everything from the budget(s) on all purchase orders; be careful not to leave anything out. Usually, the most complex purchase order or series of purchase orders are those for construction. Some designers use their floor plans and prepare the orders on a room-by-room basis.

If you intend to act as the client's agent for payment, you will usually prepare an estimate for him, and he will forward you a deposit as required. Then, you will prepare a purchase order to be sent directly to the vendor.

If the client is going to make his own purchases and payments, you will prepare the purchase order for his use in triplicate. One copy is retained for your files; another is forwarded to the vendor by the client, and a third is kept by the client for his own files. Have the client initial your copy, indicating his approval. This is extremely important.

When forwarding these purchase orders to the client, many designers wisely include a cover letter, as illustrated in the following example.

Date
Dear (Name of Client)

Attached please find enclosed purchase order #_____, dated January 15,   . Please send your check directly to the vendor and fill in the following information for our records:

    Amount of Check:
    Name of Vendor:
    Name of Bank and Check Number:
    Please process this letter as soon as possible and return a copy to our office to enable us to check on your order.

                Very truly yours,

                Name of PRINCIPAL of Design Firm

Once the cover letter has been returned to you, you will know that the order has been processed and will be able to check up on it if necessary.

Before preparing any orders, ask your client what name should be listed as the "purchaser." For example, some residential clients may instruct you to list their business as the purchaser for tax reasons. Accordingly, don't prepare the orders before checking with the client to avoid the possibility of having to redo them because the incorrect name was used.

10. *Job Supervision and Implementation of Design.* Although your letter of agreement will state that responsibility for the quality and supervision of the construction is the obligation of the general contractor, advise prospective clients that you will be at the job site as necessary with a set of design plans to make any on-the-spot changes if unexpected field conditions arise. For example, if recessed cabinets are to be installed after demolition of a wall, a beam might unexpectedly become revealed that would prohibit that sort of installation. You must, as the designer, make the necessary adaptation. However, if the adjustment is an architectural change, you must confer with the architect who prepared the plans. He must be responsible for all architectural supervision.

11. *Move-in Supervision.* A discussion of move-in at initial meetings can have a very positive effect. With a large, vague project looming before him, a client likes to feel that project completion is a foreseeable reality.

Advise your client that deliveries of furniture can be handled in two ways. It is best to warehouse all the goods at one centrally located location until you are ready to make one final installation. Clients are often confused by piecemeal deliveries. Each piece may look "wrong" until all the furnishings are put together. If your client will not allow you to do this, try at least to arrange for all major deliveries to be made within a one-week period.

Your step-by-step procedure is one of the most valuable selling tools for impressing a prospective client. If hired, of course you will request a retainer and set forth your client's financial commitments in a contract. It only makes sense to sell the client on the amount of work, time, and professional skill that is necessary to undertake and complete the job.

16

CREATIVITY AND CONFUSION:
Why Designers Don't Make Money

Many interior designers complain that they aren't making "enough" money. I am not necessarily referring to beginners, but to designers whose work appears in the best publications, whose designs are licensed for products, whose names are well known and highly respected. When asked why they have money problems, they may say, "My clients never pay the way they are supposed to" or "I had to absorb costs on the job that reduced my profits" or "I had problems with the contractor, and my client refused to pay part of my fee." In other words, they blame others for their misfortune. Since they don't want to accept responsibility, they don't correct the problems. These designers fall into the same traps again and again.

When I have tried to talk over financial matters with some of these designers, I often hear, "Please, I haven't got the energy to focus on money now. It's not really my strong point. Really, I just want to design and do my job. Why should I even have to waste my energy worrying about all those problems?"

Unfortunately, there is no way to free designers from the financial aspects of interior design. It's simply part of the business. Some designers, who work in large firms, have jobs with compartmentalized duties. For example, some design, some supervise, some are troubleshooters. However, the majority of designers have to cope with many aspects of interior design, including supervision of contractors.

Obviously, you can't be an entrepreneur in the field unless you are prepared to cope with all phases of the business. Moreover, the longer designers take to learn how to handle these phases, the harder it becomes.

Some designers try to short-circuit the problem by hiring financial experts and delegating all authority to them. That doesn't solve the problem either. Using professionals to help manage a career is a smart move. However, the designer must become involved and make all the final decisions. After all, whose career is it?

Many designers don't think along financial and legal lines. Some do not have an extensive formal design education and, even if they do, they may not have learned about business or money management. Design schools are usually unable to prepare their students to cope with the business world. Many design school graduates are incapable of preparing a purchase order.

Designers *must* begin to learn about all financial aspects of their business as early in their careers as possible. Knowledge creates awareness; awareness develops skills and expertise. There is also an important psychological reason that this education should start early.

When a designer realizes that he is unable to cope with financial and legal problems, he may, as a defense mechanism, experience apathy and disinterest. However, as his career progresses and his financial problems become more complex, he then avoids this aspect of his career because he believes that he is a failure at it.

Knowledge dispels fear. If designers concentrate on acquiring financial skills, their business abilities and acumen will become increasingly sophisticated as their creative talents continue to develop.

But how can one gain this knowledge? As mentioned earlier, generally, business courses in design schools are either unavailable or inadequate. I prefer to see students take some conventional business courses in universities or colleges that specialize in business administration. The teachers of such courses can provide a basic concept of what business is about. The student is then free to generalize and apply his knowledge to a specific area.

Business is a science, just as design is an art, and accounting is a vital area of this science. The principles of accounting show where the money goes. An understanding of one's expenditure patterns leads to financial responsibility. Other helpful courses are those in basic business management. It is useful to learn the general principles of how businesses are run and to understand the techniques used.

Another way of learning about the design business is to work for a company where one can see firsthand how to handle money and make financial decisons. Good jobs are often hard to come by, however, and salaries for newcomers are, typically, shockingly low. Often, when an employer finds that a young designer can handle a specific aspect of a job particularly well, he will be restricted to that one slot because of his productivity. It is then up to the designer to make sure that he learns as many phases of the business as possible. Young designers should experience a complete overview of a design business's financial operations.

What about designers who are well established? Experienced designers will have to reshape their attitudes. They must become involved with the professionals whom they hire to advise about financial and legal matters. Once they establish a new pattern and incorporate "business" with their concept of being a designer, it becomes a lot easier.

Some of the most successful designers are partners in major firms and have very limited design ability. Many of them hardly design at all. Their strengths are in the financial area, which includes preparing proposals and selling jobs to clients. They are proficient in project management. They understand how to deal with architects and general contractors. They are also expert at hiring top creative talent to actually create the designs.

Most designers work in smaller firms and have to be jacks-of-all-trades. This requires a certain amount of entrepreneurial skill and financial know-how. They don't have to have the genius for business that partners in major firms possess. However, they should understand how to cope in the business, legal, and financial worlds.

If a designer is uncertain of how he should evaluate his role as a businessman, I always ask him where he belongs on the "Creativity Scale of Achievement." At the lower end are the *members*. These are designers who are not motivated by artistic recognition or financial success. Being a designer is simply a job. At the middle of the scale are the *players*, the active, purposeful achievers. At the top of the scale are the *factors*. They influence others. Their accomplishments transcend their generation and leave indelible marks for the future. We all know who they are; they are at the apex.

Although many strive for such achievement, most of us never completely arrive. Recognition as a designer implies a certain amount of financial success. Designers need visibility. For example, a designer should work and live in a showcase that projects his design image. Designers have to entertain clients comfortably to gain their confidence and communicate their design philosophy. Therefore, money becomes significant as a means of perpetuating design ideas and careers.

A designer will become a *factor* only when her career blooms. If she is satisfied with her ranking on the Creativity Scale, then she has chosen the right avenue to pursue her career. If she is dissatisfied, she must evaluate the areas that need the greatest improvement. She must tackle those problems with new inspiration. The designer must consider why she doesn't make enough money.

Nothing can substitute for a good financial education or for years of experience in managing a design business of your own. To that end, I have provided a detailed guide in the previous chapters to help you become smarter and more financially informed in most residential and some corporate markets.

If you have read all the chapters, you will have no doubt noticed that little of the material has been presented as hypothetical cases. In my opinion, hypothetical cases are of limited value for interior designers. Therefore, most of my discussion has been based on actual cases that I have personally witnessed during a career spanning nearly 25 years.

In the four chapters that address preparation of letters of agreement and design proposals, I have basically presented a format for contracts with a limited explanation of their rationale. Obviously, too much detail might divert the reader's train of thought, and consistency may be lost. However, in all other chapters, there are references to these agreements. Cases have been set forth explaining their rationale.

Any opinions that I have offered are based on my own observations of the cases presented. Your conclusions may be altogether different from mine. You may be right in disagreeing with me, and I may be wrong.

However, that is really not the point. This book was not written to teach you rules of law, business, or finance for interior design. It was based on my earlier book, *How to Make More Money at Interior Design*, written in 1982, and other publications and speeches written after that period.

Basically, my approach has been as follows. Starting when I wrote my first magazine column for *Interior Design* magazine in 1978, "Business and Design," my idea was to share experiences of designers that are of interest to others to enable them to realize that they are not alone. Similar problems occur repeatedly for many designers. My suggestions or solutions may not always be ideal. I don't think that is of prime importance.

I believe that once designers confront various issues that arise in their practices, they will ultimately find solutions. You will know what works best for you, based on your own business. However, it may be very useful for you to be aware of experiences of other designers.

Regardless of your level of experience, you will find information in these chapters, by reading all the case studies, that will trigger certain memories. You'll probably recall various incidents in your practice and say, "That's exactly what happened to me. If it happens again, I know just what I plan to do."

That's my idea. If reading this entire book helps you in even two or three instances, or if you can save yourself money on just two or three jobs from learning from the mistakes of other designers, it will be well worth your time. In fact, this book may help you in another way. Along with helping you to save money by avoiding costly mistakes, it may also help to maximize your profits.

Not all of this material can be digested by reading it through once. If you have already read this book completely, I think it was a good investment. You need to be familiar with all the information contained in it. Then you can refer to specific sections that may help you to resolve a question.

However, since these cases reflect human behavior, it was very hard to categorize and compartmentalize all material in this book. A lot of it overlaps and integrates. I hope, if you have the time and patience, that you will reread this entire book every so often. Your reaction may be, "I forgot about that case when I read it the first time. I'm glad I went over it again." Repeating the process over a period of time will result in learning and developing new insights.

If you are a seasoned designer, you will realize that any number of variables can change the outcome of a problem. Therefore, in your own business you may have a situation that resembles a case in this book. If the facts are not a "mirror image," you may handle it differently from my suggestions. However, at least you can review some general principles and rationale that may assist you. They evolved from application, adaptation, and reuse.

An interior designer must develop the ability to handle money and operate a business in order to be successful. Most books on law and financial management for designers set forth a lot of rules and information. The problem is that unless designers are projected into a specific factual situation where they must apply those rules, they are quickly forgotten.

That's why I have based most of my book on case studies. Law schools and graduate business programs typically teach using the Harvard Case Method. They don't primarily use texts that recite rules; they teach by example. Students read selected cases and "brief" them. Then, professors encourage students to argue whether the decisions reached in these cases are correct. This encourages students of law and business to think.

I have tried to use a similar approach for designers in my magazine columns, courses, and, finally, this book. Many cases presented in one subject area overlap in other areas.

This book, I hope, analyzes some of your most pressing problems. Use it properly, and the operation of your own business will cease to be such a dilemma. It will become, instead, a series of manageable problem areas. You will have more time, make more money, and be more successful.

A FINAL WORD . . .

Now that you've finished my book, I hope you found it to be interesting and worthwhile. In one volume, you have seen a cross section of my entire career relating to interior design, law, and business.

Of course, I couldn't present everything that I experienced in a career spanning nearly 25 years. That wouldn't be necessary or even useful. However, you have witnessed many highlights that provoked my interest. I felt they were worthy to share with the interior design community.

I cannot predict how this book will help your business. All designers have different needs. For example, you may like my contracts and proposals and decide to use them as a basis for your own. On the other hand, if they're not suitable, you may still find information or ideas useful to modify your contracts.

The same holds true of the case studies. You may identify with some of the factual situations and be able to utilize the logic for your own business. My opinions may reinforce your current business philosophy or encourage you to change it. Yet many of the problems confronting the designers in this book may not apply to you. Even if that is the case, you will still identify with certain areas, regardless of our disparities.

If you have read this book carefully, let your subconscious be your guide. Even if you don't reread it soon or refer to it for advice, you will recall certain fragments when your business demands it. Then, return to the book for further investigation.

Developing the skill to manage your business properly is not merely a convenience or energy-saving advantage. It is worth money. Money can mean the difference between success and failure. If you earnestly attempt to analyze and apply the principles set forth here, there will be no doubt about it. You will prosper!

ABOUT THE AUTHOR

Robert L. Alderman, Esq., is an attorney admitted to practice in New York and Florida. He completed his undergraduate work at Cornell University and holds an MBA in finance and a law degree from Syracuse University. He was former trial counsel for the United States Securities and Exchange Commission.

For a number of years, Mr. Alderman wrote a column for *Interior Design* magazine, "Business and Design," and for *The Designer*, "The Legal Angle." He was a faculty member at the Fashion Institute of Technology (F.I.T.) in New York City, where he taught business and law for interior design students.

His book, *How to Make More Money at Interior Design*, was published in 1982. He also produced an audiocassette series of the same title, a library of lectures.

Mr. Alderman teaches continuing education courses for the American Society of Interior Designers and the State of Florida, which qualify for state licensing programs. He has lectured nationwide at design organizations and at design centers for educational programs.

INDEX